**Environmental Ethics
Studies of Man's Self-Destruction**

Environmental Ethics
Studies of Man's Self-Destruction

Edited by **Donald R. Scoby**
Assistant Professor of Biology
Division of Natural Sciences
North Dakota State University
Fargo, North Dakota

Burgess Publishing Company
426 South Sixth Street • Minneapolis, Minnesota 55415

Cover: Background photograph
Courtesy of Champion Papers

DEDICATION

To future human generations whose environment and
survival is the responsibility of our society. DRS

Preface

"Man is part of a natural system, the earth, and is ultimately subject to the limits of that system."

Population Curriculum Study,
University of Delaware

Ethics have long been regarded by physical and biological scientists as a field divorced from their responsibility. However, at present this attitude is being questioned, and all science is being forced to face the reality and morality of many of its discoveries and judgments. More people are questioning some of our activities related to ethical values, especially in the context of conflicts with ecological principles. Many of the ideas we have inherited and cherished, all of which are man-made, are in direct opposition to the basic cycles essential for the well-being of our biosphere. In fact, every living thing, including man, is being affected by the activities of man. These activities, if not adjusted to be in harmony with natural cycles, have the potential of changing the environment to the extent that it is hostile to our very existence.

Many of our ethical values have resulted in actions which have contributed to our rape of nature and therefore have to be challenged. Many of the ideas expressed in the articles found in this book were advanced by early Greek philosophers such as Plato and Socrates. However, we have a human tendency to accept as infallible those ideas which agree with the present system of life, but to reject, without consideration, those ideas which are distasteful or contrary to our present way of thinking.

This book of readings attempts to involve environmentally motivated individuals from all disciplines. Since the problems we face cross academic areas it is essential for each individual to appreciate and understand the results of society's as well as his own actions. Each author is responsible for the ideas that he expresses and does not necessarily reflect the opinion of the other authors.

As citizens, all of us must fundamentally accept our obligation to the natural system. The tendency has been to blame everyone but ourselves. The real issue is that we are all guilty, and as such we cannot point an accusing finger at everyone else without being able to look at our own environmental ethic. One of the most serious problems is that people have personal and unique environmental obsessions, such as condemning snowmobiles while at the same time condoning the leisure-time use of a high-powered motor boat. As I see it, the true environmental realist is one that does not endorse the massive consumption of power for leisure-time activities, an excess of growth, the encroachment on our limited available space, the production of more power to meet the wasteful demands of people in a time when waste needs to be eliminated, the unlimited use of nonrenewable resources instead of living within the limits of renewable resources, and the inherited materialistic society. The list could go on but may be summarized by saying that if one were to take all the idiosyncracies and bestow them on one person, one would then have an environmentalist. Many people misunderstand such a deep concern toward our environment. This person is really a different breed than a conservationist, a wildlife proponent, or an ecologist; however, any one of these may also be an environmentalist.

Because of the diverse nature of the problem of our environment, many challenging and sometimes offensive thoughts must be presented. Articles for this book were selected with a bias toward questioning our present worldwide procedures and values. It must be understood that questioning our attitudes does not mean they are entirely wrong. Change comes about through an interaction of ideas, and only ideas presented to an open mind will allow thoughtful, serious consideration for the development of an environmental ethic compatible with our finite earth.

The intent of this book, therefore, is to stimulate thinking, discussion, concern, and action toward the development of a living ethic compatible with nature.

Acknowledgments

I am grateful to the many authors who were willing to contribute articles reflecting their personal viewpoints in relation to the problems facing man. It must be understood, however, that the opinions expressed in each article reflect the personal convictions of the individual authors and that each author does not necessarily agree with all the thoughts expressed in other articles. Each contributor maintains full responsibility for any statement open to misunderstanding.

Special thanks are extended to Drs. Laurence L. Falk and Carol Falk for their helpful assistance with a number of the articles and with editing procedures.

Mrs. Dan Lerfald and Miss Cathy Olson initially transcribed the editor's contributions from tape recorded speeches. Mrs. Hazel Ashworth patiently typed and retyped manuscripts, assembled materials, and sent our permission forms to authors and publishers. This help is sincerely appreciated.

Acknowledgment is also extended to Drs. Warren C. Whitman, Harold Goetz, John Brophy, and Frank Cassel for their initial comments on various articles contributed by the editor and other authors.

Special appreciation is extended to my wife, Glenna, and to my daughter, Melodye, for their encouragment, understanding, sacrifice, and help in supporting my idiosyncratic efforts concerned with the environment and the survival of future human generations.

Contents

The Problem - Is There Need for Concern

Introduction

This first section discusses "popullution" as the number one problem facing man. If population is the prime problem, then none of the aspects of environmental degradation—air pollution, water pollution, soil pollution, noise pollution—can be permanently solved as long as our population continues to grow. For a positive cure of an illness doctors would prefer to treat the source of a sickness and not the symptoms. By the same analogy, pollution is the symptom of our sickness and the high number of people, and their associated life style, is the source of the infection.

Without population stability the quality of life is severely threatened both physically and aesthetically. Unless we realize our predicament immediately and set as our prime goals population stability and implementation of a life style compatible with the natural system, we take the very serious risk of committing voiceless future generations to misery and death on an overcrowded planet.

America, to many concerned and dedicated people, seems to have three alternatives regarding the population explosion:

1. perish;
2. wait a few years then desperately pass heavily coercive laws which would probably be too late;

1

3. face the problem now with individual persuasion, legislation, and personal action.

What harm will there be if our growth is stabilized? What good will there be if we continue to increase in population in a world already suffering from pollution? Which will you choose? Hopefully this section will give you challenging arguments for thoughtful consideration of the subject.

Man and His Efforts To Destroy Himself

Donald R. Scoby

Within the environmental crisis we face today, there is one major item of concern—overpopulation. The pollution problems evident in water, air, and land are simply symptoms of a central cause, namely, too many people. Facing the reality of overpopulation and the resulting pollution problem is of vital importance, but it is even more important for each individual to make necessary attitudinal changes and continue taking steps to stop overpopulation. Otherwise man, who in all probability is on the list of endangered species, will become extinct.

The first step to be taken in saving our environment, or indeed man himself, is to realize and accept the fact that there are and will be too many people for the earth to support satisfactorily. This may be hard to understand if we look at past instances. It may seem that Grandpa and his ten children did very well for themselves. In fact, men with large families were often pillars of the community and held a high position in the minds of others for their acceptance of responsibility and contributions to society. Has the world changed so much that the once revered gift to society of unlimited human life is no longer needed; or worse, not wanted? Indeed it has.

At one time in history a high birth rate was essential to man's survival. He had to utilize natality and immigration, which increase population density, to combat the more frequent mortality and emigration which decrease population and could cause extinction in a particular area, or even the world. Thus, to fight against an environment which he could neither understand or control, man simply reproduced in sufficient numbers for growth and progress. In the predominantly agrarian society it was nice for Dad to tell Joe to go farm the south forty, Sam and Bill to attend the north eighty, and Henry to make use of the southwest forty. To carry on the farming of the land, it was a profitable venture having a large family of 6 to 12 children. If the area became too populated, part of the family moved on to new lands and started anew where there was enough area and work to make large families profitable once again. Europe moved to America; the east coast moved to the west and eventually the

Presented at an Elementary Science Workshop, Fargo, North Dakota, January 14, 1970. Dr. Donald R. Scoby is Assistant Professor of Botany at North Dakota State University, Fargo, North Dakota.

land ran out. Thus, man settled into suburban areas including small backyards rather than hundreds of acres of farm land, and it was no longer profitable to have ten or twelve boys to do the dishes and carry out the garbage. Therefore, in developed countries the average family size sometimes decreased; but in underdeveloped countries which still fought many of the same problems of years before, the family size remained constant or increased. This small decrease of family size in developed countries may seem encouraging or give the false security of relative safety from overpopulation, but there is no safety in that surmise and no individual should delude himself into this belief. The facts and illustrations of man's doubling time will shatter any illusions of safety without preventive measures.

The doubling time of man refers to the number of years it takes for the number of people on the earth to double. A theoretical example using a sparrow population will clarify the term (BSCS, 1963). On an island in the spring of the year are living 5 pairs of house sparrows. Let us assume that each pair produces 10 offspring, five males and five females. This does not always occur. Sometimes it may be 6 males to 4 females or 8 males to 2 females, but the average is 5. Let us also assume that each year all breeding parents die before the following spring. Again this is theoretical since some parents live to breed again. Each year all 10 offspring survive to breed again the following spring. There is no immigration or emigration. Thus the only factors considered are natality and mortality. Under these theoretical circumstances we have rapid geometric growth and a population explosion. The 5 original pairs each produce 10 offspring resulting in 50, and the parents die. These 25 pairs in turn each have 10 offspring resulting in 250 sparrows, and all parents die. The 125 pairs each have 10 offspring equaling 1250 sparrows, and the growth spirals upward with the doubling time span decreasing. In 8 years the sparrow population has gone from 50 to 19,531,250.

Thus, if we substitute humans for sparrows the results are frightening. Even though the sparrow illustration is theoretical, man's population growth is comparable since the length of his doubling time is steadily decreasing. This is rapidly leading man toward the dangers of an environmental crisis. When man was a berry-picking, grub-eating individual, it was estimated the earth could support 2 to 3 million people. These people were literally living off the land by collecting grubs and nuts, berries and wild game for food. It took 1 to 2 million years for man's first doubling time and for him to reach a population of approximately 5 million people. During the time it took man to go from a population of 5 million to 500 million, he was doubling approximately every 1000 years. But after the mark of 500 million was reached, the doubling time decreased to approximately every 200 years, once every 80 years and, finally, once every 35 years which is the present rate (Ehrlich, 1968). By the year 2000 the number of people on earth will be theoretically doubling every 15 years to 7 years to 3½ years until it will occur every year, or even at 6 month intervals. As we all know, these huge numbers of people are impossible even though the scientific and social changes have increased the support capabilities of the earth. The following examples should show that the above figures are not merely surmise. India alone is contributing 12 to 14 million people per year on top of a population that is at present unsupportable at a quality level. In 12 to 15 years they will have added to their present population as many people as are presently inhabiting the United States. This addition of over 200 million people predicts a horrible future since they cannot feed the people they now have. In the year 2000 there is a potential for over 6 to 7.5 billion people to populate the earth if we continue at the present birth rate. The population of China alone will exceed 1 billion people by the year 2000. Taking a conservative doubling time of 35 years, 60 million billion people will exist in the year 2900 (Ehrlich, 1968).

Now, that is too many people. It's an impossibility. The earth cannot support this many people and the symptoms of this inability are fast becoming apparent in the present pollution problems facing man. Population is the crucial cause of pollution. The more people you have, the more items you have for pollution. When we were a population of 100 million in this country, nature could take care of man's stupidity. But now the numbers have increased beyond the possibility of natural control and problems acrue in nearly all areas.

One of the developments which has had an influence on agricultural advancement is pesticides. Insect control, a vital concern for every person making his living from the land, has been greatly advanced through the use of pesticides. Many of the so-called "harmless" pesticides are really poisoning the environment and endangering other organisms including the human race.

One of the most common and widely used pesticides throughout the world is DDT. This is an example of a compound that is persistent and accumulates in each organism. As it passes through each trophic (feeding) level it accumulates in the next highest level. A hypothetical situation will illustrate the point. If a martin eats 1,000 mosquitoes that each contain 1 part per million, the martin then has 1,000 parts per million of DDT. In turn, another animal will eat the martin and gain 1,000 parts per million of DDT. If this animal eats 10 martins, he will consume 10,000 parts per million. In turn this animal passes on 10,000 parts per million which accumulates in whatever consumes it. Soon the accumulation of DDT or its metabolites reaches the lethal range. This is why species such as osprey, golden eagle, and many others are endangered. The DDT concentration is high enough so that it is affecting the reproductive system of the individual. At the present time man contains 12 parts per million of DDT and other metabolites. This is a greater concentration than the U.S. Department of Agriculture allows in the beef we consume. Thus, we are theoretically unfit for human consumption. Even though it has not been proven that DDT is harmful to man, what DDT does to the environment in which man lives is drastic. Because it alters the environment in which the interrelationships of nature occur and because it is the cause of the near extinction of many species, this pesticide cannot be considered harmless.

But even if DDT and many of the other pesticides were to be eliminated, the pollution of the environment by humans would still go on. Man in his unlimited quest for knowledge discovered how to make an organic compound. There was really no serious pollution problem when the population of the world was small and organisms in nature would break down naturally occurring organic compounds, recycle and return them to the biological cycles which operate within our earth. But with the development of a man-made organic compound came materials which would not completely biodegrade and return to nature. Unlike natural compounds which are recycled through action with organisms within nature, many of the man-made organic compounds are not affected by natural organisms. Thus, when discarded into nature, these compounds remain the same for years, if not forever. This is a dangerous situation. Unable to recycle their energies, the compounds "bunch up" and collect, causing pollution which cannot be remedied.

An excellent example of a man-made organic compound is Dupont's miracle Teflon. Its major selling point is its indestructibility. When cast aside in the garbage for one reason or another, it will remain Teflon. Unlike iron which rusts and returns to nature, Teflon is forever removed from the energy cycle and is useless to both man and nature. Other examples of organic pollutants are certain detergents, many pesticides and herbicides, and plastics. Considering the numbers of these used in an individual's life can be frightening, especially when it is realized that discards of this nature are never disposed of entirely. They remain. When a person drinks apparently crystal clear water run from the tap in the kitchen sink, he is drinking many of the pollutive compounds including detergents which he ran into the water supply for disposal. In addition to pollution from each individual, industry also contributes to the problem. At the 1970 National Association of Science Teachers at Cincinnati, Ohio the Taft Research Center provided this example. Filtered water taken from an Ohio River tributary contained a tarlike residue composed of over 7,000 chemicals. Out of these 7,000 chemicals only 14 were identified and one of these was a known cancer-producing material. Of the approximately 500,000 compounds man has made, action and results with environment are known for approximately 10 per cent (Clark, 1969). Thus, the curse of ignorance is very present and one of the greatest dangers to man and his environment.

Many people succeed in detaching themselves from the pollution problem. They have no direct contact with pesticides and once the garbage leaves the premises they do not contend with it any longer. Even though each human is responsible for 5.6 pounds of trash per day at the present, he is oblivious to the vast amounts of trash his society produces and of the monumental effect this has on his environment. Perhaps a more dramatic and shocking example will awaken the public to the part each individual plays in pollution. Along with the previously discussed pollutants produced by humans (upon the environment) is human waste. In an area from Boston to Washington, D. C. there reside approximately 50 million people. Each of these people defecates approximately 2 pounds of fecal waste every day. The problem rests with the disposal of 100 million pounds of excrement per day. At present this is being mildly treated and dumped in the river, when it should be directly recycled into nature by use as a fertilizer upon the land. Allowing one cubic foot per individual, calculations show all waste, including trash, from 50 million people alone would cover the city of Fargo, North Dakota (about 7 square miles) to the depth of 180 feet in a year's time. We have 204 million people in the United States. What is to be done with all the waste? India and China solved the problem years ago when they used human waste as fertilizer for crops. Since human waste is part of nature's natural energy cycle, this sytem completed its purpose and caused little pollution. But would our society today accept food grown under such conditions? Since waste is biodegradable and a part of nature, nature would handle it, except that the population has increased so greatly that nature is in trouble and can no longer dispose of an increased deposit of human waste. Excretion cannot be eliminated from our life cycle; therefore, we must eliminate uncontrolled population growth and reuse waste as fertilizer for the land if we are to solve the problem.

For man to exist on this planet he needs air, water, and food. Air, of course, is essential. Without its supply man dies in a matter of seconds. Secondly, man needs water, for he can survive longer without food than without water. Even though these two things are most important to man's existence, he sacrifices their purity and supply for the sake of progress and convenience. By polluting the water with industrial wastes and the air with products from transportation, man is separating himself from the two most important things upon which existence depends.

Human waste is certainly a problem as was discussed previously, but it is minor when compared to the problem of industrial wastes now polluting our waters. The main cause of the problem is that man believes if he dilutes the waste enough, he ends the pollution. One gallon of pollutant is dumped into 100 gallons of water. When the 100 gallons are polluted, they are deposited into 1,000 gallons, and the never-ending spiral develops. The result of this theory is horrible. The main water bodies of lakes and rivers become the targets for industrial wastes. Thus, Lake Erie is one great cesspool at the present time. Lake Michigan and Lake Superior are following the same route. Again, the problem is not the responsibility of industry alone. Treatment is not profitable in our present economic outlook and when done by an industry is really nothing more than charity on their part. Society at present demands progress and products. The larger the society and its demands, the more volume industry produces and the greater the amount of wastes to be handled. Overpopulation – the root of still another pollution evil.

Providing convenient transportation and entertainment for our millions of people has produced the greatest pollution evil of all, transportation and the attitudes associated with the "sacred" internal combustion engine. Pesticides and industrial wastes may be controlled by law; nature would handle biodegradable human wastes if recycled as fertilizer; but, demand for the cancellation of easy transportation through removal of the private car may cause the greatest demonstration the U. S. has ever experienced. As a society we demand the convenience of the automobile and in turn are experiencing the elimination of the pure air which keeps us alive.

Vehicles of transportation contribute 65 to 70 per cent of the air pollution problem. Combustion products from all sources going into the air equal approximately 144 million tons of pollutants per year. Of this amount, approximately 88 million tons are produced by the motor vehicle. Sulphur compounds, nitrogen compounds, carbon dioxide and monoxide, unburned hydrocarbons, and lead make up the greatest percentage of pollutants. Of these pollutants tetra-ethyl lead added to eliminate the "knocking motor" is highly dangerous. Continued deposits could cause death from lead poisoning, a terrible sacrifice for a quiet car. Tetra-ethyl lead accumulates in the bones. The seriousness of this condition can be historically rationalized by looking at the Roman Empire. A lackadaisical attitude was one of the biggest causes of its ruin. This attitude, a symptom of lead poisoning, may be partially attributed to that disease. Drinking and eating vessels of the Romans were cast in bronze which gave a distinct taste to the beverages and foods. Since this condition was disliked, the rich who could afford it coated their vessels with lead to eliminate the taste of bronze. They undoubtedly suffered from lead poisoning as is deduced from the bones discovered by archaeologists years later (Ehrlich, 1969). Today's society and its selfish attitudes are partially responsible for air pollution. Tons of potential killers are put in the air daily for the sake of convenience. The same motivation was behind lead-covered vessels of Roman days which led to death and ruination.

Five years ago man invaded the last relatively undisturbed area. The northern snow-covered reaches of the continent escaped from the fate of disturbed populated areas for they had been invaded by few vehicles. The nonpolluting dog sled was the most useful and practical transportation for the area. But man and his supposed intelligence invented the motor on skis, the snowmobile. He now has speed, an easy way of traveling over snow, and a wonderful way to pass the time, which he cuts ever shorter through motor vehicle pollution. There are over 100,000 of these mechanical monsters in Minnesota alone and with such a profitable business venture, cessation of production is doubtful. Once again man has decreased his ability to escape. He has invaded the last pure frontier and is furthering his power consumption, which is also poisoning the air and mutilating the land.

Man has not limited air pollution to the earth's atmosphere. He has extended its deadly results to the upper atmosphere. Through the discovery and extensive use of the transcontinental jet, man has probably made another blunder. The noise emitted from these monsters makes human residence near airports impossible. Besides the intrusion of shattering noise, these jets are producing the same pollutants above our atmosphere as below. During flight, combustion of the propellant fuel utilizes oxygen (including ozone, which all life is dependent upon), and yields water vapor. This vapor crystallizes due to the cold temperatures of the high altitude, and the sun's rays (our energy source) can do one of three things. Some of the rays may be reflected, causing the earth to cool dramatically; all may pass through the crystals but stopping heat from escaping, may cause the earth to heat; or, the rays may cause no change in the earth's temperature. Lamont Cole supports the premise that carbon dioxide given off in our tremendous energy consumption will eventually trap within the atmosphere much of the heat normally reflected from the earth. Gradually we will warm up. This is considered a natural phenomenon; only the length of time in which this occurs is being radically changed. Under normal conditions the temperature change of the earth would take place over a period of 20 to 40 thousand years. But man, in his obsession to speed up his travel and social habits, has succeeded in accelerating changes in nature. Reid Bryson, climatologist at the University of Wisconsin, (personal communication, 1970) predicts air particle contamination from dust and energy consumption is occuring faster than the carbon dioxide accumulation. Therefore, he feels the earth is cooling and, indeed, said North Dakota would likely experience a 6 weeks longer winter within 20 years.

Scientists are confused about the results of air pollution, but they are sure of one thing. Air pollution, no matter what the result, is harmful to man and his environment. Even though the jet age is convenient for the businessmen to travel from Tokyo to New York at a faster rate, it is not safe or necessary enough to cost man his environment. It is time for man to slow down. Rather than being concerned with the shortest amount of time needed to arrive somewhere, man should pause for thought under an oak tree and decide personally what he is contributing to the environmental crisis.

A review of the transportation problem shows once again that it is not the automobile or the plane that is solely to blame for pollution. Were it not for man's increased numbers, the pollution from his transportation would not be greater than nature could handle. But as the population explodes, so do the numbers of vehicles required to move that population. Therefore, limit the people and transportation vehicles are cut down. To aid in cutting down on the number of vehicles, some definite steps should be taken. Not only do the number of vehicles increase pollution but energy consumption is increasing also.

As can be easily understood, the energy available for our use is limited and we must adjust our lives to this situation by limiting the size of cars as well as families. By imposing a stringent tax upon the weight and horsepower of cars, most individuals would tend to limit the size of their cars. As an example taxes for license plates could be a dollar per pound and ten dollars per horsepower. When vehicles are reduced in numbers and size, the pollution problem is partially solved as well as the danger of a severely depleted energy supply.

But partially solving the problem is not enough. The challenge has been presented. The earth cannot support the present population satisfactorily and if estimates of future populations materialize, by the year 2000 life on this planet will be so degenerate that man will detest his very existence. Man can either accept or reject the responsibility he has for future generations. Many believe the living pattern of today's society and the steps man has taken to solve pollution are satisfactory. If this is the case, these people must be able to honestly say they have no responsibility for future generations, because they have turned the human race into the path of eventual extinction. Since their solution to pollution is extinction, they are correct in believing today's methods of solution will solve the problem. On the other hand, if the information presented thus far has awakened man to his situation, he will accept the responsibility of ensuring the continuation of the human race and of providing an adequate environment wherein man may live.

Hopefully, assuming that man will be intelligent enough to choose the latter option and accept the responsibility, he must then analyze the reason man placed himself in this dangerous situation. Man owes his problems to the cycle of people, progress, money by which he presently lives. This cycle is an inherited "hang-up" and works in this manner. The more people in society, the more progress that society will make, and the more money the people will make from this progress. And since the rule of living in this society seems to be "keep up with the Joneses," more people are always needed to advance progress and give everyone more money to compete with each other for social position through the dollar sign. And so it goes; people, progress, money, which leads to more people, more progress, and more money; a never-ending cycle leading only to a polluted environment and eventually death.

At one time this unlimited capitalism was an advantage to man. He needed to populate and develop the country in which he lived. But we no longer need this system. We are overpopulated and unlimited expansion cannot go on for we take the risk of depleting our energy supply entirely. It is time for the population and economy to stabilize. Now man needs to limit himself and what he uses to exist in harmony with nature. For example, a newspaper in place of forever growing larger to meet the numbers of people would stabilize at a specific level of subscriptions and with a stable population would keep this level. Companies would level off at an assured and constant level of profits. Items would be reused and recycled back into the system rather than the constant and expanding search for the new. Through the limitation of the population and the leveling of the economy, the cycle of people, progress, money would come to a halt.

But again, the solution to the problem lies in limiting the population. It does no good to scream about pollution problems when the reason for those problems is never solved. When man refuses to see population control as the answer, he is merely handing the problem on to future generations. Eventually these generations will be unable to control the problem and man will become extinct. Thus, it is of extreme importance that today's generation acts immediately.

Many theories of correction have been advanced concerning overpopulation and the resulting pollution problem. Transporting the people to other areas such as the other planets has been suggested but upon study proves to be impractical. Even though the technology for such a project is now a possibility, the energy required makes the project impossible. Another impractical solution is to find another galaxy. However, if the sun is placed on a solar map where its distance from the earth equals three feet, the location of the nearest galaxy, Alpha Centauri, would be plotted hundreds of miles away from the earth on the map. It would take many generations to reach it. Again we have a ridiculous solution.

Therefore, since we cannot ship the population off the earth, we must seek to solve the problems endangering them on this earth. The first problem under consideration and in need of solution is that of feeding the people. At the present time millions are starving and this problem will continue to grow with increased population. It has been suggested that man should become a first order consumer. In nature there is a definite cycle of nourishment. The sun provides energy for vegetation which is eaten by first order consumers such as insects, mice and rabbits. In turn certain birds, snakes and weasels which are second order consumers, eat the first order consumers of insects, mice and rabbits. A third order consumer eats the second order and so on. Man being omnivorous eats something from all orders but mostly the upper ones. The problem lies in the fact that the energy, so plentiful in the green plants, lessens greatly in total quantity as it is passed from order to order through different animals. As energy is passed from level to level some of it is lost due to respiration, heat loss, and normal activity of the life process. Thus the organism can incorporate only a small percentage of the energy he consumes in his own body and he therefore can pass on only a small percentage to the next level. For example, 1000 calories produced by small oxygen-producing plants within water, the phytoplankton, may be eaten by small aquatic animals who will experience energy loss through normal activity and incorporate only part of the phytoplankton's calories. The next group eats the small aquatic animals and the energy passed on is about 150 calories. The smelt, at a higher feeding or trophic level, eat the carnivores and incorporate only 30 calories. Trout, at a still higher trophic level, eat the smelt and retain 6 calories and, finally, man eats the trout and incorporates 2 calories.

Because of the large energy loss it takes more trout to feed man than it would the organisms from other levels. Therefore, if man would eat the plankton burger and cut out the "middle man," he would obtain more calories and more people could be fed.

But there are many reasons why this theory will not succeed in solving the hunger of our rapidly growing population. First of all, man and his form of diet and nourishment are part of nature's balance. By removing the "middle man" or the uncontrolled consumption of other orders, we are interfering with nature's balance and we must face the consequences. In addition to this imbalance, overpopulation will also cause a problem. The phytoplankton of the ocean provide over 70 per cent of the oxygen supply. At the present time we are depositing a great deal of our run-off in the ocean including pesticides, herbicides, fertilizer, and waste materials. Even though man probably does not depend upon the ocean organisms for the air he breathes, he continues to endanger these organisms through his ignorance of what his run-off materials are doing to the plankton. Man will eventually kill these organisms because of extermination through waste from too many people. In addition to waste materials polluting this area of nature, we see man covering up vast areas of land with plastic, concrete, and asphalt in order to give himself a more convenient existence. In reality he is limiting that existence and endangering nature's originally adequate system.

As is usually the case, a few people will refuse to believe there will even be a food shortage. For example, the Fargo Forum in a recent editorial rationalized the seriousness of the situation by quoting one economists' magazine which stated that we will be suffering from a food surplus rather than a food shortage. This is impossible if all people are fed now or if a small percentage of the future populations will be fed. The reason for this lies in the geometric growth of population. The base changes every year. As an example, population growth may go from 2 per cent of a billion to 2 per cent of a billion and a half, growing like compound interest. In food production the base stays the same. There is only so much land to be used for production and this amount will not increase as the population increases. Hybrids may help out and increase yield but the production of food and the reproduction of people will never cross. Our agriculture practices of using pesticides and inorganic fertilizer may seem to ease the food shortage, but they only cause problems of pollution in the future. Food has no doubling time as population does; therefore, food production will never be greater than what an ever-increasing population requires.

The recent hybrid rice developed for the Far East causes a problem in the form of a polluting and nature-disturbing cycle. Hybrid rice needs additional fertilizer and protection of pesticides for their more lush growth. Insects become adapted to pesticides, so greater and stronger amounts must be added to insure protection. These products many times end up as unknown compounds which cannot be broken down and which may be far more harmful than the original product. We are even trying to replace the traditional water buffalo with a mechanical gasoline-consuming implement, again adding to the problem. No matter where man turns he succeeds only in upsetting nature's balance and leading himself into catastrophe.

Feeding the people is an impossibility. Proposals for moving the people to other planets are ridiculous. Therefore, what can be done? Man must learn to live in harmony with his environment. He cannot change it according to his every whim. To do this he must control the population and take steps to stop excessive pollution. This can only be accomplished through drastic changes in the present attitudes of today.

The first areas in need of change are those of birth and death control. Death control is highly moral, fashionable, and profitable. Heart transplants, care for the aged, and treatments for all disease are presently saving many lives. But birth control is a nasty word. We must "hush up" discussion of this very important topic because it is supposed to be private. It is of concern to no one else how many children we have. The government cannot handle anything else; they had better stay out of the bedroom. And in addition to these biases and ignorant comments, a large majority of the public will say that Christian principles cannot condone birth control. But taken directly from the book of Christian principles, the Bible, is found this statement: "Be fruitful and multiply and take dominion of the earth." The important word in this passage is not fruitful or multiply, but dominion. Dominion indicates administration, care, and most of all good stewardship. At present stewardship of God's greatest gift — life and nature — is absent in our society. We seek not to care and carefully minister to our society, but only to subdue and change our natural environment for the assurance of our convenience. We have endangered the lives of every human being through overpopulation and the pollutional results it brings. For the sake of a Christian principle which supposedly does not approve of birth control, we are murdering our fellow human beings through starvation and a poisonous environment. Is this also a "Christian" principle?

If we are to continue to save lives through advanced death control, we must assure these very lives of a secure existence by stopping the population explosion. We must preach, teach, and above all practice birth control. An example illustrating this need is taken from a movie of an authentic incident. The Eskimo culture practiced birth control which was mandatory and passed on from mother to daughter. If the first-born was a boy, the mother was to bite the umbilical cord in two, remove the embryonic covering and nurse and care for the baby as best she could. If the first-born was a baby girl, she was to immediately fill its mouth with snow and throw it out of the igloo. By our standards this was murder. But within their culture these methods were essential for their survival. The male must hunt and furnish the tribe with food, which the girl could not do.

Therefore, the Eskimo's culture evolved and provided a means of survival in accordance with his environment. The same methods were used to solve the problem of old age. When an adult no longer felt useful to a society, he in turn removed himself from the society by mounting an ice-floe and floating away, eventually to freeze to death.

These cultural practices were so offensive to us we decided to offer our humanitarian views to the Eskimo. We gave him a gun to allow him a sure food supply. He then could eliminate the harsh birth control and old age methods. But with the greater advantage of a gun and a greater population, the wildlife diminished and the Eskimo now fights starvation. How logical was it to impose upon this cultural group? We only gave them the same problems we have. We caused a culture already adapted to its environment to try to change the environment to its own purposes. We caused more people to die, a direct result of death control without birth control.

India and Mexico also suffered from our benevolence. During the 1920s we provided Mexico with our technology, allowing them to produce more food to solve the starvation problem. Within 20 years their food production increased nearly 80 per cent. But we did not provide birth control and their population increased approximately 80 per cent. The problem was not solved, in fact, there were more people starving.

In 1965 India had a starvation problem. By shipping over one-fourth of our wheat crop it is estimated that we saved 12 million people from starvation. But again we did not demand birth control. With each family having 4 children, there will be 48 million people in a generation's time. When the next famine develops we will have to send our entire wheat crop. How humanitarian were we not to demand rigid birth control and in not allowing them to starve? We saved 12 million and put 48 million on the starvation list.

Partial help for the solution may lie in improved foreign policy. Before delivering medical aid and technology to fight starvation, underdeveloped and overpopulated countries must accept birth control measures. If this is not accepted, the people must be left to starve in order to halt overpopulation. The policy is harsh; but the only way to save the human race is to practice death control only in accordance with birth control.

The above practice would make a large difference in the population explosion in other countries, but the greatest change in our country is to be found in the results of legalized abortion and sterilization. These are the most effective methods of necessary birth control. Abortion would offer an open and safe way to aid families and society of unwanted children which are only a burden on both. Sterilization eliminates the chance of an unwanted child and provides safety for those who cannot condone abortion for reasons of conscience. The time is coming when sterilization will be mandatory after parents have two children. An even stronger step may be taken should these practices fail to solve the problem. Mandatory sterilization may be required at the age of 20. Before sterilization both sperm and eggs could be deposited in a bank. Upon marriage, application will be made to have a child. At the present these practices are not socially acceptable. But if we do not practice less severe methods of birth control voluntarily at the present, it will fall upon our children to employ the severe practices endorsed above. In any event, we must have birth control to survive.

Tax laws and welfare programs are also detrimental to the population problem and must be changed. President Nixon claims that he is vitally concerned with pollution problems. Yet he seems to be oblivious to the center of the problem, overpopulation. The tax laws are indicative of this blindness. By raising the exemptions for dependents to $750, Congress provided an excellent incentive for larger families. If exemptions were graded allowing $1000 for the first child, $500 for the second and a -$500 for those thereafter, the problem would be helped. Welfare programs should be similarly programmed. Instead of supplying $50 per month for every child born, $1000 should be given for every year a child is not born. If the parents could not or would not work, they would be aided in the support of one child, two at the most. But, after the birth of the second child, sterilization would be mandatory. Short of this plan an economic bounty of $10,000 could be paid to all women after menopause for no children (or after sterilization), $5,000 for stopping at one, $2,500 for stopping at two, and no payment for more than two.

Another area of necessary change lies in our methods of burying the dead. We pollute nature with our discoveries which she cannot handle; and in turn, we rob her of ourselves when we die. We must be embalmed and placed in a steel vault. What we are saving or protecting is unknown. It is a certainty that our decayed bodies are of no use to anyone but nature wherein we are recycled into the energy cycle so necessary to the world. Burial in a wooden coffin on a hill overlooking a lake is far more sensible than today's methods.

Another illustration of the uselessness of our absurd methods follows. Recently many a town's population has been surpassed by that of the cemetery. There are more people dead in the cemetery than alive in the town. As populations increase, so do filled lots in the cemetery. This land is needed for production and use by the living. Therefore, the acceptance of natural burial is an eventual necessity.

The evils of transportation were vividly illustrated earlier and should leave no doubt in anyone's mind as to the necessity for change. Smog and air pollution are first on the list of national concerns, so elimination of this problem should be welcome; but is it? Convenience is the main reason for the existence of transportation and most people will not be willing to abide by the following recommendations. The business areas should be entered only by mass communications media, for example monorails or street cars. Absolutely no cars should be allowed in the city limits and monorails could be installed on the super-highways also. Finally, the horsepower of all vehicles should be limited. In line with transportation is recreation. Motorboats, motorcycles, and snowmobiles are responsible for a good part of today's pollution problem. To solve this problem without eliminating recreation, one or two major resort areas on every usable lake wherein all vehicles of this nature would be allowed would be a sensible plan. Not only would this reduce pollution, but it would curb the complex of "keeping up with the Joneses," which is partly responsible for inflation and financial problems plaguing the greater percentage of Americans.

Learning to live with nature rather than against it may be the key to solving most pollution problems if population is controlled. At the present time, the land in which we live has been grossly misused. This is partially due to ignorance and also for the sake of convenience and the American dollar. Industry locates by rivers and lakes. After all, water seems to be the best way to rid the area of waste. But the assumption is false since the water can handle waste for only a set period before it becomes polluted. As a result we have what were once pure and healthy water bodies turning into stagnant sewers, poisonous cesspools blotching the land. The environment and natural cycles of life are completely terminated. This is because the companies were either oblivious to obvious results or wished to take the easiest and cheapest way of handling waste materials. Rather than build the factory up and away from natural water bodies and equip it with sufficient aeration and settling beds, they chose to exploit nature. Up until this time man has been innocent until proven guilty. But in the case of pollution, industry as well as man-made chemicals should be considered guilty until proven innocent and possibly they would consider the long-range results of their action.

Residential areas are also good examples of land misuse. Excellent areas which are prime for agricultural purposes are being forever lost as they are given up daily for highways and houses. California is a prime case in point. The best orange grove lands around Los Angeles have been subdivided and sold for housing. As a result, irrigation must be employed at great cost to force unsuited land into production. The irrigation when evaporated leaves salts upon the land and turns it into a desert. Once again, man is trying to force nature into his own mold and the results are destruction and hardship for all.

The chance to solve the problems of land misuse may have already passed us by. But if there is any chance for correction, steps must be taken immediately. The ecologist, engineer, sociologist, and economist must band together and consider all areas and factors necessary for man to live in harmony with nature. Then, with correct and unselfish programs advanced, the people as a whole must band together for complete accomplishment of the task. Even though the establishment of suitable areas for residence, industry, agriculture, and recreation may be expensive and inconvenient, it is necessary if man is to stop total destruction of his environment without which he cannot live.

Death control, birth control, burial, transportation, recreation, and land usage are all areas in which vast attitudinal changes must be made if the human race is to survive. Even though we have been told time and again that our attitudes must change, advertising has stopped much progress. Every manufacturer and distributor seeks to sell his product for the sake of money. The results upon nature are not considered. Household goods of every shape and form are sold on the basis of performance: clean clothes, whiter clothes, softer hands, fewer germs, instant stain removal. No consideration is given to the fact that many chemicals do not break down and recycle into nature when they reach the river or lake. The fabulous detergent with its phosphate and enzyme content is used to clean the dishes and "soften" hands. The same chemicals run down the drain and contribute to the environmental problem. Man has clean dishes, soft hands, and white clothes; but he also consumes his own waste products because many can never be handled by nature. He does this because he is fooled into thinking the results of the products, such as detergents, are necessary for a comfortable and satisfactory existence. Man must be informed of the results these products have upon his environment and he must then establish his priorities. He must choose between convenience or the protection of the world in which he lives. It is not advocated to remove all technology, but man must be able to distinguish between the good and the bad and he must act accordingly.

Not only is advertising leading man on the road to destruction, it is blotching up the beauty of the environment. Man can find few places where signs and gimmicks are not demanding attention and robbing nature of her beauty. Stopping this gross waste and deterioration is simple. One center for advertising located at the edge of the city limits would solve the problem. Within this structure businesses could display and advertise. Man entering the city could stop, decide where to go and what to buy and finally enjoy an area native with trees and flowers rather than billboards and neon lights.

The life man leads today is not his own. At the present time it belongs to the pollutants which will eventually destroy him. Air and water fit for consumption are fast decreasing. Atmospheric pollution is fast blocking the sun and either raising or lowering the temperature of the earth, creating a problem in either case. Concrete, steel and asphalt replace the luscious pallet of nature's ever-changing colors. Man, created to breathe clean air, drink and enjoy pure water, and enjoy the adventure of his natural surroundings, has changed his environment and finds he cannot adapt. He is preparing his own mass execution.

Is there no hope? Is it possible that man, a supposedly intelligent being, could become extinct after 1½ to 2 million years?* Unless man faces the fact that his pollution problems are a result of overpopulation and life-style attitudes, he will

*This is a far cry from the 150 million year reign of the dinosaurs, creatures with a small brain capacity and no understanding of the world about them.

be extinct far before the dinosaurs met their end. Realistically our problems boil down to common horse sense. For example, our present attitudes are leading man to what many scientists consider a path toward a lowering of our environmental quality and even to complete destruction. Whereas, others predict technology (whose unquestioned use got us into our trouble) will solve the problem and there is no need to be overly concerned. If a mistake is to be made in choosing a path of destruction or caution, which one would common horse sense tell you is the most logical? Therefore the so-called "practical" people who realize the problem but do nothing about it must be convinced to face reality. Only birth control practiced by all, employment of immediate pollution remedies, and life style changes can save man now. Can he face his situation intelligently? Can he forego convenience and archaic attitudes for the sake of his own survival? He must or we have witnessed the last of the most advanced species ever to inhabit the earth.

Bibliography

BSCS 1963. Student's Manual (Green Version): Laboratory and field investigation. Chicago, Ill.:Pand McNally

Clark, W.Г 1969. Environmental responsibility. *N. Dak.Quart.* 37: 10-18.

Ehrlich, Paul R. 1968. *The population bomb.* New York, N.Y.:Ballantine

The Limit: 500 Million

Richard A. Watson and Philip M. Smith

Man is biologically but an infant in earth, having appeared no more than one or two million years ago. Many other species have survived for many millions of years. Why not man? Will the earth's most distinctive living species fulfill its biological potential, or will mankind soon become extinct?

If mankind is to survive it must maintain a healthy breeding population in ecological balance with nature. Too few individuals would make changes of survival for the species precarious, and too many would lead to the destruction of the environment or to mass madness brought on by overcrowding. The problem is to determine the optimum population for mankind. This is a biological demand. But since man has also the need and desire to exercise intelligently his capacity for culture, the optimum is determined by a compromise of biological and cultural factors. This means that the ultimate battle between man and nature is within. Each individual finds that cultural regulations restrict the full expression of his biological urges. Far from being deplorable, however, this is the state of self-consciousness that makes us human. And it is consideration of the various ways of integrating biological with cultural demands that gives rise to morality. What is the morally right way for human beings to reproduce, to develop natural resources, and to distribute manufactured goods? In answering this complex question with art and technology, man creates civilization. And the cumulative philosophies of both East and West generally agree that civilization is humane when it provides ways for every individual to obtain the basic necessities of life, and that civilization promotes human dignity when it provides democratic means for each individual to participate in the direction of his own and mankind's destiny. In an ideal civilized state, free men would come to agreement as to the best balance between resources and population size. Having decided on an optimum, they would act voluntarily to maintain a balanced society. Presumably they would consider, beyond the necessities, the desirable amenities of modern life such as rapid communication and transportation, education, books and

From FOCUS/Midwest, No. 51. Reprinted with the permission of FOCUS/Midwest magazine, St. Louis, Mo., Copyright © 1970. Dr. Richard A. Watson is Assistant Professor of Philosophy at Washington University, St. Louis, Missouri. Dr. Philip M. Smith is Deputy Head of Polar Programs at the National Science Foundation in Washington, D.C.

television and high fidelity music, pleasant homes, superb stadiums, theatres, concert halls, libraries, and restaurants, as well as carefully managed outdoor preserves for picnicking, for the protection of wildlife as well as for hunting and fishing, and for wilderness adventure. These are not simply luxuries; they contribute to the psychological health of mankind. If people could maintain themselves and the natural environment in ecological balance to these ends, then it is possible that the human species could survive healthy and happy on earth for millions of years.

RESOURCES ARE BEING DEPLETED

How are we doing so far? Badly. Famine, pestilence, and war threaten. To the extent that decisions have been made, mankind is allowing population to grow to a size that cannot be maintained, so that the earth's natural resources are being fast depleted. Those who are favored in the consumer economy have moral anxieties about its wastefulness, while the majority of mankind existing on meager goods is righteously resentful at being left out. There are about 3.5 billion people living on earth today. United Nations statistics show that 1.5 billion are undernourished, and that of these, 500 million are starving. However, 2 billion, more than half the world's population, are properly nourished. But since most men want much more out of life than a proper diet, a United Nations study poses the following question: given the present world-wide industrial and agricultural capacity, technological development, and resource exploitation, how many people could be supported on earth today with the standard of living of the average American? The answer is just 500 million. This means that to make it possible for all individuals on earth to enjoy the standard of living of the average American today *with present production,* the world's population would have to be reduced to 1/7 of its present size, from 3.5 billion to 500 million people.

Obviously the most humane goal of mankind is the improvement of the human lot. Can life be made better for everyone without wholesale population reduction. Perhaps a population of 3.5 billion could be maintained on earth if all food and goods were equitably distributed. It is generally believed, however, that *with present production,* equitable distribution would leave everyone in a state of poverty and malnutrition, such that even the present rate of production could not be continued, let alone improved. So equitable distribution to a population of the present size is not the answer. However, that 2 billion people are properly nourished on earth today does suggest that more than 500 million could lead happy, productive lives. The way of life of the average American is obviously ostentatious and wasteful in many ways. By doing away with excesses, it might seem possible *with present production* to maintain as many as one billion people at a standard of living of high quality, if not on a level of today's average

American. But it is very doubtful that present production can be continued because of resource depletion. We believe, therefore, that the present drive to increase production will not help to provide a happy life for billions on earth. Let us examine why the present production rate, let alone an increased production schedule, cannot be maintained indefinitely.

The world's present technology is almost entirely based on extracting concentrated resources from the earth, processing them, and using them in such a way that the useful elements are dispersed so widely as waste products that we cannot—with our present technology—reuse them. For example, when we burn coal and oil, we obtain energy, but we disperse great concentrations of hydrocarbons into the atmosphere. This not only wastes resources that have more valuable uses than as fuel, but also adds to the atmosphere substances harmful to mankind and destructive of the natural environment. Similarly, from ore deposits concentrated over millions of years we refine metals that after use are in large part dispersed as nonrecoverable waste. The earth is finite, and so are its concentrated resources. Whether the present rate of extractive and dispersive exploitation is maintained, increased, or reduced, resources will be used up eventually, and the environment will be perhaps irretrieveably polluted by waste products long before the human species lives out its biological potential.

TECHNOLOGY IS A FAILURE

The only way to continue to use our present technology or to increase greatly its rate of production is to develop means to extract needed raw materials from bedrock and sea water. Along with farming the sea, bedrock and sea water refineries using atomic or solar energy are favorite topics of science fiction and Sunday supplement writers, politicians, and propagandists. The facts are, however, that these possibilities are largely dreams. Any regular reader of *Science,* published by the American Association for the Advancement of Science, knows that the research and development necessary for such technological advancements can hardly be said to have begun. A basic reason is that these problems are very difficult and expensive to solve, and their solutions even more difficult and expensive to apply on a large scale. Nevertheless, faith continues in the belief that science will save us, that easy and cheap and practical ways will be found to exploit new sources of energy, resources, and food. Thus it is claimed, we will be able to support the present world population and burgeoning billions to come.

Of course, there is an aesthetic objection to this scheme. Mankind may not want to see the mountains eaten and the seas swallowed simply to allow billions of men to subsist elbow to elbow on mountains of recycled garbage and waste. But besides this, the dream is fatally flawed. First, any advanced technology of extraction must be developed on the *present* technological base of production.

The present technology is already a failure; it continues to fall behind in its ability to support the increasing world population. Before conversion and expansion can be accomplished to support the coming 7 or 14 billion people on earth, the capacity would have to be developed to support the 3.5 billion who are here now. This is becoming increasingly difficult to do. Technological "breakthroughs" such as virile wheat are described even by optimists only as means of "buying time." There is not enough for everyone. The dreamers who say that science will save us with new inventions and techniques for production are like people who stand in a heavy rain on a pile of clay talking loftily of the brick castle they will build, while the water washes the ground from under their feet. Their only hope would be in beginning to build at once. As for mankind on earth, population is dangerously close to a size that will make it impossible to survive. Famine and pestilence resulting from overpopulation in this age of atomic, biological, and chemical war could lead to the extinction of the human species.

The second flaw in the dream relates to distribution. Without belief or assurance that the present rate or an increased rate of production could provide adequately for the 3.5 billion people on earth, production managers arrange self-protective and self-perpetuating institutions of exploitation, production, and trade designed to insure the unequal distribution of goods. This is not necessarily to be condemned. As a practical matter where there are limited goods, unequitable distribution is necessary to survival. It would, for example, be species suicide to distribute all available food equitably today. These are hard facts. But even harder is the fact that before the coming 7 or 14 billion people on earth could be supported, the present distribution system would have to be converted to one that supplies the 3.5 billion now on earth. But even if we had the resources and the techniques for exploiting them, we could not increase our production fast enough to keep up with increasing population. The total effect of dwindling resources plus production that decreases proportional to population size leads to increased protectionism of inequitable distribution systems.

BIRTHS MUST BE REDUCED

To avoid disaster — given individual needs and the present world-wide state of technology, production, and distribution — the present world population must somehow and soon be stabilized at a size much lower than now exists. Population size *will* be reduced somehow, because the present imbalance is too extreme to be maintained much longer. The alternative to hundreds of millions of people dying because of famine, pestilence, and war is for mankind to decide at once to reduce the human population on earth. This can be done most humanely by decreasing the birth rate below that of the natural death rate until a population size that can be supported on earth is reached. We believe that if everyone is to have a good and healthy life, population should be stabilized at about 500 million.

Given how urgent is the need for immediate population reduction, some observers worry about the initial imbalances among age groups that will result. The only answer is that mankind will just have to cope with such imbalances for a few generations in order to survive. Mankind is, in fact, attempting to cope with such an imbalance right now, one result of the population explosion being that the percentage of young people on earth is greater than it has ever been before.

Three immediate developments, then, are necessary to save mankind as a species on earth. First, some form of world government such as a universal United Nations must be established so that mankind can consider himself as a species and manage himself as a whole. A world-wide educational program is needed to convince the people of the world of the necessity of programs to bring population and resources into ecological balance, and this can be accomplished only with international cooperation.

Second, effective techniques of birth control must be developed that are so exquisite, effective, and easy to apply that their practical value alone will recommend them to most people. The only other possible way of averting ecological disaster is the morally undesirable imposition of birth control on involuntary subjects by a totalitarian government. But this would destroy the very civilized values that make the human species worth preserving.

One can hope that the power elite of the world — the leaders of government, business, industry, and the military — will see the need of planned world cooperation for the good of the human species, and thus form a world government. And then one can hope that these leaders will see the need for population reduction, and undertake it in the fairest and most humane way possible. We fear, however, that the need will not be acted on — whether seen earlier or not — until famine, pestilence, and war strike a large proportion of the world's people. If this occurs it is possible that one of the major national powers will then impose totalitarian control over the rest of the world. And if overpopulation is seen to be the cause of the world's ills, those who rule a world government by conquest will probably reduce the world's population efficiently, but not necessarily in the fairest and most humane way.

To avoid the nightmare of racial and religious genocide, the third thing necessary to make it possible for the human species to survive in a civilized state on earth for millions of years is the development of a new technology of equilibrium that recycles resources rather than dispersing them wastefully. It is most probable that a recycling technology on the present resource base would result in fewer consumer goods than are now produced, because of the conservation techniques that would have to be imposed. Thus, to return to the United Nations figure, the new technology could not support 500 million people indefinitely at a standard of living of today's average American, but it could probably support that number at a lesser standard that still provides a high quality life for each individual.   500 million people is a reasonable world population figure, even for a science fiction future when solar energy is harnessed and practical techniques are developed for extracting useful elements from bedrock and sea water. For as we said above, besides the mere goal of being in ecological balance with nature so that everyone can enjoy the basic necessities and amenities of life, mankind desires a viable development of human culture. It is clear that huge populations curtail many possibilities of individual and social freedom and development. In mass social institutions, uniform techniques of control are necessary. People cannot be treated as individuals, and they become dehumanized. A simple and rational solution to many of the problems of mass society, then, is to have population stabilized at such size that each person can be treated as an individual. The problems that could in part be solved this way are staggering. Let us list a few: parking, unemployment, juvenile delinquency, racketeering, anomie. Please do not misunderstand; we are not raving utopians. There would still be problems. Kids might kick bums to death in parks at night for thrills, and some people would continue to harm and to cheat others. All we are suggesting is that if there were radically fewer people, then there would be not only radically fewer problems, but also these problems would be of a size and order easier to contend with and to solve than are those deriving from present overpopulated mass society. With a smaller population, human needs and capacities could better be accounted for.

LIMITED GOODS IMPOSES IMMORALITY

Moral decisions would also be easier to make if there were fewer people on earth, living in ecological balance with nature. For the good of all mankind, it would then be apparent that large portions of the earth should be maintained in natural conditions, and that some presently worn-out lands should be restored to make them useful again. It would be possible then to plan cities, towns, and farms that best fit the natural environment. Morality today is sidelined in the name of survival. For example, something over 200 million people in the United States are said to use from 50 to 65 per cent of the resources being extracted in the world today. The Western World — North America, Europe, and Russia — about a billion people — is said to consume as much as 85 per cent of the total goods being produced. This means that the remaining 2.5 billion people on earth are being sustained on as little as 15 per cent of what is produced. Now sources for these figures vary. Local agricultural and craft produce is not adequately accounted for, and we have quoted extremes. Nevertheless, it can be argued that it is morally wrong for a minority of wealthy and powerful people to maintain this imbalance. Yet, the maintenance of this immoral situation is imposed because there are not goods enough in the world for equitable distribution. As earlier remarked, it would be species suicide if the world's goods were equitably distributed now; if there were only 500 million people in the world and goods enough for all, equitable distribution of at least the necessities of life would not only be seen as the moral thing to do, it would surely be done.

A stabilized population of 500 million in balance with nature would not result in a uniform, stagnant world. Equal numbers of Caucasoids, Mongoloids, and Negroids would first of all always provide variety. Then there is a great variety of creative work in the arts, sciences, and scholarship, and practical work in production, distribution, and maintenance of the environment. And there are many governmental tasks in the many ways of life that are compatible with one another and with nature. As for worries about human advancement and progress, it is to be remembered that there were about 500 million people on earth during the 17th century, and that century of genius is not noted for lack of accomplishment in either the East or the West. The feasibility of maintaining a high technological civilization on earth with only 500 million men cannot be challenged. There are also many moral and aesthetic reasons for stabilization at this figure. It is only the means of reaching this utopian state that are in question.

Many scientists agree that if mankind does not control resource use and population size, our species is due for disaster. Many people in power are also aware of these facts and predictions. Some of them will act. However, we must not be over-optimistic. Revolutionary measures should have been taken *yesterday* if these problems were to be solved in time to avoid all trouble. It may be utopian to suggest that the power elite will or can take them today. And tomorrow may be too late. Furthermore, history shows that there are always those willing to risk all to grasp wealth and power at the expense of the misery of others, the destruction of the environment, and future generations. So it may be too much to expect good people of great wealth and power to risk their positions for the good of mankind, even if they want to. *Nevertheless* we must work and hope for this course of action, for it is almost our only hope for a moral, humane, and noncatastrophic future for mankind. Otherwise, a terrible "final solution" to the population problem may be imposed.

In conclusion, we must remember that even in the best of circumstances, it will be extremely difficult to stabilize population and to develop the technology to establish mankind in ecologic balance with nature. Any realistic examination of man on earth today shows that he is headed for the cataclysmic disasters of famine, pestilence, and war. We can only hope that it is not too late to save the human species, even if there is a chance that it is too late to save our present civilization. But if strenuous efforts are not made now, mankind may be lucky if even as many as 500 people survive the 20th century.

The Physical Impact on Our Environment

Introduction

Every aspect of our relationship with nature is being questioned, and the activities of man are far-reaching and affecting all living things on earth.

Pollution is a normal phenomenon. However, it is the type, degree, rate, and amount of pollution resulting from our numbers and life style that is placing an abnormal burden on our life-supporting systems. When man disrupts natural cycles beyond their limits of tolerance, he provides the mechanisms to destroy the very system which supports him.

This section provides different academic approaches to environmental problems. Two articles are in the form of thought-provoking scenarios, while the others involve authors trying to understand their discipline's role as it relates to human activities and nature.

Eco-Catastrophe!

Paul Ehrlich

In the following scenario, Dr. Paul Ehrlich predicts what our world will be like in ten years if the present course of environmental destruction is allowed to continue. Dr. Ehrlich is a prominent ecologist, a professor of biology at Stanford University, and author of The Population Bomb (Ballantine).

(I)

The end of the ocean came late in the summer of 1979, and it came even more rapidly than the biologists had expected. There had been signs for more than a decade, commencing with the discovery in 1968 that DDT slows down photosynthesis in marine plant life. It was announced in a short paper in the technical journal, *Science,* but to ecologists it smacked of doomsday. They knew that all life in the sea depends on photosynthesis, the chemical process by which green plants bind the sun's energy and make it available to living things. And they knew that DDT and similar chlorinated hydrocarbons had polluted the entire surface of the earth, including the sea.

But that was only the first of many signs. There had been the final gasp of the whaling industry in 1973, and the end of the Peruvian anchovy fishery in 1975. Indeed, a score of other fisheries had disappeared quietly from over- exploitation and various eco-catastrophes by 1977. The term "eco-catastrophe" was coined by a California ecologist in 1969 to describe the most spectacular of man's attacks on the systems which sustain his life. He drew his inspiration from the Santa Barbara off-shore oil disaster of that year, and from the news which spread among naturalists that virtually all of the Golden State's seashore bird life was doomed because of chlorinated hydrocarbon interference with its reproduction. Eco-catastrophes in the sea became increasingly common in the early 1970s. Mysterious "blooms" of previously rare micro-organisms began to appear in offshore waters. Red tides—killer outbreaks of a minute single-celled plant—returned to the Florida Gulf coast and were sometimes accompanied by tides of other exotic hues.

Reprinted with the permission of Paul Ehrlich. Originally published in *Ramparts*, September, 1969. Dr. Paul Ehrlich is Professor of Biology at Stanford University, Stanford, California.

It was clear by 1975 that the entire ecology of the ocean was changing. A few types of phytoplankton were becoming resistant to chlorinated hydrocarbons and were gaining the upper hand. Changes in the phytoplankton community led inevitably to changes in the community of zooplankton, the tiny animals which eat the phytoplankton. These changes were passed on up the chains of life in the ocean to the herring, plaice, cod and tuna. As the diversity of life in the ocean diminished, its stability also decreased.

— Other changes had taken place by 1975. Most ocean fishes that returned to fresh water to breed, like the salmon, had become extinct, their breeding streams so dammed up and polluted that their powerful homing instinct only resulted in suicide. Many fishes and shellfishes that bred in restricted areas along the coasts followed them as onshore pollution escalated.

By 1977 the annual yield of fish from the sea was down to 30 million metric tons, less than one-half the per capita catch of a decade earlier. This helped malnutrition to escalate sharply in a world where an estimated 50 million people per year were already dying of starvation. The United Nations attempted to get all chlorinated hydrocarbon insecticides banned on a worldwide basis, but the move was defeated by the United States. This opposition was generated primarily by the American petrochemical industry, operating hand in glove with its subsidiary, the United States Department of Agriculture. Together they persuaded the government to oppose the U.N. move—which was not difficult since most Americans believed that Russia and China were more in need of fish products than was the United States. The United Nations also attempted to get fishing nations to adopt strict and enforced catch limits to preserve dwindling stocks. This move was blocked by Russia, who, with the most modern electronic equipment, was in the best position to glean what was left in the sea. It was, curiously, on the very day in 1977 when the Soviet Union announced its refusal that another ominous article appeared in *Science*. It announced that incident solar radiation had been so reduced by worldwide air pollution that serious effects on the world's vegetation could be expected.

(II)

Apparently it was a combination of ecosystem destabilization, sunlight reduction, and a rapid escalation in chlorinated hydrocarbon pollution from massive Thanodrin applications which triggered the ultimate catastrophe. Seventeen huge Soviet-financed Thanodrin plants were operating in underdeveloped countries by 1978. They had been part of a massive Russian "aid offensive" designed to fill the gap caused by the collapse of America's ballyhooed "Green Revolution."

It became apparent in the early '70s that the "Green Revolution" was more talk than substance. Distribution of high yield "miracle" grain seeds had caused temporary local spurts in agricultural production. Simultaneously, excellent weather had produced record harvests. The combination permitted bureaucrats, especially in the United States Department of Agriculture and the Agency for International Development (AID), to reverse their previous pessimism and indulge in an outburst of optimistic propaganda about staving off famine. They raved about the approaching transformation of agriculture in the underdeveloped countries (UDCs). The reason for the propaganda reversal was never made clear. Most historians agree that a combination of utter ignorance of ecology, a desire to justify past errors, and pressure from agro-industry (which was eager to sell pesticides, fertilizers, and farm machinery to the UDCs and agencies helping the UDCs) was behind the campaign. Whatever the motivation, the results were clear. Many concerned people, lacking the expertise to see through the Green Revolution drivel, relaxed. The population- food crisis was "solved."

But reality was not long in showing itself. Local famine persisted in northern India even after good weather brought an end to the ghastly Bihar famine of the mid-'60s. East Pakistan was next, followed by a resurgence of general famine in northern India. Other foci of famine rapidly developed in Indonesia, the Philippines, Malawi, the Congo, Egypt, Colombia, Ecuador, Honduras, the Dominican Republic, and Mexico.

Everywhere hard realities destroyed the illusion of the Green Revolution. Yields had dropped as the progressive farmers who had first accepted the new seeds found that their higher yields brought lower prices—effective demand (hunger plus cash) was not sufficient in poor countries to keep prices up. Less progressive farmers, observing this, refused to make the extra effort required to cultivate the "miracle" grains. Transport systems proved inadequate to bring the necessary fertilizer to the fields where the new and extremely fertilizer-sensitive grains were being grown. The same systems were also inadequate to move produce to markets. Fertilizer plants were not built fast enough, and most of the underdeveloped countries could not scrape together funds to purchase supplies, even on concessional terms. Finally, the inevitable happened, and pests began to reduce yields in even the most carefully cultivated fields. Among the first were the famous "miracle rats" which invaded Philippine "miracle rice" fields early in 1969. They were quickly followed by many insects and viruses, thriving on the relatively pest-susceptible new grains, encouraged by the vast and dense plantings, and rapidly acquiring resistance to the chemicals used against them. As chaos spread until even the most obtuse agriculturists and economists realized that the Green Revolution had turned brown, the Russians stepped in.

In retrospect it seems incredible that the Russians, with the American mistakes known to them, could launch an even more incompetent program of aid to the underdeveloped world. Indeed, in the early 1970s there were cynics in the United States who claimed that outdoing the stupidity of American foreign aid would be physically impossible. Those critics were, however, obviously unaware that the Russians had been busily destroying their own environment for many years. The virtual disappearance of sturgeon from Russian rivers caused a great shortage of caviar by 1970. A standard joke among Russian scientists at that time was that they had created an artificial caviar which was indistinguishable from the real thing—except by taste. At any rate the Soviet Union, observing with interest the progressive deterioration of relations between the UDCs and the United States, came up with a solution. It had recently developed what it claimed was the ideal insecticide, a highly lethal chlorinated hydrocarbon complexed with a special agent for penetrating the external skeletal armor of insects. Announcing that the new pesticide, called Thanodrin, would truly produce a Green Revolution, the Soviets entered into negotiations with various UDCs for the construction of massive Thanodrin factories. The USSR would bear all the costs; all it wanted in return were certain trade and military concessions.

It is interesting now, with the perspective of years, to examine in some detail the reasons why the UDCs welcomed the Thanodrin plan with such open arms. Government officials in these countries ignored the protests of their own scientists that Thanodrin would not solve the problems which plagued them. The governments now knew that the basic cause of their problems was overpopulation, and that these problems had been exacerbated by the dullness, daydreaming, and cupidity endemic to all governments. They knew that only population control and limited development aimed primarily at agriculture could have spared them the horrors they now faced. They knew it, but they were not about to admit it. How much easier it was simply to accuse the Americans of failing to give them proper help; how much simpler to accept the Russian panacea.

And then there was the general worsening of relations between the United States and the UDCs. Many things had contributed to this. The situation in America in the first half of the 1970s deserves our close scrutiny. Being more dependent on imports for raw materials than the Soviet Union, the United States had, in the early 1970s, adopted more and more heavy-handed policies in order to insure continuing supplies. Military adventures in Asia and Latin America had further lessened the international credibility of the United States as a great defender of freedom—an image which had begun to deteriorate rapidly during the pointless and fruitless Viet-Nam conflict. At home, acceptance of the carefully manufactured image lessened dramatically, as even the more romantic and chauvinistic citizens began to understand the role of the military and the industrial system in what John Kenneth Galbraith had aptly named "The New Industrial State."

At home in the USA the early '70s were traumatic times. Racial violence grew and the habitability of the cities diminished, as nothing substantial was done to ameliorate either racial inequities or urban blight. Welfare rolls grew as automation and general technological progress forced more and more people into the category of "unemployable." Simultaneously a taxpayers' revolt occurred. Although there was not enough money to build the schools, roads, water systems, sewage systems, jails, hospitals, urban transit lines, and all the other amenities needed to support a burgeoning population, Americans refused to tax themselves more heavily. Starting in Youngstown, Ohio in 1969 and followed closely by Richmond, California, community after community was forced to close its schools or curtail educational operations for lack of funds. Water supplies, already marginal in quality and quantity in many places by 1970, deteriorated quickly. Water rationing occurred in 1723 municipalities in the summer of 1974, and hepatitis and epidemic dysentery rates climbed about 500 per cent between 1970-1974.

(III)

Air pollution continued to be the most obvious manifestation of environmental deterioration. It was, by 1972, quite literally in the eyes of all Americans. The year 1973 saw not only the New York and Los Angeles smog disasters, but also the publication of the Surgeon General's massive report on air pollution and health. The public had been partially prepared for the worst by the publicity given to the U.N. pollution conference held in 1972. Deaths in the late '60s caused by smog were well known to scientists, but the public had ignored them because they mostly involved the early demise of the old and sick rather than people dropping dead on the freeways. But suddenly our citizens were faced with nearly 200,000 corpses and massive documentation that they could be the next to die from respiratory disease. They were not ready for that scale of disaster. After all, the U.N. conference had not predicted that accumulated air pollution would make the planet uninhabitable until almost 1990. The population was terrorized as TV screens became filled with scenes of horror from the disaster areas. Especially vivid was NBC's coverage of hundreds of unattended people choking out their lives outside of New York's hospitals. Terms like nitrogen oxide, acute bronchitis and cardiac arrest began to have real meaning for most Americans.

The ultimate horror was the announcement that chlorinated hydrocarbons were now a major constituent of air pollution in all American cities. Autopsies of smog disaster victims revealed an average chlorinated hydrocarbon load in fatty tissue equivalent to 26 parts per million of DDT. In October, 1973, the Department of Health, Education and Welfare announced studies which showed unequivocally that increasing death rates from hypertension, cirrhosis of the liver, liver cancer and a series of other diseases had resulted from the chlorinated hydrocarbon load. They estimated that Americans born since 1946 (when DDT usage began) now had a life expectancy of only 49 years, and predicted that if current patterns continued, this expectancy would reach 42 years by 1980, when it might level out. Plunging insurance stocks triggered a stock market panic. The president of Velsicol, Inc., a major pesticide producer, went on television to "publicly eat a teaspoonful of DDT" (it was really powdered milk) and announce that HEW had been infiltrated by Communists. Other giants of the petrochemical industry, attempting to dispute the indisputable evidence, launched a massive pressure campaign on Congress to force HEW to "get out of agriculture's business." They were aided by the agro-chemical journals, which had decades of experience in misleading the public about the benefits and dangers of pesticides. But by now the public realized that it had been duped. The Nobel Prize for medicine and physiology was given to Drs. J. L. Radomski and W. B. Deichmann, who in the late 1960s had pioneered in the documentation of the long-term lethal effects of chlorinated hydrocarbons. A Presidential Commission with unimpeachable credentials directly accused the agro-chemical complex of "condemning many millions of Americans to an early death." The year 1973 was the year in which Americans finally came to understand the direct threat to their existence posed by environmental deterioration.

And 1973 was also the year in which most people finally comprehended the indirect threat. Even the president of Union Oil Company and several other industrialists publicly stated their concern over the reduction of bird populations which had resulted from pollution by DDT and other chlorinated hydrocarbons. Insect populations boomed because they were resistant to most pesticides and had been freed, by the incompetent use of those pesticides, from most of their natural enemies. Rodents swarmed over crops, multiplying rapidly in the absence of predatory birds. The effect of pests on the wheat crop was especially disastrous in the summer of 1973, since that was also the year of the great drought. Most of us can remember the shock which greeted the announcement by atmospheric physicists that the shift of the jet stream which had caused the drought was probably permanent. It signalled the birth of the Midwestern desert. Man's air-polluting activities had by then caused gross changes in climatic patterns. The news, of course, played hell with commodity and stock markets. Food prices skyrocketed, as savings were poured into hoarded canned goods. Official assurances that food supplies would remain ample fell on deaf ears, and even the government showed signs of nervousness when California migrant field workers went out on strike again in protest against the continued use of pesticides by growers. The strike burgeoned into farm burning and riots. The workers, calling themselves "The Walking Dead," demanded immediate compensation for their shortened lives, and crash research programs to attempt to lengthen them.

It was in the same speech in which President Edward Kennedy, after much delay, finally declared a national emergency and called out the National Guard to harvest California's crops, that the first mention of population control was made. Kennedy pointed out that the United States would no longer be able to offer any food aid to other nations and was likely to suffer food shortages herself. He suggested that, in view of the manifest failure of the Green Revolution, the only hope of the UDCs lay in population control. His statement, you will recall, created an uproar in the underdeveloped countries. Newspaper editorials accused the United States of wishing to prevent small countries from becoming large nations and thus threatening American hegemony. Politicians asserted that President Kennedy was a "creature of the giant drug combine" that wished to shove its pills down every woman's throat.

Among Americans, religious opposition to population control was very slight. Industry in general also backed the idea. Increasing poverty in the UDCs was both destroying markets and threatening supplies of raw materials. The seriousness of the raw material situation had been brought home during the Congressional Hard Resources hearings in 1971. The exposure of the ignorance of the cornucopian economists had been quite a spectacle—a spectacle brought into virtually every American's home in living color. Few would forget the distinguished geologist from the University of California who suggested that economists be legally required to learn at least the elementary facts of geology. Fewer still would forget that an equally distinguished Harvard economist added that they might be required to learn some economics, too. The overall message was clear: America's resource situation was bad and bound to get worse. The hearings had led to a bill requiring the Departments of State, Interior, and Commerce to set up a joint resource procurement council with the express purpose of "insuring that proper consideration of American resource needs be an integral part of American foreign policy."

Suddenly the United States discovered that it had a national consensus: population control was the only possible salvation of the underdeveloped world. But that same consensus led to heated debate. How could the UDCs be persuaded to limit their populations, and should not the United States lead the way by limiting its own? Members of the intellectual community wanted America to set an example. They pointed out that the United States was in the midst of a new baby boom: her birth rate, well over 20 per thousand per year, and her growth rate of over one per cent per annum were among the very highest of the developed countries. They detailed the deterioration of the American physical and psychic environments, the growing health threats, the impending food shortages, and the insufficiency of funds for desperately needed public works. They contended that the nation was clearly unable or unwilling to properly care for the people it already had. What possible reason could there be, they queried, for adding any more? Besides, who would listen to requests by the United States for population control when that nation did not control her own profligate reproduction?

Those who opposed population controls for the U.S. were equally vociferous.

The military-industrial complex, with its all-too-human mixture of ignorance and avarice, still saw strength and prosperity in numbers. Baby food magnates, already worried by the growing nitrate pollution of their products, saw their market disappearing. Steel manufacturers saw a decrease in aggregate demand and slippage for that holy of holies, the Gross National Product. And military men saw, in the growing population-food-environment crisis, a serious threat to their carefully nurtured Cold War. In the end, of course, economic arguments held sway, and the "inalienable right of every American couple to determine the size of its family," a freedom invented for the occasion in the early '70s, was not compromised.

The population control bill, which was passed by Congress early in 1974, was quite a document, nevertheless. On the domestic front, it authorized an increase from 100 to 150 million dollars in funds for "family planning" activities. This was made possible by a general feeling in the country that the growing army on welfare needed family planning. But the gist of the bill was a series of measures designed to impress the need for population control on the UDCs. All American aid to countries with overpopulation problems was required by law to consist in part of population control assistance. In order to receive any assistance each nation was required not only to accept the population control aid, but also to match it according to a complex formula. "Overpopulation" itself was defined by a formula based on U.N. statistics, and the UDCs were required not only to accept aid, but also to show progress in reducing birth rates. Every five years the status of the aid program for each nation was to be reevaluated.

The reaction to the announcement of this program dwarfed the response to President Kennedy's speech. A coalition of UDCs attempted to get the U.N. General Assembly to condemn the United States as a "genetic aggressor." Most damaging of all to the American cause was the famous "25 Indians and a dog" speech by Mr. Shankarnarayan, Indian Ambassador to the U.N. Shankarnarayan pointed out that for several decades the United States, with less than 6 per cent of the people of the world had consumed roughly 50 per cent of the raw materials used every year. He described vividly America's contribution to worldwide environmental deterioration, and he scathingly denounced the miserly record of United States foreign aid as "unworthy of a fourth-rate power, let alone the most powerful nation on earth."

It was the climax of his speech, however, which most historians claim once and for all destroyed the image of the United States. Shankarnarayan informed the assembly that the average American family dog was fed more animal protein per week than the average Indian got in a month. "How do you justify taking fish from protein-starved Peruvians and feeding them to your animals?" he asked. "I contend," he concluded, "that the birth of an American baby is a greater disaster for the world than that of 25 Indian babies." When the applause had died away, Mr. Sorensen, the American representative, made a speech which said essentially that "other countries look after their own self-interest, too." When the vote came, the United States was condemned.

(IV)

This condemnation set the tone of U.S.-UDC relations at the time the Russian Thanodrin proposal was made. The proposal seemed to offer the masses in the UDCs an opportunity to save themselves and humiliate the United States at the same time; and in human affairs, as we all know, biological realities could never interfere with such an opportunity. The scientists were silenced, the politicians said yes, the Thanodrin plants were built, and the results were what any beginning ecology student could have predicted. At first Thanodrin seemed to offer excellent control of many pests. True, there was a rash of human fatalities from improper use of the lethal chemical, but, as Russian technical advisors were prone to note, these were more than compensated for by increased yields. Thanodrin use skyrocketed throughout the underdeveloped world. The Mikoyan design group developed a dependable, cheap agricultural aircraft which the Soviets donated to the effort in large numbers. MIG sprayers became even more common in UDCs than MIG interceptors.

Then the troubles began. Insect strains with cuticles resistant to Thanodrin penetration began to appear. And as streams, rivers, fish culture ponds, and onshore waters became rich in Thanodrin, more fisheries began to disappear. Bird populations were decimated. The sequence of events was standard for broadcast use of a synthetic pesticide: great success at first, followed by removal of natural enemies and development of resistance by the pest. Populations of crop-eating insects in areas treated with Thanodrin made steady comebacks and soon became more abundant than ever. Yields plunged, while farmers in their desperation increased the Thanodrin dose and shortened the time between treatments. Death from Thanodrin poisoning became common. The first violent incident occurred in the Canete Valley of Peru, where farmers had suffered a similar chlorinated hydrocarbon disaster in the mid-'50s. A Russian advisor serving as an agricultural pilot was assaulted and killed by a mob of enraged farmers in January, 1978. Trouble spread rapidly during 1978, especially after the word got out that two years earlier Russia herself had banned the use of Thanodrin at home because of its serious effects on ecological systems. Suddenly Russia, and not the United States, was the *bete noir* of the UDCs. "Thanodrin parties" became epidemic, with farmers, in their ignorance, dumping carloads of Thanodrin concentrate into the sea. Russian advisors fled, and four of the Thanodrin plants were leveled to the ground. Destruction of the plants in Rio and Calcutta led to hundreds of thousands of gallons of Thanodrin concentrate being dumped directly into the sea.

Mr. Shankarnarayan again rose to address the U.N., but this time it was Mr. Potemkin, representative of the Soviet Union, who was on the hot seat. Mr. Potemkin heard his nation described as the greatest mass killer of all time as Shankarnarayan predicted at least 30 million deaths from crop failures due to overdependence on Thanodrin. Russia was accused of "chemical aggression," and the General Assembly, after a weak reply by Potemkin, passed a vote of censure.

It was in January, 1979, that huge blooms of a previously unknown variety of diatom were reported off the coast of Peru. The blooms were accompanied by a massive die-off of sea life and of the pathetic remainder of the birds which had once feasted on the anchovies of the area. Almost immediately another huge bloom was reported in the Indian ocean, centering around the Seychelles, and then a third in the South Atlantic off the African coast. Both of these were accompanied by spectacular die-offs of marine animals. Even more ominous were growing reports of fish and bird kills at oceanic points where there were no spectacular blooms. Biologists were soon able to explain the phenomena: the diatom had evolved an enzyme which broke down Thanodrin; that enzyme also produced a breakdown product which interfered with the transmission of nerve impulses, and was therefore lethal to animals. Unfortunately, the biologists could suggest no way of repressing the poisonous diatom bloom in time. By September, 1979, all important animal life in the sea was extinct. Large areas of coastline had to be evacuated, as windrows of dead fish created a monumental stench.

But stench was the least of man's problems. Japan and China were faced with almost instant starvation from a total loss of the seafood on which they were so dependent. Both blamed Russia for their situation and demanded immediate mass shipments of food. Russia had none to send. On October 13, Chinese armies attacked Russia on a broad front . . . . .

(V)

A pretty grim scenario. Unfortunately, we're a long way into it already. Everything mentioned as happening before 1970 has actually occurred; much of the rest is based on projections of trends already appearing. Evidence that pesticides have long-term lethal effects on human beings has started to accumulate, and recently Robert Finch, Secretary of the Department of Health, Education and Welfare expressed his extreme apprehension about the pesticide situation. Simultaneously the petrochemical industry continues its unconscionable poison-peddling. For instance, Shell Chemical has been carrying on a high-pressure campaign to sell the insecticide Azodrin to farmers as a killer of cotton pests. They continue their program even though they know that Azodrin is not only ineffective, but often *increases* the pest density. They've covered themselves nicely in an advertisement which states, "Even if an overpowering migration (sic) develops, the flexibility of Azodrin lets you regain control fast. Just increase the dosage according to label recommendations." It's a great game—get people to apply the poison and kill the natural enemies of the pests. Then blame the increased pests on "migration" and sell even more pesticide.

Right now fisheries are being wiped out by over-exploitation, made easy by modern electronic equipment. The companies producing the equipment know this. They even boast in advertising that only their equipment will keep fishermen in business until the final kill. Profits must obviously be maximized in the short run. Indeed, Western society is in the proces of completing the rape and murder of the planet for economic gain. And, sadly, most of the rest of the world is eager for the opportunity to emulate our behavior. But the underdeveloped peoples will be denied that opportunity—the days of plunder are drawing inexorably to a close.

Most of the people who are going to die in the greatest cataclysm in the history of man have already been born. More than three and a half billion people already populate our moribund globe, and about half of them are hungry. Some 10 to 20 million will starve to death *this year*. In spite of this, the population of the earth will increase by 70 million souls in 1969. For mankind has artificially lowered the death rate of the human population, while in general birth rates have remained high. With the input side of the population system in high gear and the output side slowed down, our fragile planet has filled with people at an incredible rate. It took several million years for the population to reach a total of two billion people in 1930, while a *second two billion will have been added by 1975!* By that time some experts feel that food shortages will have escalated the present level of world hunger and starvation into famines of unbelievable proportions. Other experts, more optimistic, think the ultimate food-population collision will not occur until the decade of the 1980s. Of course more massive famine may be avoided if other events cause a prior rise in the human death rate.

Both worldwide plague and thermonuclear war are made more probable as population growth continues. These, along with famine, make up the trio of potential "death rate solutions" to the population problem—solutions in which the birth rate-death rate imbalance is redressed by a rise in the death rate rather than by a lowering of the birth rate. Make no mistake about it, *the imbalance will be redressed*. The shape of the population growth curve is one familiar to the biologist. It is the outbreak part of an outbreak-crash sequence. A population grows rapidly in the presence of abundant resources, finally runs out of food or some other necessity, and crashes to a low level or extinction. Man is not only running out of food, he is also destroying the life support systems of the Spaceship Earth. The situation was recently summarized very succinctly: "It is the top of the ninth inning. Man, always a threat at the plate, has been hitting Nature hard. It is important to remember, however, that NATURE BATS LAST."

The Destruction of North Dakota

Robert L. Burgess

The destruction, devastation, and deterioration had been going on for a long time, but the death, the actual, final, and uncompromising death still came sooner than expected. Most scientists had figured that the portion of North America that would survive the longest lay in the northern plains, including most of North Dakota, eastern Montana, and the Prairie Provinces, hence when North Dakota ceased to function in the late summer of 1997, much of the remaining world population was deprived of a large share of its existence. New York had died in 1984, the first of the metropolitan areas to go. Emigration had already cut the city's numbers to six million, but a series of tragic smog days in June and July had taken two-thirds of the remainder, and two million survivors flowed west and north, abandoning the great city to the rats and the roaches.

New York City started it, but southern California and New Jersey went in 1987, Pennsylvania, Illinois, and Ohio in 1988, Texas, Michigan, Wisconsin, and the Gulf States in 1989, and the remainder of the Atlantic seaboard in 1991. The remnant population was crowded, of course, into the mid-continent and mountain states and the loss of North Dakota was a crushing blow.

At the time of Lewis and Clark, the area that was to become North Dakota was a magnificent land of beauty, productivity, and equilibrium. The first pioneers in the 1870s found game plentiful and the prairie soil deep and rich. Crops were good, water abundant, and the people prospered. With statehood and the advent of bonanza farming, the young giant was on its way to becoming a self-sufficient member of the community of states.

But the ominous signs were already evident to those who took the time to read them. In 1882, 1887, and 1897, eastern North Dakota was swept by raging floods. The Sheyenne and the Red now flowed gray with sediment, where 20 years before the water had run clear and cold. And in the early 1900s, sawmills were established near Lisbon and in the Turtle Mountains.

Originally presented in a Symposium "Environmental Crisis: Focus North Dakota," sponsored by the Action Committee for Environmental Education, Bismarck, North Dakota, February, 1970. Dr. Robert L. Burgess is Associate Professor of Botany at North Dakota State University, Fargo, North Dakota, and Deputy Director of the Eastern Deciduous Forest Biome Project, International Biological Program, Oak Ridge National Laboratory, Oak Ridge, Tennessee.

By 1910 virtually all of the state had been settled and the unending cycle of plow, plant, harvest, and plow was the order of the day in the east while white faces, thousands upon thousands, had supplanted the bison in the rich and rolling grasslands to the west of the wide Missouri. As the deep soils of the eastern valleys were no match for the moldboard plow and hybrid durum, so the fragile, unglaciated western hills were no match for cattle and sheep, but in both regions the real menace was modern man's constant and insidious quest for the dollar. Nature could not be spared if another buck could be made. Plow closer to the fenceline and through the shallow pothole! Another hundred head can't hurt the range! And then came the thirties.

The dependable rains were no longer dependable. Topsoil left Dakota bound for Cleveland and Baltimore. The Red dried to a trickle and in thousands of potholes, the cattails shriveled and died. And people suffered, and the winds still blew, and people migrated and the rains never came. But the New Deal did, and alphabetical conservation was abroad in the land, NRA, FHA, WPA, CCC, and SCS—all contributed, and in time the rains returned and the rivers flowed, crops grew and cattle fattened, but a billion tons of North Dakota fertility had gone eastward, and an empathy for the land had left the soul of the people. No longer was nature something to endure, to enjoy, to husband and cherish, but something to be whipped, beaten, and subdued, never again to challenge the supremacy of man.

In the late 1930s and early 1940s, a series of shelterbelt plantings was established, particularly in the eastern part of North Dakota. These increased landscape diversity, softened the horizon, AND kept valuable land out of crop production. When some trees began to die in 1964, and deterioration, disease, and decay were evident in many belts, some were bulldozed and burned, their owners oblivious to the ecological lessons of the 1930s.

In 1880, there were 3,790 farms in North Dakota, totaling 2.3 raging floods. The Sheyenne and the Red now flowed gray with sediment, where 20 declined to 43,000 in 1969 and 31,000 in 1976. But since 1940, when the last major railroad land sale was consummated, almost 43 million acres, 96 per cent of the state, was in farms, and 26 million acres were under increasingly intensive crop production.

Machinery got bigger—it had to. By 1966, 6- and 7-bottom plows were common, and at the Winter Show in Valley City in March of 1974, Melroe unveiled its 15-bottom gang plow, capable of a section a day. Giant tractors stalked like prehistoric dinosaurs across the land, furrowing, dragging, planting, while the dust clouds towered higher and higher, eventually to soil the washing in Fargo and Grand Forks, create magnificent sunsets in Minneapolis, and filter imperceptibly into the china cabinets of Milwaukee and Indianapolis. And a little more prairie fertility went with it.

Fertilizer application had begun slowly, during and shortly after World War

II. In 1951 only 17,000 tons were used, mostly on small grains. Quantities climbed steadily, as natural fertility waned. One hundred thousand tons in 1960, 200,000 in 1965, 300,000 in 1969, and a half million by 1975. Wheat yields crept past 20 bushels to the acre, 25, 30, 35 bushels in 1973. Barley was up over 50 bushels in the Red River Valley, and the politicians and the Greater North Dakota Association had a field day extolling the virtues of the state. All restrictions on crop acreages had been lifted the year before, and 31 million acres were plowed in 1973. There appeared to be no limit to what North Dakota's love affair with agriculture could do.

In addition to the fertilizers, the state was also supporting the pesticide industry on a grand scale. Again, after a slow start, farmers discovered that wholesale application of pesticides increased yields still more. Back in 1964, 84 million pounds of herbicides were used in the state, 60 per cent of it on small grains. Even then, some were prone to spray on windy days, and the effects of the drift began to show in the shelterbelts. In that same year, we used 156 million pounds of insecticide, 92 per cent of it on crops, and about 76 per cent of it was hard, nonbiodegradable, mostly DDT. Of course, DDT was banned in 1970, but not before three-quarters of a million tons of residue lay in the soil, coursed through the ecosystem, and invisibly entered the fat and the liver of the people. As late as 1969, in the face of overwhelming evidence of its deleterious effects, the city of Fargo had used DDT for mosquito control, solely because it was cheaper. Three members in one Fargo family died, and the autopsy confirmed accumulated DDT poisoning. Their back yard abutted the large county drain on the southwest edge of the city. And that drain had been for years a favorite target for the mosquito abatement program. Also in 1964, 170 million pounds of fungicide were used, 98 per cent on crops, 47 million pounds of miscellaneous biocides, 85 per cent on cropland, and, as a vehicle, 313 million pounds of petroleum products. By 1972, the total of all biocides being used on the land was in excess of 800,000 tons. In 1970, scientists from both universities documented pesticide pollution in all of the rivers and many of the lakes in the state, but oblivious to the ominous warnings from all over the world, chemical agriculture was still being fostered by the Extension Service, and the state Commissioner of Agriculture and USDA.

In the western part of the state, the livestock industry scarcely noted the general decline in production. The state had hit a high of 2.4 million cattle in 1964, dropping to 2 million head in 1969. But fewer ranchers grazing larger holdings masked the drop in overall production. Sheep dropped by almost 40 per cent from 1965 to 1970. Hogs, while never in large numbers in North Dakota, followed suit. Chicken and turkey production also suffered, but more from intensive competition by other states than from a deterioration of the land resource. The animals also were subject to the chemical panacea, and a million cattle and a quarter of a million sheep and hogs were sprayed in 1964, and the total rising to almost 99 per cent of all animals by 1972.

But the western ranges were losing their battles with the ruminant stomach. Established grazing rotations were gradually eroded as ranchers moved the cattle into pastures 4 days early, then a week, then 2. The vegetation never really had a chance, and when the drought of 1976-77 came, with less than 5 inches of rain at Dickinson, 6 at Bowman and Williston, 6½ at Bismarck, the range stopped working. Feed lots in the eastern part of the state took up some of the slack, but thousands of cattle died, and many were shipped to market little more than skin and bones.

Primeval North Dakota was a beautiful place, not overly diversified, but blessed with magnificent prairies, fine forests, and an abundance of wetlands. The prairies went first, and where giant blue-stem and Indian grass had, each fall, waved their tasselled heads as the last of the plovers set wing for the Argentine, mile after mile of black furrow now faced the winter winds. In a few secluded spots, one or two railroad rights-of-way, a back corner in an old cemetery, and an occasional forty that had somehow escaped the plow, the grasses still grew and the prairie flowers still sprinkled their blessings of color on all who cared to look, but the lands in the Red River Valley, some of the most fertile agricultural soil the world had ever seen, had parted forever with the very vegetation that had given them birth. Certainly in the '50s the soil bank law had been a step in the right direction, but a prairie, hundreds of years in the making, does not regenerate and recreate four feet of topsoil in a decade, just because Washington wishes it. So when the soil bank program expired, the last chance for the native ecosystem went with it.

Farther west, in the mixed grasslands of the Missouri Coteau and the unglaciated regions beyond, many unplowed acres still remained in the mid-1960s. But all of these had been heavily grazed, some of them fertilized, and of all things, many seeded to introduce grasses whose yield was high but whose longevity in native pasture was a stark unknown.

The wetlands were next. With dragline, draintile, ditch and culvert, and a liberal serving of federal money, a large portion of the mid-American duck factory went express to the Gulf of Mexico and Hudson Bay. A million and a half acres of beauty, serenity, stability, and productivity were being compromised at the rate of 20,000 acres a year. The giant tractors were too large to go around potholes, the dollar too precious to ignore, so the wetlands had to go. Drain, burn, fill, level, plow, plant, harvest—the cycle was dizzying. The Department of Interior and the State Game and Fish Department tried valiantly to preserve wildlife habitat through their acquisition and easement programs— while the Department of Agriculture continued to offer cost-sharing for "conservation practices." The carrot was mightier than the prod, and the Starkweather sellout of late 1969 marked the beginning of the end. The Starkweather Watershed project near Devils Lake had been a battle for 20 years. The Bureau of Sport Fisheries and Wildlife believed that the public had a stake in wetland preservation if public funds were to assist private owners with wetland drainage. But the landowners, economically and politically more powerful than either the Bureau or the general public, succeeded in forcing approval of a plan that prostituted the intent, if not the letter of the law. Of 18,000 original acres of wetland, less than 10,000 remained by the fall of 1970. In the state forty thousand acres were drained in 1971, 43,000 in '72, 48,000 in '73, until the land lay raped and mutilated by men and machine and the monotony of the North Dakota landscape was rivaled only by the ecological stupidity of the people. The lesson that an environment that harbors ducks is also one that nurtures people was never really learned.

North Dakota was a prairie state, but it had its forests. Rich bottomland forests bordered the Red, Sheyenne, Souris and Missouri; oak, ash, elm and aspen clothed the Turtle Mountains and the Pembina Hills; and in the west, watersheds were verdant with cedar and pine. Half a million acres in 1920, a fifth of that gone by 1970 and most of the remainder jeopardized. Dams on the Missouri at Garrison and Oahe had taken most of the great valley, vast acreages in the Pembina gorge were bulldozed for tax relief, and, incredibly, in 1969, the United Methodist Church in the Dakotas was buying bulldozers so that Indians in the Turtle Mountains could clear more land! In a state where less than 1 per cent of the land was forested, there was a "need" to clear more land. Proposed dams on the Sheyenne, Goose, and Turtle rivers threatened further loss of native forest, but again, politicians were oblivious to the ecological consequences of their acts.

In 1969, North Dakota had only 52,800 acres of public park, and 48,000 of these were in the western Badlands, at Theodore Roosevelt National Memorial Park. A series of postage stamp state parks comprised the remaining 4,700 acres. The Bureau of Outdoor Recreation was recommending a minimum of 45 acres of state park per 1,000 people, so North Dakota was considerably short, but the really feasible park locations, the Turtle Mountains and Pembina Hills, plus the lower Sheyenne Valley, were being destroyed before park acquisition had a chance.

Oil had been discovered at Tioga in 1951, and by 1965 2,000 wells were producing 26 million barrels of oil and almost 40 billion cubic feet of natural gas. Meanwhile, 40 mines produced 2.8 million tons of lignite in 1965, up to 3.9 million tons in 1967, and 5.5 million tons by 1973, all coming from the enormous 350 billion ton deposit in western North Dakota. Much of the lignite was strip mined, and despite legislation that required restoration, the mining landscape continued to be one of desolation.

These resources did, however, attract industry to the state. Lockheed Aircraft established in Minot in 1971, Holly Sugar north of Fargo in 1972, and by the late 1970s a flood of industry into the northern plains was evident. The Fargo Area Industrial Development Corporation, formed in 1970, had been amazingly successful in attracting both heavy and light industry. There were two major reasons for the attraction. In spite of the environmental concern expressed by the President, evident in the news media, and culminating in a nationwide Environmental Teach-In in April of 1970, North Dakota successfully passed the most lax air and water pollution regulations of any of the fifty states. When U. S. Steel Corporation left Duluth after a battle with the Minnesota Pollution Control Agency, North Dakota was not inclined to replicate the stringent but effective laws of its eastern sister. As a result, a tractor manufacturer moved in in 1972, a steel mill and an automobile assembly plant in 1973, two electronics firms, a long overdue macaroni factory, three breweries and a distillery, along with a second aircraft plant in 1974. And of course, people came, too.

Since the 1930s, North Dakota had undergone a rather steady population decline, but as environmental conditions in the eastern states deteriorated, more and more people were attracted to the state that, in 1968, the governor had proclaimed to be "cleaner and greener in the summer, and whiter and brighter in the winter." Population reached 700,000 by 1973, a million in 1975, and in spite of the drought, 1.5 million by 1979. Fargo was a thriving, if smogbound, community of 300,000, Grand Forks, Bismarck, and Minot all over 100,000, and even Dickinson and Jamestown were pushing 85,000 people.

By 1979, it was evident that the state could not keep up. Sewage facilities at all the major cities were grossly inadequate, and in spite of their new technologies to handle garbage, the urban centers were drowning in their own refuse. Clean water was a thing of the past, and both the Red and the Missouri were posted all along their length with signs warning against contact with the water. Bacterial counts were running 500,000 per cubic centimeter or better, and the chemical load approached 2500 parts per million. The Souris, James, and Sheyenne were not much better off.

With the advent of irrigation from the Garrison Diversion Project, increasing quantities of chemical laden water flowed down the Sheyenne. By 1981, Lake Ashtabula was a putrid mess, and by 1985 had parted with its last fish. Two years earlier, 47 people in Valley City had died from botulism, brought in, it was suspected, by an errant duck who happened to die in the lake. Waterfowl were by this time a rare sight around the reservoir, but with the closing of all hunting seasons in 1981, no one paid much attention. In the 1960s, three million ducks and geese were bred and raised in North Dakota, but now it was a rare flock that clove the murky skies of the prairie flyway. It had been 2 years now since a Canada goose had been seen in the state, and 4 since the last report of a whooping crane. The latter were presumed extinct, due in part to the filling and subdividing of about 60 per cent of their winter refuge at Aransas, Texas, providing housing for people fleeing the Atlantic seaboard.

Other types of wildlife were also dwindling. The deer population, cut in half by the loss of the lower Sheyenne Valley in 1975, was down to under 10,000 by

1980, most of these in the Badlands and the Turtle Mountains. The last cougar report had been way back in 1968, and the reestablished bison herd, 300 strong in 1979, had been slaughtered for food in 1977, the second year of the drought.

Robins had not been seen in Fargo or Grand Forks since 1980, and the Bismarck Audubon Club reported only six species of birds in the Christmas count of 1981. Hawks and owls had almost vanished (DDT accumulation again), resulting in population explosions of field mice, and when all pets were banned in 1984, Grand Forks was immediately plagued with house rats. The obvious solution to both eruptions was more poison and 1149, the successor to the famous 1080 predator and rodent control was heavily used. By the end of the year, 17 children and 6 adults had died from accidental contact with the lethal chemical, while there was only slight evidence of diminished rodent numbers.

In 1974, despite heroic efforts by concerned citizens and ignoring the pleas of 100,000 petitioners, the Kindred Dam was built. Almost immediately, all discussion of wildlife and recreational benefits was dropped by the Corps of Engineers. From the day the gates were closed, the reservoir began to accumulate the excess polluted water that had been temporarily stored in Ashtabula, and when the lake, filled with dirty water and possessing no semblance of a tree-studded shoreline, failed to attract users, the Corps went to great lengths to search out, confiscate, and destroy the numbered copies of the Interim Survey Report of 1968 that had assured the politicians of 350,000 man/days of recreational use on the reservoir by 1980. By 1976, the first adverse economic effects of the dam were appearing. The Sheyenne Grazing Association, that by a combination of hard work and bold and imaginative management had pulled the region from the depths of drought and depression to the pinnacle of economic stability, was in financial difficulty. Kindred Reservoir had driven an economic wedge into southeastern North Dakoa, sundering ranches and school districts, disrupting taxation, marketing and banking patterns, and affecting the social ecology of the entire region. But this wasn't all.

Hydrostatic pressure caused lateral seepage through the vast deposits of porous, deltaic sand in which the reservoir was situated, and, almost simultaneously, water appeared in the basements of Leonard and Walcott. The following spring, high water tables doubled the wetlands area in the sandhills, but halved the crop and pasture acreage.

In addition, riverbank erosion along the Sheyenne in West Fargo tumbled two homes into the stream and threatened several others. An urgent call went out to the Corps of Engineers to rectify the problem. They responded with a recommendation to pave the banks with old automobile bodies, an ugly and temporary measure that had failed 15 years earlier in the Bismarck-Mandan area. The river of course, had dumped its sediment behind the Kindred Dam, and the awesome erosive power of the silt-free water released below the dam was inexhorably destroying the city that the dam was built to save.

If all this constituted a nagging irritation, the flood of 1979 did not. After 2 low water years during the drought, the river roared back in fury. Heavy snow cover in the upper watershed began to melt in late March. Three and a half inches of rain fell on April 7th and 2 more on the 12th. The reservoir level climbed toward elevation 1016 at an alarming rate. On April 21st, the spillway gates were opened for 36 hours, unfortunately coincident with the crest on the Maple River a few miles to the northwest. Despite warnings that the dam would not provide absolute flood control, no counter measures of any consequence had been accomplished in West Fargo. When the water hit, the West Fargo City Commission, in emergency session, was still commandeering trucks to haul sand, and in a matter of hours, water was two feet deep in most living rooms in the city.

Even before the debris had been cleared away, the Corps of Engineers announced preliminary plans for high dams on the Sheyenne at Lisbon and Fort Ransom, which (they were certain) would provide adequate flood protection for Horace, West Fargo, and downstream communities.

The first major crop failure came in 1985, when an epidemic of sawflies hit the small grains. Seven million pounds of Thanodrin were sprayed, but the insect proved to be a pesticide-resistant strain, and an estimated 28 million bushels were lost in the Red River Valley. Two years later, 4.5 million acres of wheat were wiped out by a mutant stem rust that paid no attention to the fact that it was attacking rust resistant wheat. And then, in the spring of 1988, thousands of acres of seeded land failed to germinate, eventually traced to a synergistic action among chemical residues in the soil.

Until 1985, overall crop production had increased almost every year. From between seven and eight million tons in the 1950s, to a bumper of 12.2 million tons in 1965, the yield jumped to 18 million tons in 1974, a record year. The two years of drought in 1976 and 1977 saw drastic reductions, but 1978 hit 17 million tons. Production fluctuated around 20 million tons through 1984, dropped to 15, in 1985, and by early summer of 1991 it was evident that yields would be under 8 million tons for the first time in 37 years.

Cattle production in the 1970s and '80s had continued the slump begun in the late 1960s. By 1987 beef prices were out of reach for most people, and the slackened demand paralleled the rising incidence of protein deficiency symptoms in the general population. In the fall of 1988 and through most of the following year, cattle began to die in large numbers, older ones first, then yearlings. It was some time before scientists from northern New Mexico arrived to make a diagnosis. Back in 1970, a dean at the state university, by the simple expedient of setting his own subjective promotion policy, had succeeded in drastically cutting the state's supply of qualified scientists. The handful that remained were tragically overworked in the population centers, with no time to investigate the problems in the hinterland. With the arrival of the New Mexico ecologists, the finger again pointed at pesticide accumulation, and examination of fetal calves at the Dickinson Experiment Station showed fat concentrations between 80 and 300 parts per million. Calves were now being born with virtually lethal, congenital chemical loads. Spraying could not be curtailed, even though more and more insect species were showing increased resistance. To do so would be to invite an almost immediate arthropod takeover. Thus the only available solution was to terminate the livestock industry, and North Dakota lost its last cow on November 10, 1990.

Air and water pollution were now taking their toll. Over 1500 had died in Fargo in July of 1986, when horrendous smog hung for days in 100 degree heat. A month later 56 died in Bismarck in one afternoon. In 1987 both Minot and Williston suffered epidemics of typhoid that killed thousands, traced eventually to a mutant strain probably spawned in the mountains of garbage that now surrounded both cities. A year later, both Fargo and Grand Forks rationed water for domestic use after scientists ruled the water purifying systems were inadequate to keep out the chemicals in a single run. Hence both cities went to a double cycle, automatically cutting the water supply in half. The same year Dickinson began trucking water from Colorado.

Psychological deaths were becoming common. For no apparent reason, people began dropping dead. Autopsies showed nothing more than the standard pesticide load, no cancer, no heart disease, no lung or kidney ailments. A plausible explanation was offered by a sixth grader who had picked up an ancient copy of LIFE, dated February 20, 1970, containing a segment of "The Social Contract," by Robert Ardrey. Density strain and environmental stress were simply more than man could take—so he died. There was a tremendous physio-psychological need for natural beauty, green trees, open spaces, clean air and water, but none remained. The Turtle Mountains and the Pembina Hills now produced meager yields of rye and barley, while the Sheyenne Valley, once the garden spot of the state, lay drowned from Cooperstown to Kindred. The International Peace Garden had been plowed in 1981, Teddy Roosevelt's old ranch fell victim to strip miners in 1982, and a year later Lindenwood Park, the last public park in Fargo, went into high-rise apartments.

Thus there were no respites from the smog, the garbage, the people, the concrete and asphalt, steel and glass, the pollution, decay, and death. For a couple of months each spring the endless grain fields would green, but the monotony of the unbroken rectangularity under dirty skies was little relief. So people died.

After 1991, events went rapidly. Jamestown was abandoned in 1992 after it was apparent that both air and water in usable condition were not likely to last the year. Fargo and Bismarck suffered major smog disasters in 1993, the same year that water contamination killed thousands in Grand Forks and Minot. In 1994, 7,563 farm workers died from chemical accumulation, and agricultural production ground to a halt. In 1995, only two million acres were seeded, but the harvest was pitiful.

In the spring of 1996, Valley City was already under four feet of water when Baldhill Dam let go. The wall of water scarcely slowed as it demolished the city, raced the length of Fort Ransom Reservoir, and cascaded into Lake Lisbon. After spreading over most of the city of Lisbon, the crest headed for Kindred. But the reservoir was full, and when the spillway opened, West Fargo was doomed. The city never lived to see the year 2025, when over 50 per cent of the economic benefits of the Kindred dam were supposed to accrue.

Two weeks later, Minot went the same way, but the Corps of Engineers, busy with sewage treatment and water supply in the mountain states, scarcely noticed.

In January of 1997, the legislature convened in Bismarck, debated the question for two weeks, and then abolished the state on a roll call vote in joint session. The governor reluctantly signed the bill and forwarded all state documents to the national capitol in Denver.

Emigration began almost immediately, a third of the people assigned to western Wyoming, a third to Colorado, and a third to New Mexico. By late August, only a housekeeping contingent of National Guardsmen were left in the state.

North Dakota was dead.

POSTSCRIPT

I am deeply indebted to Paul Ehrlich, whose article "Eco-Catastrophe," in the September 1969 issue of *Ramparts,* provided both the inspiration and the model for this scenario. As in the model, all events and statistics quoted prior to early 1970, are true.

Pollution and Disease

M. C. Bromel

Man's environment has always influenced his susceptibility to bacterial and viral disease. Long before the Golden Age of Microbiology when the agents of infectious disease were finally identified, perceptive men recognized the correlation between crowding, filth, and disease. Battles and wars were won or lost, peoples and continents subjugated because of debilitation of the losing side by agents of disease working in conjunction with a disrupted environment.

While the people of the developed countries presently congratulate themselves on the eradication of infectious disease through the use of sanitation procedures, antibiotic drugs and insecticides, there is nevertheless a growing suspicion that all is not as rosy as it seems. The population pressures of an increasing birth rate over a declining death rate, the depletion of land, air and water resources, (not to mention the poisoning of these resources by agricultural and industrial chemicals and industrial and domestic sewage respectively), and the appearance of drug-resistant strains of the very microbes and insects thought to be forever vanquished—all these factors combine to cause concern that the "benefits" of civilization may be Damoclean swords so far as infectious disease and degenerative disease is concerned.

The aborigine in Australia, lacking the most elementary rudiments of sanitation and modern medicine, nevertheless has a life expectancy of 65 years, rivaling that of the American worker or the Swedish businessman. The ceaseless search for food and water keeps these primitive peoples on the move, and they never remain long enough in one place to foul it with the pollution of more advanced societies. It is the population in transition between the Stone Age man and the "civilized" man that suffers most. The farmers of India, Africa, Asia and South America are culturally far ahead of the aborigines. They live in houses, they till their fields, they wash their bodies; but they keep their domesticated animals in their houses, their crops are woefully lacking in proteins and vitamins because of depleted soils, and they drink the water they have used for sanitary purposes. Because of their poor nutritional state they are subject to many

Written for this volume. Dr. M. C. Bromel is Associate Professor of Bacteriology at North Dakota State University, Fargo, North Dakota.

contagious and parasitic diseases and their life span is shorter than that of the aborigine. The people in transition therefore, do not live long enough to suffer from degenerative disease.

In prosperous countries, however, the average life expectancy has increased as a result of control of infant deaths that used to be caused by infectious disease. In contrast many of the diseases most characteristic of our times find their origins in economic affluence and pollution. Vascular disease, certain types of cancer, chronic ailments of the respiratory tract, are among the ailments of persons in advanced societies. It may be that many medical problems today are the results of industrial man's failure to adapt to the conditions of his environment generated by his civilization. Only 1 of 23 cancer-stricken children in Uganda and Nigeria have leukemia while 4 out of every 10 children with cancer in the U.S. suffer from this disease of civilization. Could this new epidemic of degenerative disease so conveniently listed on death certificates as due to "natural causes" be at least partially due to Western man's use of mercury, lead, nickel, nitrates, and nitrites, radiochemicals and other poisonous insecticides and herbicides?

It should be noted that many of the metals, with the exception of lead and mercury, are absolutely essential to the good health of man as well as of plants and animals. But, only in trace amounts, not in the ever increasing quantities that our industries are pouring into the environment. There are 51 metals known to be present in man in varying concentrations. Without the iron in hemoglobin, oxygen could not be carried throughout the body in the blood. Without magnesium in chlorophyll, plants could not utilize the energy in sunlight to synthesize carbohydrates. Other metals form portions of the enzymes, the all important catalysts of life processes. Over the eons of evolutionary time organisms have developed delicate balancing mechanisms for regulating the amount of these essential trace metals in their tissues. But no organism, including man, can long tolerate toxic amounts of the heavier metals such as mercury and lead or some other metallic pollutants that have recently become objects of concern. Damage to respiratory systems can be caused by beryllium emitted by some processing plants. Respiratory difficulties can also result from nickel—toxic amounts of which are present in the air from the burning of coal and oil as well as an unburned fuel additive. There is some evidence that cadmium, which can be present in drinking water from particles flaking off of galvanized water mains and pipes, can be a cause of high blood pressure. However, by far the most dangerous of the heavy metals are lead and mercury. Both metals, highly toxic in their elemental form, are considerably more dangerous in their organic form since they tend to concentrate in nerve tissue in the body and the brain.

Documentation of the toxicity of lead is very extensive; some scientists have implicated lead in the downfall of the Roman Empire. Lead was used in wine flasks and in cosmetics and medicines—thus in this case the more affluent classes were affected rather than the poor who could not afford such luxury. Large amounts of lead have been found in the bones of ancient Roman leaders and, according to those historians who implicate lead as a prime cause for the gradual deterioration of the upper classes, this lead poisoning brought about widespread stillbirths, deformities and brain damage.

The most tragic examples of lead poisoning occur today among slum children who eat the deceptively sweet flakes of old paint peeling from walls and windowsills. But the most widespread threat of lead poisoning comes from the increasing levels of lead in the air. Unfortunately there are no lead-free people in the world today so it is very hard to judge what blood level is to be considered dangerous.

Dr. Robert Kehoe of the University of Cincinnati Kettering laboratory found no overt signs of lead poisoning in adults if the blood lead levels were below 80 μg (80 millionth of a gram) per 100 grams of blood. However, in children visible symptoms of poisoning have been observed with blood levels of 60 μg and in some adults twice the 80 μg levels are innocuous.

Some facts are known: primarily the fact that the closer people get to exhaust fumes, the more lead shows up in the blood. The U.S. Public Health Service in 1963 performed a survey of Cincinnati, Philadelphia and Los Angeles and found that garage mechanics, parking attendants and traffic policemen showed highest concentrations with people living near busy highways the next highest levels. This year another survey of the air in these three cities showed a 50 per cent increase in atmospheric lead in the Los Angeles survey over that found in the study of 1963. Comparing a study of lead in the bones of Peruvian Indians of six centuries ago with what modern man carries in his bones, scientists found 10 times as much lead in contempory skeletons. Dr. Isabel Tipton of Oakridge National Laboratories has recently reported that lung tissue of Americans contained twice as much lead as that of Africans.

The big unanswered question is, what are these increasing levels of lead doing to human health? Given to mice and rats in doses sufficient to reproduce the amount of lead now found in human tissues, the metal has significantly shortened the animal's lifetime by inducing general weakness and fatigue. In man the early symptoms may easily be mistaken for a number of maladies since they include a loss of appetite and weight, fatigue, headache, and anemia.

The other metallic element causing much furor and many headlines is mercury. The term "mad hatter" comes from the occupational hazard attendent to the old time hand manufacture of fur and felt hats. The poor unfortunate workers often suffered mental instability and tremors as a result of inhaling vapors from metallic mercury, used in processing these materials.

Today the scientific concern is more directed at methyl mercury, the organic compound, since it can penetrate biological barriers with great ease. If it reaches the brain it may not show up for months or years. Methyl mercury is often the product of biological action by microorganisms in nature and it is then released into water or soil where it is taken up by successively larger organisms. Thus with each step in the food chain it becomes more and more concentrated so that the tissues of some fish high up in the chain show a 3000-fold concentration compared to the surrounding H_2O.

It is interesting to note that the FDA has recently stated that the smaller types of tuna may be eaten with impunity but that swordfish may not. Could it be that the younger and smaller the fish the less mercury has accumulated? Thus can we not hypothesize that American affluence and technology may actually be contributing to the decline of a civilization, and may not this decline be hastened by epidemics brought about by the very microorganisms thought to have been eradicated by modern medical science?

The history of infectious disease is a history of the disagreeable tendency of some living things to save themselves the bother of building, by their own efforts, the food and shelter they require. Thus, life on earth may be viewed as an endless chain of parasitism with plants dependent on the sun and microorganisms of the soil, animals dependent on plants, and man, the biggest parasite of all, dependent on both. Yet, unlike many of the more efficient parasites that have evolved throughout eons of time into a harmless if not mutually beneficial relationship with their hosts, man appears to be the least efficient parasite as he devours his host—the Earth.

The great pestilences that have swept the Earth from prerecorded time such as typhus, cholera, plague, tuberculosis, syphilis, and malaria are mistakenly judged by many persons to be under control if not entirely eliminated. And while it is true that man, in the industrialized nations at least, is better able by means of the wonder drugs, chemicals, and immunizations to cope with infectious disease than were his ancestors in medieval Europe, nonetheless the major gains in public health have resulted principally from social measures not from a decrease or disappearance of virulent microorganisms. Modern sanitary methods attempt and usually succeed in making it impossible for the most pathogenic microbes to reach their human targets. Drinking water is chlorinated to kill off the disease bacteria óf intestinal origin while controls over food production and preparation, where effective, greatly minimize bacterial contamination. Insect vectors of diseases such as malaria, yellow fever and bubonic plague are attacked with insecticides and similar chemicals. Vaccinations of populations where given, not just individuals, have increased resistance to such ancient diseases as smallpox, cholera and typhoid fever.

The impact of such social measures on the health of Western man may be measured against the disease rampant today in the underdeveloped countries where the dual lethality of poverty and population is all too apparent. Lack of protein in the daily diet of these unfortunates greatly lowers resistance to infection. The life expectancy of only one out of three East Indians born in 1964 is a mere 50 years. Multiple infections and infestations by parasites kill 20 per cent of the children before they are 5, and many of the surviving adults are perpetually weak. Even such technological advancements as the Aswan dam in Egypt, the completion of which was thought to herald increased food supplies through irrigation, is a dubious blessing since these irrigation ditches have served to spread the parasitic worm disease—schistosomiasis. Until proper sanitary measures and adequate and balanced food supplies are provided the people of the have-not nations, the mortality rates will continue to be appalling.

Yet, even in the industrial nations at the dawn of the present decade, the frightful evidences that some omnipresent but usually quiescent disease organisms are still capable of causing epidemics is all too real. The presence of cholera, endemic in the Far East and Near East for years, suddenly spreading to the southern vacation shores of the USSR and across Africa to Guinea in only a few months brought a shudder of alarm to health officials in Europe and America. The last cholera epidemic struck the U.S. in 1873, reaching from the Gulf of Mexico to the Great Lakes. The institution of off-shore ship quarantines along with advances in chlorination and sanitation prevented any further spread of this most swiftly-striking of the great plagues. Yet, one wonders if in these days of jet travel with its accompanying phenomenon of being hijacked to an endemic cholera area, exposed to the disease, and then returned to a nonresistant population, the citizens aren't just as vulnerable as our forefathers.

Many communities in the U. S. still dump raw, untreated sewage into streams and lakes. Those municipalities that do remove the suspended solids often do not remove the dissolved material which is costly. Even treated effluent is not an elixir one would relish—it is simply plain sewage effluent, stepped down in potency and lethal quantities. For example, with secondary treatment, the sewage effluence from a city of 100,000 is still equal to the raw sewage of 20,000 persons. Any of the water-borne infectious diseases such as cholera, hepatitis, typhoid, or dysenteries ranging from mild intestinal upsets to severe and prolonged prostration or even death are continuing public health hazards so long as we continue to use our rivers and streams as domestic sewers. In the case of the hepatic or polio viruses even chlorination of sewage water is not efficacious since many viruses are resistant to such treatment. Adsorption of pollutants on activated charcoal as is performed in many water purification plants only serves to concentrate these agents of disease. Whenever population pressures or torrential downpours overload existing sewage treatment facilities in the larger cities, no treatment at all is given the wastes in the sanitary sewers and the appalling mixture flows undisturbed into the nearest river or lake. According to the United States Public Health Service there has been an 11 per cent increase in *reported* infectious hepatitis cases in 1970 in the nation as a whole with the New England area reporting a 60 per cent increase!

The U.S. has been spared the ravages of the Black Death, or bubonic plague, that swept Europe during the Middle Ages killing an incredible total of 25 million people and that, as recently as 1910, killed 60,000 in Manchuria and China. Yet the bacterium that causes the plague, *Yersinia pestis,* may be found in the fleas that parasitize ground squirrels and other rodents in 15 of the western states. In 1970 New Mexico and California reported 7 cases of plague in humans, the highest number since 1965. Epidemiologists are particularly watchful because the field mouse, known to carry plague fleas, often shares quarters with domestic rats during severe winter months and could set up the deadly flea-rat-man cycle of the disease. Pollution in the rat-infested metropolitan slums due to solid wastes and garbage presents yet another perilous potential for disease.

Flies and roaches, both mechanical vectors of disease, are developing resistance to even the most powerful of insecticides. Mosquitos carrying the dread falciparum malaria in Viet Nam are resisant to DDT, and the malaria organism they carry is developing resistance to Atabrine and other anti-malarials. Even immunizations have turned out to be less than the perfect answer. There are over 100 different strains of the pneumonia and septic sore throat organisms—the pneumococci and the streptococci—and it is impossible to vaccinate whole populations against all of them. These agents of disease may be air-borne particularly under conditions of crowding and stress such as prevails in any city ghetto. The greatest pandemic of modern times, due to a mutant influenza virus strain in 1918-1919, killed between 10 and 20 million people throughout the world. However, an influenza vaccine developed in the 1950s gave hope that such a killer virus was defeated. A less virulent but even more rapidly spreading pandemic due to another mutant, the Asian flu virus, occurred in 1960, and a third mutation occurred as recently as 1968 when the Hong-Kong strain spread around the world in a matter of weeks. While it is true that the secondary bacterial invaders accompanying all these viral pandemics were usually eradicable with chemotherapeutic drugs, almost none of the virus-caused diseases are treatable with such drugs. Moreover, in 1960 a group of Japanese workers under Watanabe reported that the dysentery bacillus, *Shigella dysenteriae,* had developed resistance not merely to one antibiotic but multiple resistance to many antibiotics and, further, could transfer this multiple resistance to the common colon bacillus. Since that time the bacteriological literature is replete with reports of multiple drug resistance and transfer of this resistance among all members of the intestinal group of bacteria parasitizing man and his domestic animals.

Thus since the secondary host for many of these intestinal bacteria is man, we are in danger of becoming infected from the food we eat or the water we drink with bacteria already resistant to the very antibiotics our doctors would use to treat our disease. It is felt by many scientists that one of the causes of so much drug-resistance in bacteria is due to the practice of supplementing the feed of domestic animals—sheep, swine, chicken, cattle—with such antibiotics as the tetracyclines, penicillins, sulfa compounds, or streptomycin. These antibiotics are given to increase the animal's weight gain before marketing by repressing those microorganisms that would slow or inhibit this rate of gain. Even if man creates a risk of drug-resistant organisms because of his careless use of antibiotics in human medicine, there is no justification for augmenting the risk by a similar lack of prudence in the use of antibiotics in animal medicine.

Most recently, hospital strains of deadly, highly penicillin-resistant staphylococci have been discovered to be able to transfer their resistance by means of a bacterial virus to sensitive strains of the same organism. The syphilis spirochaete and the gonorrhea organism are also showing signs of resistance to pencillin, and with the wide-spread dependence on the oral contraceptive and the decline in use of the protective sheath, a rise of antibiotic-resistant venereal disease organisms seems inevitable. These examples of drug-resistant pathogenic bacteria demonstrate the dangers inherent in the indiscriminant use of any chemical however beneficial it may appear when first used.

It is a widely held tenet of epidemiology that populations are only resistant to the infectious diseases native to their region with which they have been in contact all their lives. Occasionally, for reasons of lowered resistance such as fatigue or ill health, these native microorganisms can and do overwhelm the natural defenses of the individuals. But this balance of power between microbes and man may be upset on a much grander scale. A foreign microbe may overwhelm a community of sensitive individuals or great numbers of people may undergo some stress or change unfavorable to their powers of resistance. This close connection between infectious disease and a stressful environment is nowhere more evident than in the crowded confines of a city ghetto or in the more dangerous ranks of an army at war. (Hans Zinsser has written that the body louse and the rickettsial disease it carries (typhus)—along with its brothers and sisters—plague, cholera, typhoid, and dysentery—"have decided more campaigns than Caesar, Hannibal, Napoleon, Hitler, and all the inspector generals of history.")

The stress by pollution on modern living undoubtedly contributes much to the degenerative diseases of the more affluent countries where emphysema, atherosclerosis, cancer, arthritis, and diabetes were the chronic diseases of the aged but are now appearing in much younger persons. The incidence of respiratory disease such as emphysema and bronchitis, both infectious and noninfectious, always goes up after an intense smog settles over a city, and such killer smogs as the London smog of 1952 spares no age group.

The most startling fact about combined bronchitis and emphysema is the rapid spread of this disease throughout the industrialized societies. Dr. John Hanlon, Assistant Surgeon-General of the U. S. Public Health Service, recently informed a meeting of the American Medical Association in Boston that "environmental pollution is the reason the life expectancy of the average adult male in America has not significantly increased in the last 50 years." There was, according to Dr. Hanlon, a 500 per cent increase in the death rate from emphysema in New York City in the past 10 years with a 200 per cent increase in the death rate from chronic bronchitis. Relatively rare 25 years ago, it is now the most prevalent respiratory ailment and afflicts nearly 10 million Americans. Cigarette smoke and polluted air from automobiles and industrial smog are seriously implicated as causative agents in this type of disease just as the same agents are suspected to initiate many lung cancers. In other types of cancer, virus infections of a hidden nature are suspected. These viral invasions are thought to occur at an early age, lie dormant for years, and then are triggered into explosive growth by external agents such as radiations or chemicals in the environment. Atherosclerosis or hardening of the arteries is the number one killer among diseases in the U.S. today, claiming close to a million lives each year. It is rare among undernourished populations, and some experts feel that it is the overindulgence in rich food, so characteristic of the average American, that predisposes us to this disease. Stress is also thought to contribute to the progress of the illness, thus the frequency of this malady among business executives suggests to many that this is but one more degenerate disorder linked to modern civilization. In fact, Dr. Hanlon told the physicians that threats from unsafe foods, water, drugs, chemicals, and a variety of consumer products are rapidly causing the quality of American life to deteriorate. Unfortunately, the Public Health Service, by law, has authority to adopt standards for water and food *only* for the purpose of controlling the introduction or spread of communicable disease. It has no legal authority to deal with the kind of noncommunicable chronic disease that may be induced by some chemicals. It is clear that this law should be up-dated.

Our affluent society has become an effluent society, and these effluents are killing us. If humans were the only life to suffer it could be termed a fitting penalty for our carelessness, but we are taking many of the plants and animals of the biosphere with us. As René DuBos had told us, "...children born and raised in a modern environment are handicapped for the future—they will pay the consequences in the form of what we call the diseases of civilization"—a slow, silent, but pervading deterioration of human health. No less a person than the President of the United States stated recently: "Today we are certain that pollution adversely affects the quality of our lives. In the future it may affect their duration."

BIBLIOGRAPHY

Abinante, R.R. 1967. Role of microorganisms in the chronic degenerative diseases of man. *Annual Review of Microbiology,* Vol. 21: 467-494.

Anderson, E.S. 1968. The ecology of transferable drug resistance. *Annual Review of Microbiology*, Vol. 22: 131-180.

DuBos, René. 1968. *So human an animal.* New York, N.Y.: Scribner.

Fortune Magazine. 1970. The environment: a national mission for the seventies. Chicago, Ill.: Time Inc.

Smith, T. 1963. *Parasitism and disease.* New York, N.Y. and London: Hafner.

Zinsser, H. 1963. *Rats, lice and history.* Boston, Mass.: Little Brown.

Pesticides in the Freshwater Ecosystem

B. T. Johnson

In "Pesticides and Their Relationship to Environmental Health," the Secretary of the Department of Health, Education and Welfare stated that some 900 pesticidal chemicals are formulated into over 60,000 preparations readily available in the United States. If the current rate of development continues, in the near future a billion pounds of pesticides per year will be used in this country. Most of these pesticides which are chiefly insecticides and herbicides find their way to our streams, lakes and rivers either from runoff, from direct application or from industrial sewage. What effect do these pesticides have on the freshwater ecology? Acute effects as measured by fish kills or decline in bird population are relatively simple to detect; but what of the long range chronic effect of low level exposure? What about the fish that disappears and that we don't see. What are the physiological or behavioral effects of the chemicals? Mutagenic? Teratogenic? What effect do pesticides have on the flow of energy and the cycling of matter in an aquatic food chain? Are chemicals undergoing biological magnification at one trophic level and transferred to another with serious deleterious effects? Most, if not all of these questions remain nearly unanswered.

I will limit myself to three areas of the freshwater ecosystem that may be affected by pesticides. These are areas that we in microbiology at the Fish Pesticide Research Laboratory in Columbia are currently investigating. They are: the influence of pesticides on primary productivity, the biological magnification of pesticides by consumers, below the vertebrate trophic level and finally the interaction of pesticides and decomposers. All of these topics, as you can readily see, involve the flow of energy and the cycling of matter—they involve food chains. I will also for simplicity reduce our discussion of pesticide chemicals to one—the insecticide DDT. For our purposes this evening this is an excellent choice. Why? It is probably the most ubiquitous synthetic chemical known to man with global distribution. It has been estimated that 1,000,000,000 pounds of DDT have been used in the last thirty years. It is a valuable insecticide with a

Taken in part from an address given to the Annual Meeting of the Association of Midwest College Biology Teachers at Cedar Falls, Iowa, October 9, 1970. Dr. B. Thomas Johnson is at the Fish Pesticide Research Laboratory, Fish and Wildlife Service, Bureau of Sport Fisheries and Wildlife, Columbia, Missouri.

broad spectrum of activity. It is a biocide. It has controlled arthropod vectors that have plagued man with some of the most devastating diseases. It is persistent. It is cheap. It is a household word associated with insecticides. It has been banned or drastically reduced in usage in the United States. Why? Is the government placating the capricious whim of a small segment of vociferous ecological sentimentalists longing for the "good old days of pristine water and air." Are we acting from "ecophobia," rashly dooming millions to the ravages of malaria as predicted by the World Health Organization (WHO)?

We in the Bureau of Sport Fisheries and Wildlife are an advisory agency, we do not make policy, we do not make laws, we do not make public moral judgements, we are directed by law to gather information through research and advise concerning fish and their environs. These are the data we have gathered on DDT as it affects the freshwater ecology. These data should not be considered as an all-encompassing review of the literature, but, in general, the personal research experiences of the speaker. These I will explain and hopefully, if necessary, successfully defend.

How does DDT affect producers? It is well known that essentially all energy flows into an aquatic food chain via plants. All energy that sustains living systems is solar energy fixed in photosynthesis and held for a finite period in the biosphere. The total amount of life on this planet is limited by the photosynthesis process—the size of the biosphere is finite. Any alteration of the photosynthetic process will ultimately be reflected in altered production at all trophic levels of the aquatic community. Studies with freshwater algae exposed to DDT showed a marked decrease in cell number, biomass and carbon assimilation. What conclusions can one draw from this research? One must consider the long term effect of DDT in freshwater ecology as well as animal species, the latter is frequently overlooked. Our observation with freshwater algae suggest that small additions of persistent organochlorine insecticides (DDT) may cause a reduction in population density and suppression of carbon fixation. It is quite easy to postulate a more drastic effect on lowered productivity at all trophic levels. Remember: *DDT residues are a widespread occurrence in freshwater communities.*

What effect does DDT have on consumers? The magnification of organochlorine insecticides by biological components of terrestrial and aquatic ecosystems has been documented by numerous studies. The concept of biological magnification implies the increased accumulation of a pesticide at each succeeding trophic level. The ultimate result is the accumulation of residue levels in predators which may be 100,000 to 1,000,000 X the concentration in water. For example, in Lake Michigan DDT concentrations of 1 to 5 pptr are found, yet DDT residues of 10 ppm in coho salmon occur, a 1 million fold increase above water concentration. How does the magnification occur? From food? From water? After exposing prime fish food, crustacea and insect larvae species, to ^{14}C-labeled DDT at concentrations less than 100 pptr for 24 hours, we found DDT residues 10,000 to 100,000 X higher than those found in the surrounding water. Continued exposure revealed little evidence of the DDT residue reaching a plateau level. In addition, evidence of marked degradation of pesticides would seem not only to be a rapid direct route for massive passage of many micropollutants but also an important source of pollutant proliferation.

What effect do microorganisms have on DDT? How are decomposers affected? It is frequently regarded as axiomatic in microbial ecology that all organic molecules regardless of complexity are degraded by microorganisms. Modern organic chemistry in agriculture has unfortunately shown microorganisms to be quite fallible. DDT is an excellent case in point. This organochlorine molecule is neither an energy source or C substrate for microorganisms. DDT does degrade however under suitable environmental conditions. It undergoes co-oxidation with attack concentrated solely on the ethane moiety of the molecule. There exists little evidence that biological clevage of the biphenyl linkage occurs. *For all practical purposes DDT is not readily biodegradable. Microbial attack of DDT in actuality increases the number of biphenyl molecular species in the environment.*

I feel that emphasis in the past has been too heavily weighed in favor of the parent pollutant with minimum, if any, concern for their degradation products. If the compound lost its pesticidal property it was considered "degradable." Unfortunately the spectrum of pesticidal activity and our definition of pest are not synchronous. In our studies on DDT we found that not only magnification of DDT occurred but also an increase in the number of pollutants occurred both through microbial and invertebrate activity. We feel that the presence of these degradation products and their magnification pose both a short and long range threat to the aquatic community. Recent investigations of DDE, a degradation product of DDT strongly suggest the need for concern. Hickey and others have shown the strong correlation between DDT-DDE residues and bird reproduction. The decline of the bald eagle, the precipitous decrease in the number of peregrine falcons, and the failure of the pelicans to produce hatchable eggs due to thin-walls has been correlated with DDT-DDE pollution.

Should DDT be banned? The answer unfortunately is painfully obvious. But this is not the real question. Have we mortals learned anything? What can we teach others about chemical pesticides to avoid the pitfalls of DDT. Perhaps we are all falling prey to "ecophobia," that topical malaise characterized by the paranoia of an insidious sense of decay and deterioration through industry technology. A certainty that man is being deluged with an encompassing rain of chemicals...insecticides, fertilizers, herbicides, fungicides..."–icide" *ad infinitum*. As always there are many calls to action but few noteworthy proposals. Neither the atavistic romantist cry "Ban it!," nor the chem-agro complex anthropocentric statement, "What problem?" offer much hope in answering the chemical pollution problem. Perhaps man is doomed to wallow in his technological waste but I prefer to believe that there is still a chance, still hope for the best of the two—high productivity with clean air and water.

Somebody Fouled Up/Birds and Bees

Daniel Zwerdling

Americans dump and spray 1.2 billion pounds of pesticides each year on their gardens, lawns, forests, pastures, farms, lakes, and rivers; the amount grows 14 per cent every year. Literally thousands of pesticide formulations used every day around the home have potentially harmful effect on humans. One Philadelphia man died early this year after household termite spray with chlordane poisoned his bone marrow. The government places very limited restrictions on consumer pesticide use. Anyone can buy the poisons and use them as he pleases, endangering both himself and his entire community. Lawn pesticides travel up to three miles on a calm day, settling on water which ends up in kitchen pipes and on plants which nourish the animals we eat. Major pesticides such as DDT—organochlorines—persist for years in the soil and atmosphere, accumulating in animal and human tissue. Scientists studying the effects of human exposure to these chemicals have barely broken the surface. Government researchers have looked at a handful in the past several years only because pending ecological disasters have brought them to public attention. "The field of pesticide toxicology," wrote a special HEW Commission on Pesticides last December, "exemplifies the absurdity of a situation in which 200 million Americans are undergoing life-long exposure, yet our knowledge of what is happening to them is at best fragmentary." The government response to the crisis indicates that it has not learned its lesson.

When a suburbanite sprays weed killer on his lawn, the chances are great that he is using 2,4,5-T, the same herbicide that the Defense Department has dropped in enormous quantities to defoliate the jungles of Vietnam. Since it was first developed as a chemical warfare agent in the late 1940s, 2,4,5-T has remained a popular all-purpose herbicide. But now scientists fear it may cause fetal deformities in pregnant women.

The government had not thought much about the side effects of 2,4,5-T until Sen. Philip Hart's environmental subcommittee probed herbicides in several hearings this spring. As early as 1966, studies by the Bionetics Laboratory for the National Cancer Institute showed 2,4,5-T is teratogenic in rats. Cleft palates

Reprinted with permission from *New Republic*, October 31, 1970. Daniel Zwerdling is senior editor of *The Michigan Daily*, Ann Arbor, Michigan.

and kidney abnormalities among the offspring raised the frightening possibility that such defects among human babies may sometimes result from overzealous use of weedkiller in daddy's garden. The findings were not publicized until the HEW pesticide commission revealed them last winter, and called for immediate restriction of 2,4,5-T to minimize human exposure. Surgeon General Jesse Steinfeld apparently felt worried enough about the chemical to promise that the government would ban it by January. In April, 2,4,5-T production was still growing.

Spurred by Hart's hearings and embarrassing publicity, the Agriculture Department announced suddenly in April that it was suspending uses of 2,4,5-T in liquid formulations around the home and on water, and would cancel several other uses. Agriculture's actions will not go very far. There's a bureaucratic catch: all pesticides sold interstate must be approved and registered for specific uses by the Pesticides Regulations Division of USDA. *Suspending* a chemical revokes its registration, in effect banning further manufacture and interstate transport. USDA's suspension of 2,4,5-T in liquids around the home and on water accounts for only a fraction of the herbicide's total market. Dow Chemical Corp. (associated in most minds with napalm) estimates that the ban will affect no more than 10 per cent of its 2,4,5-T sales. USDA barely touched the 2,4,5-T used around the home in granular powder form, or dumped by the thousands of tons on food crops which end up on the dining room table. FDA considers 2,4,5-T to be so toxic that it will seize foodstuffs with any trace of the chemical. Investigators have occasionally found contaminated food samples, but could not stop the entire shipments in time. Instead, it *cancelled* these uses, a sluggish administrative mechanism which allows the chemical to be shipped and sold while manufacturers petition for advisory committees, hearings, and finally appeal the case in court—a process that can take years. Major 2,4,5-T producers filed their first round of protests in May; five months later USDA has not yet formed an advisory committee.

Agriculture Department officials have refused to take any action against 2,4,5-T used on range and pastureland which account for 80 per cent of its use. They say it is enough to warn farmers not to turn cattle loose on sprayed land for a "reasonable" time after treatment and to make certain the poison does not get into their milk, and eventually into human stomachs. What is a "reasonable" time? Former Presidential science adviser Lee DuBridge recommends 30 days. Chemists have found 2,4,5-T persists on land for eighteen months in dry conditions.

Why doesn't the government suspend all uses of 2,4,5-T? Under the Federal Insecticide, Fungicide and Rodenticide Act, USDA may suspend any pesticide which poses an "imminent hazard" to human health. Spraying 2,4,5-T on food crops does not pose an imminent hazard, department officials reason, since six months may pass between the time the crops are grown and the time a person actually eats them. (That view, though not the 2,4,5-T policy, has changed slightly. Imminent no longer means "threatening to happen now." USDA linguists now admit that a chemical causing cancer 20 years after its ingestion is an "imminent" hazard.)

Even under the suspenions, and even if the cancellation proceedings are completed, 2,4,5-T will still continue to be sold in hardware stores across the country in spray cans and plastic bags which every lawn buff can purchase as he pleases. Federal laws do not cover retail dealers who sell, and consumers who buy, contraband pesticides. The government can fine only the firms that ship them interstate—and then a minuscule $1000. The government can also seize pesticide stocks, but it employs exactly 32 inspectors to roam the entire nation. 2,4,5-T producers, furthermore, can continue legally selling existing stock as long as they merely change the package labels to conform with new government restrictions. That does not guarantee that the consumer will follow the directions. Agriculture officials won't warn the public about the dangers of 2,4,5-T. There are 300 2,4,5-T home products: "Publication of such a long list might be more confusing than helpful," says a department spokesman. (On October 17, the National Association of Broadcasters attacked a Federal Trade Commission plan to warn consumers of the dangers of pesticides. The warning—"this product can be injurious to health; read the entire label carefully and use only as directed"—is too cumbersome, said the NAB. It could not be gotten into a five-second commercial.)

Five environmental groups have filed suit in federal court asking for immediate suspension of all uses of 2,4,5-T. USDA science and education assistant director T. C. Byerly, however, insists "there are no reasonable doubts" about the safety of the pesticide to warrant further restrictions.

The White House announced with great fanfare last November that the government would forbid certain uses of DDT. Interior Secretary Walter Hickel later declared that DDT was taboo on Interior controlled lands, and Agriculture chimed in, banning the chemical from its government programs. DDT has symbolized the pesticide pollution problems since Rachel Carson's *Silent Spring* first revealed in 1962 that it kills wildlife and accumulates in almost everything and everybody (DDT residues have been found in Arctic seals). So the government seemed to be taking a significant step toward a healthier country. In fact, the elimination of DDT in government programs accounts for a minor fraction of the DDT used. In the private domain, the government only *cancelled* uses of DDT around the home, in waterways, on tobacco and on certain shade trees—mere fragments of the DDT market. USDA sneezed at conservationists' demands to eliminate DDT's major uses in agriculture, until a federal court suit by the Environmental Defense Fund spurred it two months ago to extend cancellations to non-citrus fruit trees, some vegetables and livestock. And these uses may be perfectly legal for at least several more years while manufacturers exhaust administrative and court appeals. Meanwhile, more than 400 million pounds of the poison will have been added anew to the nation. USDA has taken no action whatever to restrict the use of DDT on citrus trees and cotton, and they consume more than 80 per cent of all DDT produced. The District Court of Appeal has not yet issued a decision on the Defense Fund's suit, but it is likely that the court will simply remand the case to USDA for further study, order a public hearing, or dump the matter in the lap of a lower court. (On October 22, EDF sued California's Montrose Chemical Corp., the largest DDT maker, claiming that massive dumping of the poison into Los Angeles sewers contaminates ocean marine life.)

"We have used DDT safely for 40 years," declares Agriculture's Byerly. An FDA study released in August shows that DDT causes mutations in laboratory rats. Earlier research demonstrated that DDT induces cancer in mice. DDT poisoning in nature is so common that it scarcely surprises anyone anymore: Virginia has banned the sale of shellfish and crabs caught on its shores because of DDT contamination. (The state's agriculture department plans to ban all DDT use save for those instances in which there is "no suitable substitute.") And Interior Department investigators recently reported, with some bewilderment, that the entire white ibis bird population around Brigham City, Utah, has been suddenly wiped out—probably due to DDT used in nearby mosquito control programs. USDA asserts that such bird mortalities are only "temporary."

USDA scientists are testing a new form of DDT which they claim degrades almost immediately. That would help prevent more poisoning in the future. As the disastrous effects of DDT on the American environment become more evident, however, the government is increasing its shipments of the chemical to underdeveloped countries— mostly in Asia and South America—under the aegis of the Agency for International Development and the World Health Organization. Exports topped 100 million pounds in 1968, a 30 per cent increase over 1967. AID officials claim that DDT is essential for malaria control. They note that the DDT is usually sprayed inside houses, minimizing its leakage in the environment; they fail to add that such spraying maximizes DDT contamination of the people who live there. Vast quantities of the insecticide are also used on crops. Indiscriminate spraying has reportedly killed some wildlife, and Argentina is concerned over growing DDT accumulations in its prized cattle. But, says one top AID official, "we have seen very few instances where harmful results of DDT are ... permanent."

While the Agriculture Department battles conservationists who attack its sanctions of 2,4,5-T and DDT, it is quietly preparing a $200 million, 12-year program which will dump 450 million pounds of the insecticide Mirex over cities and fields in nine southeastern states. Government officials bill the program as the last phase of the fire ant eradication program, authorized by Congress in 1957 on a cost-sharing basis with the states. The government started its aerial bombardments last month, over the cries of scientists who fear Mirex will poison millions of acres, possibly killing wildlife.

"The history of the fire ant program makes your hair curl," says Ray Johnson, assistant director of research at the Interior's Bureau of Sport Fisheries and Wildlife. USDA began battling the fire ant (famed for its sting and the dirt mounds it lives in) 13 years ago, using dieldrin and heptachlor. The fire ant population spread, but thousands of animals died. In 1962 the government switched to Mirex, which tests in the Interior's Gulf Breeze, Fla., laboratories showed had no harmful effects on animals. They were wrong. In 1968 millions of blue crabs and shrimps died from Mirex poisoning off the Atlantic coast from North Carolina to Florida, putting many fishermen out of business. Last year, a curious chemist repeated the laboratory experiments watching the test animals for 10 days rather than the standard 96 hours. A minuscule one part per billion of Mirex in sea water killed 11 per cent of the shrimp tested. In another experiment, 78 per cent of mallard ducks tested died after 10 days.

Since 1957 federal government and various states have already spent $70 million trying to kill the fire ant, but it is alive and thriving in the South. The new and supposedly final phase of the program calls for treating 120 million acres, applying three separate treatments six months apart over one area at a time. Old bombers drop the Mirex in the form of a corncob grit bait doused with soybean oil—about 757,000 granules per acre. Convinced that Mirex actually *does* kill shellfish, program directors have agreed to stop spreading the insecticide over estuaries and waterways. "The accuracy of the planes is the best I've ever seen," exclaims Johnson—although he notes that Mirex is still showing up in water. On land, officials are not worried that animals may inadvertently eat the bait and die of Mirex poisoning or pass it on to humans. "The ants will remove most of the bait, and haul it into their mounds," says USDA agricultural research director Leo G. K. Iveson. Animals are eating the Mirex somehow: zoologist Denzel Ferguson discovered 150 parts per million in songbirds, as long as one year after an area had been treated with Mirex. (FDA will confiscate meat with more than 7 parts per million). The Agriculture Department is still waiting for results of a field testing program, to see if animals might die from Mirex after all. The studies will not be completed for eight months. Researchers haven't found any Mirex contaminated carcasses yet, but as Interior Department investigator Tom Carver points out, "if an animal is killed in nature, its predators dispose of it quickly."

While no one has conclusively proven that Mirex poisons animals in nature, opponents of the program argue that far too much doubt exists to justify continuing what will be the most massive insect eradication campaign in the nation's history. "There are too many things we don't know about Mirex," says Ferguson, "sophisticated biological data like its effect on hormones, enzymes, and metabolism." Studies by the National Cancer Institute found that Mirex induces cancer in mice; the HEW Research pesticide commission accordingly urged that the pesticide be used only where advantages to human health clearly outweigh the potential hazards. A scientist-dominated conservation group called CLEAN (Committee for Leaving the Environment of America Natural) and the Environmental Defense Fund are seeking a court injunction to suspend the program pending more research, but Iveson has declared flatly that the project can't be delayed. "Research has not developed data showing that Mirex has caused significant harm to a nontarget environment," Iveson told CLEAN; he adds, "a delay in the program would give advantage to the pest which may never be recaptured."

Prominent etomologists do not think the ant can be eradicated under any conditions. A report by the National Research Council of the National Academy of Sciences—commissioned especially by USDA in 1967—concludes that "an eradication of the fire ant is not now biologically and technically feasible." That report has never been released.

One colony of fire ants can reproduce and repopulate several square miles in less than three years, according to Harvard entomologist Edward Wilson, who pioneered research on the ant in the 1950s. No aerial bombardment could ever come close to hitting every mound, which ants often hide in thickets. "If one colony is missed, the entire ant population would spring back in a couple of years," says Wilson. Even if it *were* feasible to wipe out the ant, the Academy expressed "grave doubts" whether any attempts to eradicate it would be justified. Most entomologists don't consider the fire ant a pest worth bothering about. "The fire ant doesn't damage crops, unlike other pests," concedes one USDA official. In fact, the ant eats insects that do harm crops, such as the boll weevil. Fire ants do not hurt farm animals, either. The ant is primarily a people pest: it has a strong bite. William Murray, chairman of an interagency committee that reviews federal pesticide programs, insists the ant can make life hellish for Southern people. "I saw for myself," he says. "I kicked off the top of a mound, stuck my hand in and let it get stung ten or twelve times."

Mississippi, North and South Carolina have already started dumping Mirex over their countryside and cities. "Some of us don't think the program is nearly as necessary as the people in the states think it is," one top USDA official concedes now, but the department is determined to forge ahead nonetheless. "The people through elected representatives in Congress have asked for the program," declares Byerly. Murray calls it the department's "mission." Byerly isn't worried the program will be stopped in court. "Any damage which Mirex might do to the environment should be temporary. It should recover within 18 months," he says. "The balance is in favor of Mirex."

The public might get some better protection against pesticides if Congress passes Senator Hart's new bill, which would require immediate suspension of any pesticide whenever there is reasonable doubt about its safety, and which would penalize retail dealers who sell, and homeowners who buy, the banned chemical. But legislation is only a small part of the story. DDT, 2,4,5-T, and Mirex are only three of thousands of pesticides which the government is scarcely looking at. What is the use of new laws if the government doesn't even know which pesticides are dangerous? USDA is currently reviewing two old-time insecticides, dieldrin and aldrin, both used widely in government programs as well as in homes across the country despite the fact they have caused massive animal kills. HEW's pesticide commission wanted dieldrin and aldrin severely restricted, but Agriculture will not act hastily. The department isn't even considering 2,4-D, the nation's most popular weedkiller (often mixed with 2,4,5-T or with fertilizer) although National Cancer Institute and FDA tests show that it causes fetal deformities in laboratory animals. All of these chemicals continue in use.

One thing the government *has* done is form a commission to look into ways of disposing of pesticide containers once we have already discharged their poisons. For example, 100 million bug bombs sit on the nation's shelves. "How do you get rid of them?" asks Byerly. "The problem hasn't been faced up to very well."

The Impact of Industry Upon Our Environment

Oscar W. Johnson

With varying degrees of enthusiasm, most people these days are concerned about our environment. The more fervent (and I would like to consider myself in that category) vacillate along a scale of relative pessimism depending upon what ecological disaster or crisis happens to be occurring at a given time. The situation is not hopeless, but until the majority becomes absolutely committed to maintaining a quality environment, victory is less and less likely. Nothing is as sobering to me as contemplating the sort of world my children will inherit, and their chances of survival.

All of us have experiences in which we come face to face with the effects of industry upon environmental quality. It is repulsive to drive through the clean air of Wisconsin only to enter a grey pall known as Chicago. I can remember Salt Lake City at Christmas a couple of years ago when the surrounding mountains were completely obliterated by smoke from industrial operations. Then there is the little town of Columbia Falls, Montana with its Anaconda Aluminum plant. Fluoride emissions from the latter have annihilated the vegetation on a mountain overlooking the town, and the destruction now extends for several miles in the direction of Glacier Park. We read of massive water pollution far exceeding present efforts of our government to clean it up, and of the possibility of global weather changes induced by air pollution. The list goes on and on *ad nauseum.*

My topic is not the population explosion as such, nonetheless, I must touch upon it. This phenomenon (a net increase of 5500 new Americans per day) is, of course, the basis for growing industrial pollution U.S. style. We do everything big here. We have about 6 per cent of the world's population, yet we consume about 40 per cent of the world's resources and energy. We live an incredibly good life, and in consequence place a fantastic burden upon our environment.

SOME HISTORICAL TIDBITS

I make no pretense of being a historian; nevertheless, we can gain perspective on the industrial impact by reviewing the highlights of The Industrial Revolution.

Written for this volume. Dr. Oscar W. Johnson is Professor of Biology at Moorhead State College, Moorhead, Minnesota.

Prior to 1750, farming was mankind's major occupation. In small towns, craftsmen made hardware goods, cloth, etc., in their own shops. Conditions were often unpleasant, hunger was commonplace as were epidemic diseases.

In about 1750 changes began, particularly in England. The commonfolk were anxious for a better way of life, and a few enterprising souls with a vision toward the future started to manufacture cotton cloth. These early mills were probably the world's first factories.

With the water wheel as an energy source, iron mills, textile plants, and pottery works were well established by the late 1700s. In 1769 Watt invented the steam engine, and the latter gradually replaced water power as industries expanded. To fire the boilers of steam engines, coal mining assumed massive proportions.

The Age of Steel dawned about 1870, and the world's first billion dollar company—United States Steel—was founded in 1901. With all of this industrial growth came roads, railways, and improved communications networks. Generally peoples' lives were enriched as industrial development forged ahead. Between 1815 and 1939 average per capita income in England increased about thirty-fold. Standards of comfort grew more rapidly than ever before in the history of mankind.

In 1878, Edison produced the incandescent lamp, and shortly thereafter he designed the world's first electrical power plant. Now the industrial giant had a new source of energy, and even greater vistas emerged.

In the early 1900s machine tools were introduced—tools with which one could manufacture precision parts in large quantities. The parts could then be brought together on an assembly line, and the finished product mass produced. The industrial world of the 20th century was in flower.

DECEIT, DECLINE, DEMISE

Ecologists have warned of impending environmental problems for many years. Politician and layman alike have remained apathetic, preferring to touch-up the X-rays rather than coming to grips with the situation. We have been deceiving ourselves with unfounded complacency largely ignoring the environmental decline apparent to those who care to look. Admittedly, there have always been the prophets of doomsday—but generally they have not been reputable scientists.

It is now probable that sufficient environmental degradation exists in certain areas of our country to produce unprecedented calamities. With appropriate weather conditions, a massive build-up of air pollutants in a metropolitan center could kill or severely injure thousands. Perhaps this is the sort of jarring experience necessary to stimulate social and political action on the scale necessary to prevent ecosystem collapse. Barry Commoner has suggested that our government declare a state of ecological emergency and begin to react within that context. I would heartily agree with such an approach.

Although the problems are manifold, I must, within the confines of this paper, restrict myself to only a few critical areas. Hence, I will focus upon the automobile, the power industry, certain effects of the mining and chemical industries, and problems associated with the extraction and processing of oil. Only the basics will be treated—an indepth discussion of any one of the above would be the subject of a book.

The Automobile

The eternal, infernal, internal combustion engine (as Ralph Nader puts it) is an enigma to modern man. Each of us enjoys the luxury affored by this marvelous machine. Encompassing everything from trips to the supermarket to one's love life, it is a cornerstone upon which our society rests. Yet this convenience factor is a monster in disguise. In aggregate, motor vehicles are responsible for the major share (about 60 per cent) of air pollution in our country.

Some 90 million motor vehicles presently spew forth exhaust wastes in the United States. In almost human-like fashion, the automobile is experiencing a population explosion of its own. Estimates indicate that there will be about 200 million "cougars," "impalas," "falcons," and other assorted mechanical animals on our highways by the year 2000. Perhaps future survival amidst boa-constrictor traffic will require one to drive a supercar—let's call it the "rhino!"

Thus far the automobile industry has applied very little of its engineering talent toward the development of a minimum pollution engine. Pollution control devices are now being used, but only as a result of legal compulsion. The devices are not outstandingly effective, and require frequent servicing if they are to perform adequately. The average motorist does not maintain this equipment in top-working condition.

The National Air Pollution Control Administration (NAPCA) has the responsibility of certifying that the pollution control devices are doing their intended job. Thus far, this has been handled in an ineffective way with the automobile companies submitting carefully tuned prototype vehicles for the tests. It is obvious that tests should be done on production-line cars chosen at random. Incidentally, tests on the latter generally show that they fail to meet the pollution abatement standards. Here is a statistic which should frighten anyone: 2.5 million production-line cars were certified AOK after the antipollution devices on a sample of *twelve* carefully tuned prototypes were checked by NAPCA. Tougher laws may be on the horizon. Serious consideration is being given to a deadline of 1975 at which time cars could release not more than 10 per cent of the pollutants presently allowed under existing standards.

According to some, such cleanliness cannot be achieved with the internal combustion engine.

Automobile exhaust is a potent vaporous brew wherein the primary constituents are carbon monoxide, a variety of hydrocarbons, nitrogen oxides, and lead. All of these materials pose certain potential threats to human health.

Carbon monoxide (CO) is an insidious material since it is colorless and nonirritating. CO is one of the most important pollutants amidst the congested traffic of big cities. Fantastic quantities are released daily—for example, about 8.3 million pounds in New York City, and about 20 million pounds in Los Angeles. When inhaled, CO passes across the moist membranes lining one's lungs and enters the blood. Carbon monoxide in the blood is a "no-no"! The normal function of hemoglobin in red blood cells is to transport oxygen throughout the body. Unfortunately, hemoglobin has about 200 times greater affinity for CO than for oxygen. As hemoglobin becomes saturated with CO, oxygen transport is impaired. Such a situation has an immediate effect upon those tissues with the highest oxygen demand, namely the brain and spinal cord. Reduced oxygen would be expected to cause changes in normal brain function. Some preliminary studies indicate the CO levels in heavy traffic are sufficient to depress one's discrimination of time. Such an impairment while driving has obvious safety aspects, and should be evaluated further.

One of the most reassuring things that I know of is the knowledge that one's chest contains a happy and healthy heart humming along in a robust manner. Less reassuring is the fact that some investigators view long term exposure to low levels of CO as a possible factor in the development of heart disease. Anyone with cardio-vascular problems may overtax an already weakened heart and blood vessels by inhalation of CO. In other words, when hemoglobin is transporting less than a normal load of oxygen, the heart must work harder to pump additional blood so as to make up the deficit.

If you have ever stood in the middle of Los Angeles or some other major city, and wondered where the buildings went you probably were experiencing smog. Historically, the term "smog" was coined about 1905 in London to denote an atmospheric mixture of smoke and fog. In this country the word has a different meaning—it refers to reactions between various hydrocarbons and nitrogen oxides (both coming primarily from motor vehicle exhaust) which are brought about under the influence of sunlight. The materials produced in the smog reaction are complex and diverse. An accompanying bluish-gray haze in the air obscures vision, and one feels a burning sensation in the eyes and throat.

Two of the most important and damaging components of smog are peroxyacetyl nitrate (abbreviated PAN) and ozone (O_3). Both materials are extremely toxic to plants which are sensitive to minute quantities of these pollutants—levels measured in hundreths of parts per million (ppm) in the air. The full economic impact of crop damage can only be estimated, but it is generally conceded that many millions of dollars are lost annually in Southern California and elsewhere, particularly in the eastern states. Perhaps even more important than the loss of crops is the apparent relationship between smog and human respiratory distress. Every year several thousand people are advised by their physicians to leave Los Angeles as a result of respiratory illness (generally acute bronchitis) probably triggered by sensitivity to smog. Some medical people feel that smog is a likely causative factor in the induction of lung cancer.

It used to be thought that smog was a local problem essentially confined to metropolitan areas. This is no longer true, and California has the dubious distinction of demonstrating this to the nation. Enough smog now spills over and out of the Los Angeles basin to cause ecological upset many miles away. Trees in the San Bernardino National Forest (60 to 100 miles east of the city) are being damaged and killed in large numbers by the fumes of Los Angeles traffic.

I hesitate to make the picture even gloomier, but the automobile is also responsible for other goodies in our air—such as minute particles of asbestos (from brake linings), glass dust (ground by the incessant passage of tires over the pavement), rubber dust (from the same source), and aerosols of lead (from burning leaded gasolines). All of these are extreme health hazards. Lead is especially frightening because of its damaging effects upon blood cell formation and nerves function. It is estimated that 200,000 tons of lead are being spewed annually from automobiles in the United States.

A particularly shady chapter in the annals of the automobile industry was brought to light about a year ago following a grand jury investigation. There is good evidence to suggest that the "Big-Four" (Ford, G.M., Chrysler, American) agreed to a pact in 1953 whereby they would not compete in the development of pollution control devices for their vehicles. Essentially, this curtailed research and engineering in this crucial area for about 15 years. In fact, the automakers did not respond to the need for pollution suppression until forced to do so by recent passage of federal and state laws. The whole situation almost resulted in a federal lawsuit against the automotive industry, but the proceedings were dropped under the veil of a consent decree. The latter is an agreement that the automakers will not continue to impede progress in the area of pollution control. As one author put it, "The industry received a slap on the wrist." It would be interesting, probably shocking, to know what went on behind the scenes in this legal wrangle.

There is no question that automobile induced pollution will have to be curtailed drastically in the immediate future. The auto industry has a tremendous economic and engineering commitment tied to the internal combustion engine. Industry has taken the position that a pollution-free version of the latter can be produced. There are many who feel that this is impossible and that any improvements in engine performance will be offset by greater numbers of vehicles in the future.

The internal combustion engine may have reached a point where it is simply obsolete. A number of competent engineers have voiced the opinion that the Rankine cycle (steam) engine would be an attractive alternative to the present Detroit product. A steam system produces but a small fraction of the pollutants emitted by the standard internal combustion engine. Thus far the automakers have not applied their tremendous engineering resources toward the development of alternative engines.

One thing is clear—we cannot continue to pollute our air simply because the automobile and oil industries are unwilling to assume responsibility. Changes must be made or we will be forced to erect roadsigns like one I saw depicted in a cartoon—it said, "Caution, Breathing May Be Hazardous To Your Health." Some recent work states these hazards in a particularly drastic manner. According to Lane and Seskin, a 50 per cent reduction in air pollution would result in a 25 per cent decline in death from lung cancer and other respiratory diseases, and 20 per cent less disease and death due to cardiovascular problems. Aside from the value of lives, over 2 billion dollars would be saved annually. Unless all common sense and morality are to be sacrificed, no individual or industry can oppose a realistic and vigorous campaign to clean up America's air. After all, even polluters have to breathe.

The Power Industry

Society's demand for electrical energy is growing at an incredible rate—doubling about every 10 years. Over the next 20 years it is anticipated that the U.S. will need 340 new electrical generating plants and 200,000 miles of new transmission lines. This complex would cover an area about twice the size of the state of Delaware.

Some of the new plants would produce electricity by burning coal, many would be nuclear ("nukes" for short). Each of the latter requires monstrous quantities of water to cool the reactor in which is housed a controlled nuclear reaction. The easiest and cheapest way for power companies to cool such a facility is to circulate water through it from a nearby river or lake. Unfortunately, when the water is discharged, it is carrying a load of heat. Dumping this water back into a river or lake causes ecologic alternations, since aquatic organisms are generally intolerant to such temperature changes. The overall effect is to disrupt the aquatic ecosystem, and to degrade it from an aesthetic and recreational point of view. In two words, this is "thermal pollution."

Projections concerning the next several decades make one cringe. Within 30 years, at present rates of expansion, the power industry would require about 1/3 of all flowing waters (rivers and streams) in the United States to cool its plants. The latter figure is calculated on an average annual basis—during periods of low water flow (late summer) the demand would approach 100 per cent of our flowing waters. The trend is toward multiple generating facilities spaced out along major rivers. It does not require much imagination to visualize an ecological change of great magnitude affecting an entire river system.

But before we give Ol' Man River a heat rash two very important points should be made. First, massive thermal pollution will probably not be tolerated by the general public or allowed under federal water quality standards. Secondly, much of the thermal pollution effect can be avoided through the use of certain engineering techniques (cooling towers, for example) which cool the water prior to final discharge. The mechanics of these facilities are beyond the scope of this paper. They are expensive, and hence industry (trying to maximize income for its stockholders) has not rushed headlong into needed research and development. One final point on this matter—cost analyses generally indicate that effective cooling towers increase the consumer's electric bill by only 1 to 3 per cent. This is a small price to pay for minimizing the thermal impact.

Of a much different nature is the radiation hazard posed by the large number of "nukes" projected for construction during the next couple of decades. There is as yet no "clean" reactor—certain quantities of radioactive material are given off to the environment. Investigations have revealed that these substances find their way into food chains where they can be tremendously concentrated and possibly passed along to man. A great deal more research in this food chain aspect is needed urgently.

Radioactive wastes which do not escape to the environment must periodically be removed from the reactor and "disposed" of. Generally, they are kept in underground storage facilities where radiation gradually dissipates. During this period of decline, great care must be taken to insure that no leakage or contamination of the environment (ground water, for example) occurs. We now have stored waste materials which will have to be policed by the next 15-20 generations of human beings in order to insure safety. This is a questionable legacy!

A major reactor accident causing widespread damage and death could be an unfortunate adjunct to the growth of the power industry. Reactors are extremely complex, and they are subject to human error in design, construction, and operation. The Pacific Gas and Light Company proposed to build a reactor over an earthquake zone north of San Francisco. Consolidated Edison wanted to locate a plant in the heart of New York City. Both of these projects were stopped by concerned citizens who asked some fundamental and embarrassing questions. In either case an accident could have assumed hideous proportions.

The key to the environmental impact of the power industry is in the hands of our society. If we continue to allow population expansion coupled with a demand for the ultimate in creature comforts, then we are undoubtedly going to trade much environmental quality for electric tooth brushes and can openers.

Let's ask ourselves a very basic question—can we really have *all* the electric power we want and a decent environment too?

Mining and Chemical Industries

Environmental problems associated with these industries have as many facets as Liz Taylor's diamond rings. All I can hope to do is describe a couple of situations, and I have arbitrarily chosen taconite and mercury.

Lake Superior presently is the cleanest of the Great Lakes. Over much of its area it is clear and unpolluted, and as such represents a tremendous natural resource. Enter the villain who would sacrifice such quality for personal profit. The Reserve Mining Company near Duluth processes low-grade iron ore called taconite. After extraction of the iron, there are tremendous quantities of useless "tailings" left over. Somehow, the "tailings" must be disposed of, and Lake Superior is handy—so splash! At present, the company dumps about 60,000 tons per day into the lake. Although arguments rage on both sides, the simple fact is that the ecological impact of this venture upon the lake's ecosystem is not understood. We have here another classic example of a large scale experiment (akin to the use of pesticides, atomic testing, etc.) where the environment is used as a guinea pig without any real knowledge of the potential result.

At this time, the whole situation has become a complicated legal entanglement wherein the State of Minnesota is attempting to halt the dumping. The federal government is also in the fracas since interstate waters as well as federal water quality standards are involved. How long it will take to resolve the legal aspects of the situation is a moot point—meanwhile 60,000 tons per day!

Disposal of mercury into our nation's lakes and rivers is an indefensible affront to society. Those who operate and control chemical companies are well aware of the extreme hazards associated with mercury. Yet without apparent moral reservation large quantities of mercury have been flushed into the Great Lakes system, and into many other rivers and lakes across the United States.

Minute quantities of mercury in one's food or water cause brain and kidney damage. One develops symptoms such as muscular tremors, dizziness, headaches, fatigue, and blindness. Mercury crosses the placenta in pregnant women and can induce fetal malformations. If one ingests enough mercury, the effect is fatal. In short—mercury is one of the most toxic materials known to man.

When elemental mercury is dumped into a lake or river, it is acted upon by bacteria in the bottom sediments and converted to methyl mercury. The latter is soluble in water, tends to be concentrated by small organisms, and thus enters the food chain. In fish, methyl mercury appears to pass directly from the water across the gills and into the body. Lake Erie pike have been found to contain mercury in excess of 3000 times the concentration present in the water around them.

No one really knows what constitutes a "safe-level" of mercury in our food and water. The Food and Drug Administration says that fish is dangerous to eat if it contains over 0.5 ppm (parts per million) mercury. Fishes from Lake Erie typically contain 1 ppm with some going as high as 5 ppm. The Public Health Service has set a tentative "safe-level" of 5 ppb (parts per billion) in drinking water. Downstream from a General Electric battery manufacturing plant in Michigan the water contained about 1000 ppm!

Currently, a number of corporations (such as Allied Chemical, Olin, Weyerhauser, etc.) are facing federal lawsuits in the battle against mercury pollution. Each of these companies was discharging many *pounds* of mercury per day into nearby lakes and rivers. Try the following for a grim statistic: the total amount of mercury which was being daily added to Lake Erie by a number of companies around its perimeter was estimated at 300 pounds! And this went on for years. In some respects, it is unfortunate that in our legal structure we can sue only the guilty *corporations.* Actually, the *individuals* who allowed this to happen should also be sued, and they should be given stiff jail sentences appropriate to their disdain for moral responsibility. The mercury story could be made into a super-polluted "X" rated movie titled, "I'll Do It Until You Catch Me."

The Oil Industry

Tampa Bay, the Santa Barbara Channel, the Louisiana Gulf Coast, the coastline of Southeast Alaska, and the Knife River in North Dakota all have something in common. Each has been polluted with crude oil. Some cases were much worse than others, but in each place living things were killed and ecosystems dramatically altered.

Even a casual survey of the problem reveals that the cases above are but a small fraction of the total impact of oil pollution in the modern world. There are countless spills and accidents, most of which never make the news. The total quantity of oil annually spilled at sea is not known, but one expert, Max Blumer of Woods Hole Oceanographic Institute, estimates the amount at up to 100 million tons. Dr. Blumer also points out that certain fractions of this oil (often toxic materials) are soluble in sea water, and are taken up by marine organisms. Here then is another situation where dangerous compounds appear to be entering food chains, and might ultimately be passed on to man himself.

There are many subtle and inconspicuous aspects within the workings of an ecosystem. It appears that marine creatures often depend upon chemical signals to release behavior associated with finding food, locating a mate, or avoiding predators. Many of these reactions seem to be governed by chemical substances at levels of ppb (parts per billion) in the sea water. According to Blumer, certain fractions of oil resemble some of these natural messengers. Hence pollution even at extremely low levels might change behavior patterns in various marine organisms Alterations of this sort could disrupt a complex ecosystem. This is an unfortunate possibility in view of the importance of the sea as a food producing resource for our expanding human population.

To me, the most disheartening specter of potential oil disaster today exists in the state of Alaska. For decades it was assumed that tundra regions of the far North were safe from the ravages of "civilized" man. Now all that is changed—look closely, the aurora borealis bears a strong resemblance to shimmering dollar signs!

At Prudhoe Bay on the North Slope of Alaska (and at other sites in Arctic Canada) massive deposits of oil have been discovered. Transporting this oil to markets will be one of the biggest environmental gambles in the history of mankind. Two modes of transport have been proposed—pipeline and supertanker. Present plans call for construction of an 800 mile pipeline from the oil fields in the north to the port of Valdez on Alaska's south coast. The pipeline would traverse many river systems (including the Yukon), cross a number of earthquake zones, and negotiate a huge expanse of tundra underlain by permafrost. It is unlikely that such a pipeline can be maintained without eventual breaks. A broken water pipe in your backyard is one thing, a break in a pipe 48 inches in diameter carrying hot crude oil is quite another. Such an event could create an environmental nightmare of unprecedented scale. Consider for example, the consequences of a major spill into the headwaters of the Yukon River.

The supertanker approach is equally grim. Massive vessels are being developed to sail the Arctic Ocean (via the Northwest Passage) and deliver oil to refineries on the East Coast. Based upon our record so far, it is only a matter of time before one of these vessels does the "Torrey Canyon" routine, spilling a colossal quantity of oil. Whenever oil is spilled, it is gradually degraded and cleaned up by bacterial action. In the cold climate of the far north, bacterial effects are slow, and the damage inflicted would probably persist for decades.

Recently, in a speech before the Moorhead Chamber of Commerce, an executive of the Standard Oil Company made an interesting observation. He said that anticipated oil consumption in the 1980s is so great that the Prudhoe Bay field contains less than a two-year supply of petroleum for the U.S. Certainly such a statement prompts some basic questions: Is oil extraction in the far North really worth the probability of massive environmental deterioration? Do we really need that particular oil? Despite the immediate economics of the situation, what ethics should guide our course from a long-range point of view? Is it our responsibility to maintain a quality environment for generations yet unborn?

There are some rays of hope on the Alaskan scene which may at least delay an eco-oil catastrophe. The oil companies assumed with frontier zeal that their pipeline could not be stopped. In fact, they purchased low-bid pipe from Japan even before obtaining the necessary federal permit to cross public lands. Construction was to begin in the fall of 1969, essentially without any research on the ecological impact of the project. Three organizations (Friends of the Earth, Wilderness Society, Environmental Defense Fund) decided to fight, and they succeeded in getting a legal injunction which thus far has blocked the project. It is possible that the injunction will not be lifted until completion of detailed ecological studies on the pipeline's environmental impact—this could mean a lengthy delay. Furthermore, the Canadian government has viewed the use of an arctic route by oil tankers with considerable alarm. Canada has much to lose in the event of an oil spill along her northern coastline. Perhaps oil extraction in Alaska will be retarded long enough to allow more intelligent planning such that pollution can be lessened. However, two things are certain: political-industrial pressure will be relentless until the oil somehow is brought to market; and this cannot be done without ecological damage of unknown proportions in the far North.

A PLEA FOR A NEW PHILOSOPHY

Why do we mistreat the environment which sustains us? I have shown a gross lack of environmental conscience on the part of industry, but the same attitude exists in many, perhaps most, individuals. I recently stood at a scenic overlook viewing the blue Pacific off the island of Oahu in Hawaii. I glanced down at the rocks below, and was astonished by an indescribable array of trash. Why had people knowingly defiled one of the most beautiful seascapes in the world?

Lynn White, a noted historian, feels that the basic cause of our heavy-handed treatment of nature lies rooted in fundamental Christian beliefs. The concept that it is God's will for man to exploit nature and to exert dominion over other living things is a basic Christian tenet. This philosophy in our forefathers, coupled with the challenge of the frontier, has fixed in society a view of "progress" which is incompatible with our ecosystem. To most people the building of a dam, the construction of a highway, a new shopping center, or a growing industry is "progress." Every Chamber of Commerce in the U.S. has as its holy writ the attraction of people and industry. A well-known biologist, Garrett Hardin, warns that we cannot regard the environment as a "commons" to which we all are entitled. If we hold this view, the individual will attempt to overexploit for his own benefit to the detriment of society.

It is no longer heretical to suggest that our traditional view of "progress" has to change. Our planet is finite; we cannot expand our industries and our GNP to infinity. To continue in such an attempt will mean the complete loss of freedom and quality in human existence. Our first great hurdle is to stabilize population growth which is the major force pushing us down the hill toward environmental collapse. If this can be done, perhaps we will enter a whole new technological age—one in which we recycle instead of exploit, where we emphasize quality of experience and existence, and attempt to maximize per capita opportunity and potential. As Gaylord Nelson said, "Survival and quality are much more important than progress and quantity." To accomplish such a change in attitude will require education leading to a general awareness of ecological concepts by society. It will necessitate massive programs of pollution abatement and research in new technologies. War will have to become obsolete if the human species intends to meet the economic demands associated with becoming a member of a self-sustaining ecological system. Perhaps this last requirement will be the most difficult of all, if man (as some experts propose) is by his very genetic make-up an aggressive creature.

Aside from his scientific achievements, Aldo Leopold was perhaps the most eloquent philosopher of ecology that this country has produced. I think it is appropriate to close with a quote from his writings: "We abuse land because we regard it as a commodity belonging to us. When we see land as a community to which we belong we may begin to use it with love and respect." Let us hope that it is not too late to establish such an ethic as a foundation for our society during the perilous decades ahead.

BIBLIOGRAPHY

Air Conservation. 1965. Publication No. 80 of the American Association for the Advancement of Science, Washington, D.C. 335 pp.

Carter, L. J. 1969. North Slope: Oil Rush. *Science,* 166: 85-92.

Clark, J. R. 1969. Thermal pollution and aquatic life. *Scientific American,* 220: 19-27.

Cole, L. C. 1968. Can the world be saved? *BioScience,* 18: 679-684.

Esposito, J. C. 1970. *Vanishing air.* New York, N.Y.: Grossman, 328 pp.

Goldsmith, J. R. and S. A. Landaw. 1968. Carbon monoxide and human health. *Science,* 162: 1352-1359.

Greenberg, D. S. 1969. Pollution control: Sweden sets up an ambitious new program. *Science,* 166: 200-201.

Hardin, G. 1968. The tragedy of the commons. *Science,* 162: 1243-1248.

Holcomb, R. W. 1969. Oil in the ecosystem. *Science,* 166: 204-206.

Holcomb, R. W. 1970. Power generation: The next 30 years. *Science,* 167: 159-160.

Laycock, G. 1970. *The diligent destroyers.* New York, N.Y.: Doubleday, 225 pp.

Leinwand, G. 1969. *Air and water pollution.* New York, N.Y.: Washington Square Press, 160 pp.

Leopold, A. 1949. *The Sand County Almanac.* New York, N.Y.: Oxford Univ. Press.

Love, L. B. and E. P. Seskin. 1970. Air pollution and human health. *Science,* 169: 723-733.

Macinko, J. 1970. The tailpipe problem. *Environment,* 12: 6-13

Marine, G. 1969. *America the raped.* New York, N.Y.: Simon and Schuster, 312pp.

The Crisis of Survival. Entire issue of *The Progressive,* April 1970.

Wagar, J.A. 1970. Growth versus the quality of life. *Science,* 168: 1179-1184

White, L. 1967. The historical roots of our ecologic crisis. *Science,* 155: 1203-1207

Cultural Specialization Versus Living Space

Laurence Falk

Man is uncertain about how to judge his cities. Some persons view urban concentrations of people as the ultimate of all that is good, true and beautiful. Others view cities as places that stimulate and give rise to all the baser emotions and activities of man. Whatever the view, the city has been the social and cultural base for millions of people through hundreds of years. As soon as man freed some of his time from food gathering activities, he collected himself into cities and began to expand his technologies.

The chain of technological-agricultural-production to efficient- food-distribution to concentrations-of-people to increased-specialization continues intact though the linkages are not always apparent nor precise. The link between concentrations-of-people and increased specialization is an important though not invariable one. Perhaps a demonstration of this link will serve to clarify this relationship.

As we know, specialization implies something which is unique and which occurs with low frequency. Let us say that an individual needs to use a large capacity electronic computer. Usually the individual does not require as constant a use of such a tool as he would of a typewriter. Since the computer requires a much higher investment than a typewriter and is used comparatively less, he is unlikely to purchase this tool for his individual use. Instead, he seeks others who also require the partial use of one and shares in its cost through a co-operative purchase, or he hires the service from a computer center that provides the needed service for him and others. Only in this way can he afford to use this specialized instrument.

Computer users are not isolated from other populations. They share the needs for shelter, food, clothing, etc., with other people. Concentrations of people include, therefore, persons who share common general needs as well as persons with special needs. If persons with specialized needs were completely randomly distributed in a population there would be a direct and positive relationship between the size of a population and the number of specialized services provided. However, it is possible for persons with the same specialized needs to

Written for this volume. Dr. Laurence L. Falk is Associate Professor of Sociology at Concordia College, Moorhead, Minnesota.

collect in a given location. In most populations, though, specialized needs are neither wholly randomly distributed nor are they highly concentrated. Persons with specialized needs tend to be sufficiently randomly distributed within a population so that there is a general correlation between specialized services and the size of a population. Specialization, then, is in part a function of needs and numbers of people (Hoover, 1968). Stated as a simple formula, $Sp = f(Pn + N)$ where Sp = specialization, Pn = personal needs and N = number of people.

An important factor in the provision of specialized services is the distance at which one can obtain the service. One is much less likely to utilize a service that is 250 miles distant than one that is five. It is reasonable to assume, therefore, that the most efficient use of a service could be obtained only if that service were in a location central to the population requiring the service. This notion is known as that of " mean location." Its principal can be demonstrated by the following example.

Let us suppose that a service is located at the midpoint of a ten block area (5 4 3 2 1 . 1 2 3 4 5). If a person located in each of the blocks travelled to the point (.) of service, the total number of blocks travelled would be 30 blocks. That is, the person in area one would travel one block, the person in two, two blocks, etc. By shifting the service one block to the left or right we increase the total number of blocks travelled by all the persons to obtain the service, e.g. (4 3 2 1 . 1 2 3 4 5 6). The total distance travelled in this second example is 31 blocks. Now, if the service were to be located at the left or right extreme of the area, we maximize the distance travelled by all persons to obtain the service (. 1 2 3 4 5 6 7 8 9 10) = 55 blocks. This is similar to the situation that occurs when services are moved to the suburban areas of a community. If we incorporate the distance factor into the formula stated above, this formula becomes $Sp = f(Pn + N)/D$ where Sp = specialization, Pn = personal need, N = number of people and D = distance.

Obviously there are many factors that this formula omits. It does not consider differentials in transportation efficiency, in the socio-economic status of persons seeking service or in the motivations for use of the service, just to name a few. Nevertheless, it does demonstrate the principal that the more specialized the service, the more likely it is to occur within larger population centers simply because of its maximum accessibility to the highest number of potential users.

The exponential growth of technology has permitted man to concentrate his populations ever more densely. The technology that permits man to produce greater amounts of food with less manpower also permits man to surround himself with numerous manufactured devices for his comfort and pleasure. Occupational specialization has increased concomitantly with technological development. As a consequence urban life has become a fabric of interwoven specialities that comprise a symbiosis of mutually interdependent components.

Urban man exists because his technologies exist, and these technologies permit his concentrated populations. On the basis of current theory, it appears that the balance between population and technology is a delicate one (Bronfenbrenner and Buttrick, 1960). Certainly present technologies permit a concentration of populations that was not possible with hunting and gathering societies existing at the time of European colonial expansion.

It is awesome to consider what could happen if there were a major, nation-wide collapse of the communication and transportation system. It is estimated that about 50 per cent of our traffic flow is concentrated on about ten per cent of our transportation system. Accidents and defective traffic signals are sufficient to create major delays in the flow of traffic. The flow of foodstuffs into our major cities each day is impressive. If certain commodities can be priced beyond imagination in Chicago because of a snowstorm and if a power outrage in New York inspires special artistic creations, then certainly a total national power failure of several months would make living in most of our major cities virtually impossible. Such a catastrophe could create a thoroughgoing fight for survival. If the reader thinks this to be an overstatement, he may make the point by listing all components in the average home that are directly powered by electricity. Then, he may list all services that are secondarily dependent upon electricity. What is being suggested is simply that we have created a way of life which concentrates people in urban areas and that these concentrations of people survive through their dependency on technologies. It is also suggested that any major interruption in the flow of services could have a staggering impact on the survival of these populations.

It is difficult to determine exactly how much living space man "naturally" requires. A review of anthropological literature reveals that man lives in a wide variety of spatial circumstances. One can perform experiments which test the effects of a spatially controlled environment on rats, fruit flies, and monkeys, but one cannot perform the same kinds of experiments with humans (Freeman and Giovannoni, 1969; Calhoun, 1969). Studies of animals display wide varieties of spatial accomodations (Scott, 1969), some displaying unusual responses to controlled crowding in their environment (Calhoun, 1969). Earlier studies of humans in crowded urban areas suggested higher rates of mental illness and some other aberrant responses. Because of problems in control, however, the effects of urban crowding on man are as yet not precisely determined (Freeman and Giovannoni, 1969). Nevertheless, there are certain observations that one can make about population density and man. It has already been noted that concentrations of people create a complex system of social interdependencies and a reliance on technology to satisfy daily requirements for food, shelter, clothing, etc. There are important changes in the social system that accrue within such urban concentrations.

Simply because there are more people in a given space it is more difficult for any person to know all others in that location. For instance, the number of different two-person relationships in a group of ten persons is 45. The formula for determining this is $N(N-1)/2$ where N is the number of persons in the group. For 1,000 people the number of different pairs is 499,500; for a city of 100,000 persons it is 4,999,950,000. Obviously this bit of mathematics has important implications for the ongoing social processes in the community. As population densities increase, the likelihood of a single person knowing all other persons in the community dramatically decreases. It is little wonder that persons are likely to meet only strangers in their excursions outside their daily routine or that getting acquainted with people has become an art or science with many people.

Large populations are associated with numerous factors, some contributing to the satisfaction of man's basic needs and some inhibiting such provision. With more people man does have to compete more intensely for his daily foods, goods and services. Jonassen (1959) has correlated 82 factors with percentages of urbanization in populations in an attempt to determine the inter-relation of urbanity and such factors as amount of education, welfare services, industries and kinds of dwelling units. What emerges is a profile of urbanity that creates greater opportunity and potential for stress but also supplies accompanying provisions for handling stress, though they are generally available only for those who compete more successfully.

It is less difficult to determine what kind of living space people prefer than to determine what is optimum for healthy survival. It is obvious that people prefer more living space than they have. Michelson (1968) reports that building trades are producing housing that will require persons (1) to live in multiple dwelling units, (2) to have smaller home lots, (3) to live closer to the center of the city, and (4) to select public over private transportation. The study found no one individual in their sample whose desires matched all four of these requirements. The interesting thing is that there is a rapid increase in the proportion of multiple dwelling units that are being built in spite of these incompatible personal preferences.

Those who can afford to do so move to areas where there is more living space (Schnore and Pinkerton, 1966). It is a cliche in America that the population of the central areas of most of our major cities is decreasing or remaining stable while the population of their fringes is rapidly increasing (Hawley, Duncan and Goldberg, 1964). This trend intensified during the past two decades because the depression of the thirties and the war of the early forties drastically slowed down the construction of housing. Many persons, though certainly not all, do not want to live in the core of the cities. Those who do live there often do so because of economic or social factors that prohibit their living elsewhere (Schnore, 1964). Housing construction is now running well behind what is needed. If home construction were to catch up to demand it likely would not change the flight to the metropolitan fringes. Available information indicates that the diffusionary trend of the '50s and '60s will continue into the '70s unless some major social change interrupts this process.

Various stereotypes have emerged about persons who move to the outer fringes of the city. Assumptions are that suburbs attract white, middle-class, politically conservative, married persons with children (Fava, 1966). Others question whether these persons are predominant in suburbs (Berger, 1966). Some have argued that the flow to the suburbs is a carry-over of rural values (Rogers, 1960) and that urban people continue to hold the assumed virtues of rural living (Vidich and Bensman, 1958). There seems to be a contradiction in that if rural values are so important, why do persons leave the rural areas in the first place? Of course, the primary reason for leaving is economic—there simply is not sufficient economic opportunity in rural areas to provide employment for as many persons as are reproduced there (Beale, 1964).

Another explanation comes from the notion that persons are able to have specialized services only in relation to the number of people who desire those services. Since many of these services are not available in rural areas, persons live close to areas where they are available. One can say then, whether the flight to the suburbs is dependent on a nostalgic attitude toward country life or whether it is due to other preferences associated with more living space, the preference for the fringe is real. Persons are availing themselves of opportunities to obtain the kind of living space provided in the fringes of the cities. This establishes the basic dilemma posed in this chapter, that the preference for specialized services and technology is at odds with preferences for living space.

Two alternatives are usually suggested as partial solutions to the problem of meeting present needs for adequate living space. One solution seeks the redistribution of peoples from highly concentrated urban centers to rural areas (Doxiadis, 1968). It is supposed that this redistribution would relieve pressures in urban areas and provide better economies in rural communities. However, this process diminishes the availability of specialized services that are provided in the more concentrated living areas. Furthermore, this will likely have little direct effect in reducing the overall population pressure simply because the vacant space created by the people leaving the city would be rapidly filled by the offspring of those remaining in the area. The migration of people to reduce population pressure is at best only a stop-gap solution. The accompanying problem of converting more and more land, including agricultural land, to housing and service-industrial uses reduces the amount of land available for the production of food. The building of new cities leads either to their expansion into larger cities, or if growth is controlled, to the continual construction of additional cities. Logic leads to the conclusion that the available land supply would eventually be depleted.

The second frequently suggested solution for providing adequate living spaces proposes that the city dweller squarely face his urban environment and create an inhabitable living space within the present urban confines. Certain processes are occurring that may be creating this kind of solution. The cost of new housing continues to increase. The price of land, materials and labor has reached a point that prohibits many families from purchasing a home. Consequently, there is an increase in the sale of mobile homes. Their total cost is generally less than stationary dwellings and they are crowded into less space. They permit their owners to take them along as they pursue better economic opportunities elsewhere. The competition for land has increased the costs for all types of commercial home buildings. Multiple units are increasing in proportion to single units because the cost per unit is lower and returns on investments are higher. Therefore, more families are forced to live in apartments either because that is all they can afford or because there are no single dwelling units available.

The primary difficulty with forcing people to stay in their present urban confines is that persons are not provided the kind of living space they prefer. We are far less than fully aware of all of the psychological implications of crowded urban living. Multiple dwelling units more often reflect economic than aesthetic concerns though there are notable exceptions. Some persons are concerned with the environment and are attempting to carry out innovations in design that take into account human needs and the natural habitat (McHarg, 1969). Nevertheless, modern man does face exceedingly important problems in creating an urban setting commensurate with his desires for an adequate living space.

The basic dilemma between man's desire for specialized services in our technological society and his desire for adequate living space remains. Are there other solutions than those of redistributing people into new areas or of heaping them up in their old ones? Either a reduction in the need for specialized services or a reduction in the desire for more living room would ameliorate the problem. Even though persons are actually accepting less living space than they desire, it does not mean that they will not go on desiring more. But, if one shifts the discussion from one of spatial quantity to spatial quality, the situation becomes more complex. If quantity and quality of living space are directly related, the solution becomes more problematical. It is apparent that if the quality of modern man's environment is not improved he is in serious trouble. It is not possible to reduce our concern for a higher quality of living space. We need to know a good deal more about how that quality relates to the amount of living space—certainly there is an important connection.

Then, what about reducing man's need for specialized services? It is evident that segments of the American population are becoming disillusioned with technological gadgetry. The subsequent rejection is expressed through continuing experiments in communal living, the interest in the more aesthetic eastern religions, intensive experimentation in personal communication and its meaning, and a basic questioning of man's dependency on and increased use of the variety of manufactured chemical products. It is not likely that man will give up all of this gadgetry since he is so dependent upon it. In fact, the massive concentrations of people could not permit this situation to change rapidly or drastically. It is this technology that has given Americans their long life expectancy as well as their mechanical flights from reality.

What other alternative is possible? An obvious way to ameliorate the dilemma of living space demands and technological specialization is to reduce or stop population growth. This would temper the drain on the natural resources and permit a greater expenditure of dollars and effort on the creation of a more inhabitable environment. It would reduce the need for taking over more land for living space and would permit its continued use for food or other production. It would serve to stabilize the need for contaminating manufactured products and permit experimentation for alternatives. By reducing population growth, the intensity of the conflict between demands for specialized services and demands for an inhabitable environment can be diminished. Without this reduction man will necessarily have to accept a more massive crowding or a reduction in his more specialized technologies.

BIBLIOGRAPHY

Beale, C. L. 1964. Rural depopulation in the United States: some demographic consequences of agricultural adjustments. *Demography* 1: 264-272.

Berger, B. M. 1966. The myth of suburbia. *In* Roland L. Warren (ed.) *Perspectives on the American community,* pp. 167-178. Chicago, Ill.: Rand McNally.

Bronfenbrenner, M. and J. A. Buttrick. 1960. Population control in Japan: an economic theory and its application. *Law and Contemporary Problems.* 25 (summer): 536-557.

Calhoun, J. B. 1969. Population density and social pathology. *In* Garrett Hardin (ed.) *Population, evolution and birth control,* pp. 101-105. San Francisco, Calif.: W. H. Freeman.

Doxiadis, C. A. 1968. Ecumenopolis: tomorrow's city. *Britannica Book of the Year 1968,* pp. 17-38. Chicago, Ill.: Britannica Press.

Everett, M. R. 1960. *Social change in rural society.* New York, N.Y.: Appleton-Century-Crofts.

Fava, Sylvia. 1966. Contrasts in neighboring. *In* Roland L. Warren (ed.) *Perspectives on the American community,* pp. 161-166. Chicago, Ill.: Rand McNally.

Freeman, H. E. and J. M. Giovannoni. 1969. Social psychology of mental health. *In* Gardner Lindzey and Elliot Aronson (eds.) *Handbook of social psychology,* Vol. 5, pp. 660-719. Reading, Mass.: Addison-Wesley.

Hawley A. H., B. Duncan and D. Goldberg. 1964. Some observations of changes in metropolitan population in the United States. *Demography* 1: 148-155.

Hoover, E. M. 1968. The evolving form and organization of the metropolis. *In* Harvey S. Perloff and Lowdon Wingo, Jr. (eds.) *Issues in urban economics,* pp. 237-284. Baltimore, Md.: Johns Hopkins Press.

Jonassen, C. T. 1959. Community typology. *In* Marvin B. Sussman (ed.) *Community structure and analysis,* pp. 15-36. New York, N.Y.: Thomas Y. Cromwell.

McHarg, I. L. 1969. *Design with nature.* Garden City, N.J.: Natural History Press.

Michelson W. 1968. Most people don't want what architects want. *TransAction* 5 (July/August): 37-43.

Schnore, L. F. 1964. Urban structure and suburban selectivity. *Demography* 1: 164-176.

Schnore, L. F. and J. R. Pinkerton. 1966. Residential redistribution of socioeconomic strata in metropolitan areas. *Demography* 3: 491-499.

Scott, J. P. 1969. The social psychology of infrahuman animals. *In* Gardner Lindzey and Elliot Aronson (eds.) *Handbook of social psychology,* Vol. 4, pp. 611-642. Reading, Mass.: Addison-Wesley.

Vidich, A. J. and J. Bensman. 1958. *Small town in mass society: class, power, and religion in a rural community.* New York, N.Y.: Anchor Books.

Stress and Overpopulation
Psychological Aspects of Overcrowding

Norma Flem

Approaches to the problem of overpopulation vary, but most emphasize food production, education, and fertility control, and to a lesser extent, environmental pollution and poverty. More recent approaches have focused on the quality of life with regard to overpopulation in terms of esthetics, or the form, color, and shape of the environment, and in terms of personal freedom. The present paper stresses a third approach to overpopulation: overcrowding in terms of the psychological effects it produces. The purpose of the paper is to investigate overpopulation with regard to its accompanying psychological aspects in the areas of animal studies, human stress, attitudes and values.

The irony of overpopulation and overcrowding is that it originates not in failure but in success; that is, it is the result of man's mastery of the earth. Overpopulation is due to the technology involved in food production, medicine, and public health, without the concomitant necessary changes in values and behavior. That the world is already, or is rapidly becoming, overpopulated is evidenced in the growth rate of 2.1 per cent, or the 190,000 people added to the earth each day. As early as 1927, when the world was relatively uncrowded, the problems of population pressure, defined as the "difficulty experienced in normal times by the industrious and frugal in obtaining the necessaries of life" (Ross, 1927), were being studied. Although a slight change in meaning and emphasis has evolved since 1927, the signs of population pressure delineated by Ross are still relevant: (1) laborious agriculture to extend food-growing areas; (2) completeness of land utilization; (3) extreme utilization and economy of materials; (4) exhausting labor for very little; (5) low standard of living; (6) difficulty in maintaining existence; (7) low value on human life; (8) dependence of the individual upon his group; and (9) neglect of play and recreation (Ross, 1927). Many of these signs of population pressure do not exist in the United States, but they are clearly evident in many overpopulated, underdeveloped countries of the world. The total interdependence of the nations of the world necessitates an immediate concern for overpopulation and overcrowding. For example, the United States contains only 6 per cent, or 1/17, of the world's

Written for this volume. Norma Flem is a Sociology-Psychology Majors student at Concordia College, Moorhead, Minnesota.

population, and yet it consumes 35 per cent, or 2/5 of the world's raw materials (Life, 1970). Therefore, the relative lack of crowding and pressure in the United States is still heavily influenced by, and dependent on, the conditions of overpopulation and population pressure existing in other areas of the world.

But even in the United States, population pressure is manifest in some areas. Using density, or the number of persons per square unit of area in a certain place (Heer, 1968), as the indicator of population pressure and overcrowding, the ten most densely populated areas of the world, in persons per square mile, as of 1960, are: (1) Netherlands—906; (2) Rhode Island—812; (3) New Jersey—806; (4) Belgium—773; (5) Massachusetts—654; (6) Japan—650; (7) Republic of Korea—637; (8) United Kingdom—554; (9) Federal Republic of Germany—551; (10) Connecticut—522 (Day and Day, 1964). Thus, although the United States as a whole is not considered overcrowded, four of its states rank in the top ten with the nations of the world in people per square mile.

Overcrowding, in the form of very densely populated areas, does exist. Studies of the effects of overcrowding, however, are few. That population growth, in the United States at least, has meant increasing control from external sources, less flexibility for individual behavior, greater centralization in government, crowded schools and recreation areas, vanishing countryside, air and water pollution, endless traffic jams, and a steady loss in time, solitude, and peace of mind (Day and Day, 1964), is a well-known fact, and similar consequences may be applied to other areas of the world where the population is large. But investigations of the psychological effects of population growth and overcrowding have centered mainly on studies of lower organisms, indicating the ways in which animals react to the stress of overpopulation, and the various methods employed for controlling population growth. Although caution must be exercised in applying animal studies to human conditions, some ethologists agree that certain aspects of animal behavior relate to the problems of human behavior.

A balance exists between the reproductive rates of a given species of organism and hazards of existence for that species. Even microorganisms, for example, multiply rapidly until the accumulation of toxic products causes the growth rate to decline. In this way, the microorganisms maintain a fairly constant balance between growth and death due to toxins (Hoaglund, 1968). Thus, the balance teeters, with shifts in abundance and hazards: when the hazards are greater than the reproductive rate, the species becomes extinct; when reproduction exceeds mortality to the point of overpopulation, a catastrophe such as disease or mass suicide ensues. Many animals have ways of anticipating their population densities, however, and these mechanisms of population control are the origins and roots of all social behavior in animals. The prevailing hypothesis is that negative natural controls check population growth, such as predators, starvation, disease, and accidents. According to Wynne-Edwards (1968), however, a new hypothesis more correctly applies to the situation: animals restrict population density by means of an artificial device related to food supply, such as territorial systems and group membership; a device related to social behavior, as in dominance, peck-order, and noise; or a device related to the functioning of the endocrine glands. An example of the use of territoriality in promoting population control can be found in certain species of song birds, which automatically limit their number without starvation by a division of good and poor territory from the standpoint of food supply. The birth rate is determined automatically by the amount of food that is available, simply because there is no breeding among the poorly fed (Day and Day, 1964). Similarly, social behavior works in controlling population densities in the area of noise, for example. A chorus may provide the species with an index of population density, so that any overcrowding leads to the expulsion of the surplus population (Wynne-Edwards, 1968).

Studies have also shown that the population density of a species affects the endocrine gland functionings of its members. An interaction exists between population density, endocrine functioning, and behavior, with population density positively related to adrenal hypertrophy and adrenocortical activity, and negatively related to gonadal and mammary activity. Therefore, the population size of some mammalian species is self-limiting; pituitary-adrenal-gonadal effects are produced by general stressors and are in proportion to the severity of the stress. Overpopulation, as a stressor, decreases gonadal activity and so decreases the size of the population, usually as the result of a decrease in the survival of infants due to deficient lactation of the mothers. This population control device can be studied simply as a function of the weight of the adrenal glands: increased adrenal weight is associated with increased densities, and since adrenal size correlates with adrenal activity, there is a progressive increase in stress and in endocrine response to it as the population increases (Thiessen and Rodgers, 1961).

Other species of animals do consistently overproduce, however. The snowshoe hare, for example, seems to follow ten year cycles in which the peak population density is reached every tenth year. Following a period of high population, the hares decline dramatically. Some authors have implicated overcrowding and stress; however, field evidence is lacking (Keith, 1963). Other species, when overcrowded, suffer from symptoms of enlarged adrenal glands and heart disease; studies of chickens and woodchucks at the Philadelphia Zoo have demonstrated an increase in fatal heart attacks when too many were put in a cage (Carrighar, 1968). Thus in crowded conditions, animals are killed more often by stress than by starvation; they adapt well to an increased density up to a certain point, but there seems to be a density beyond which they cannot go.

Studies on rats and mice have been conducted by Calhoun. In an article entitled "Population Density and Social Pathology," Calhoun reports the effects that overcrowding has on rats. In two series consisting of three experiments each, the rat population increased to approximately twice the number that could occupy the available space with only moderate stress from social interaction. Calhoun observed each of the colonies for 16 months in order to obtain records of modifications of behavior induced by population density. The animals were placed in four interconnected pens, each of which was a complete dwelling unit with unlimited food and water. To encourage differential use of the pens, the partitions between the pens were electrified to prevent climbing them, ramps went across three partitions, but not across the fourth, and the burrow in pen four was elevated to discourage its use. These factors skewed the probabilities in favor of high densities in pens two and three. Thus, in the end pens, where population density was nearer to normal, the behavior of the rats differed greatly from the behavior of the rats in the crowded middle pens. One dominant male would take over the area of the pen as his territory, establishing dominion and control over a harem by preventing the subordinate males from returning. Some subordinate males inhabited the area, however, but these respected the dominant male and hid in the burrows with the females, although they attempted no sexual activity with them. The harem females were good mothers, and the mortality rate was lowest in these end pens (Calhoun, 1962).

In the middle pens, where the population density was extremely high, many forms of behavior pathology were present. In the first series of experiments, the behavior disturbances were directly related to the development of a behavioral sink in which as many as 75 per cent of the rats would assemble during periods of eating. The development of the behavioral sink was fostered by the feeding arrangements; food pellets, which took considerable time to eat, were used, and feeding eventually became associated with the presence of other rats. In time, eating and other biological activities were transformed into social activities, the principal satisfaction of which was interaction with other rats. Thus, although the rats secured adequate nutrition, this pathological "togetherness" disrupted other vital modes of behavior. In this series of experiments, where the behavioral sink developed, infant mortality was 96 per cent.

In the second series of experiments, powdered food was used and no behavioral sink developed. The social pathology was less extreme in this series, but 80 per cent of the infants died.

Thus, behavior pathology was severe in both series of experiments. Among the females, nest-building eventually ceased and the litters were born on the sawdust in the burrows' bottom. Many females were unable to carry their pregnancies to full term, or to survive the delivery of their litters; those who did often were unable to transport their litters, and the scattered infants were usually abandoned and eaten by the adult rats. The very high rate of mortality in the middle pens, therefore, was the result of disorders in pregnancy and parturition.

Behavior disturbances among the males ranged from sexual deviation to cannibalism and from frenetic overactivity to pathological withdrawal. Four types of males in the middle pens became evident: (1) aggressive, dominant males who were the most normal and seldom bothered the females or the juveniles. These sometimes went berserk, however, attacking females, juveniles, and the less active males. They also had the abnormal predilection of biting other rats on the tail. (2) Homosexual males, or more accurately pansexual, since they could not discriminate between appropriate and inappropriate sex partners. (3) Passive males who appeared to be the healthiest and most attractive rats, for they were fat and sleek, but who ignored others and were ignored by them. Social disorganization among these rats was nearly complete. (4) The most active of all the male rats were the probers. They took no part in the status struggle, but they were hyperactive, hypersexual, homosexual, and often cannibalistic.

At the end of the first series of experiments, eight of the healthiest rats, four male and four female, were permitted to survive. Although they were no longer in an overpopulated environment, they produced fewer litters than normal, and none of those born survived. Thus, the effects of the social behavior of a species on population growth, and the effects of population density on social behavior, are clearly evident.

In another experiment Calhoun placed 2600 mice in a box nine feet square. Although the pen was well-supplied and had unlimited food and water, this was 16 times as many mice as there would be under the most ideal conditions. The behavior pathology resulting from these extremely crowded conditions was in the form of a hierarchy. The top mice were in the higher burrows nearest to the food and water, while the lower grade mice were in the less desirable burrows, and the lowest mice, the proles, had no burrows at all. All of the mice were affected by a "withdrawal syndrome;" only the proles, who were the rejected males and viciously aggressive females, retained the capacity for little bursts of violence, in which they chewed on one another. The top grade mice became completely unstressed and simply ate, drank, and slept. They did nothing else; they built no nests, never fought, never foraged, reared no young, neither copulated nor conceived. They seemed completely withdrawn, as evidenced by the fact that no live births took place for six months (Alsop, 1970).

Applications of studies like these by Calhoun to the human situation are necessarily speculation, but parallels between the unstressed mice and the people in the drug culture are interesting to consider. That the experience of overcrowding did something to the programming of the central nervous system of the surviving rats and mice was evident in their inability to produce live offspring; a similar experience of overcrowding will be felt by the present generation of youth if birth rates continue as they now are, and any relationships between animal studies and the human situation will be revealed. For example, Desmond Morris, author of *The Naked Ape* and *The Human Zoo*, has reported that animals manifest behavior similar to humans with stereotyped patterns presumably from the pressures of overcrowding. Morris parallels animals eating their young to the analogous situation of the "battered babies" syndrome of the cities today, both possibly having their roots in overcrowding. Similarly, he contends that animals either succumb or adjust to overcrowding, and that humans adjust to a similar situation with tranquilizers or vacations.

It seems evident that a bigger population may mean increasing urbanization and urban sprawl, which in turn causes overpopulation and overcrowding, resulting in aggression and frustration. The consequences of life in the more crowded areas of cities point toward tighter social controls; increasing centralization; decline in the quality of life in terms of less space, devaluation of the individual, and reduction of human dignity; and the need for mass production, which tends to stifle individuality and diversity in life. The factors created by urbanization seem to have psychological, as well as economic, foundations: the city has been envisioned as exciting and alluring, besides being a place in which jobs may be found. But this revolutionary change of social environment from rural to urban, which changes more rapidly as the population grows, necessitates a revolutionary psychological adjustment of human nature (Toynbee, 1966). This, in the city, is where the problems of overcrowding first came into existence, and where they are still primarily concentrated.

A change in population figures necessarily results in a change in way of life. Before a physical lower limit of survival is reached, a psychological limit is transgressed beyond which life in the social sense becomes impossible. This is an indicator of an insufficient population density. Inversely, when a person is forced to subject to the collectivity to such an extent that he loses individual attributes, the upper limits of population density are reached (Querido, 1964). This second condition is closely connected with the high population densities of cities, in which the psychological factors of close contact with many people must be adjusted to by individuals.

These aspects of city life that must be adjusted to were studied as early as 1938, when Louis Wirth wrote "Urbanism as a Way of Life." Defining the city as a "relatively large, dense, and permanent settlement of heterogeneous individuals," Wirth cited two factors as changes which must be adjusted to in the city. These factors are the absence of intimate, personal acquaintanceship, and the segmentalization of human relationships into anonymous, superficial, and transitory relationships, or the change from primary relationships to secondary ones. This large number of superficial contacts and fewer primary relationships in high densities may contribute to mental stress, loneliness, and anomie, which are related to social void, disorganization, and freedom from the personal and emotional controls of intimate groups (Wirth, 1938). An example of the lack of primary social controls and the social pathology seeming to result from high population density is the 1964 murder of Catherine Genovese in New York. Miss

Genovese was stabbed in three separate attacks and finally killed, while none of the 38 neighbors who witnessed the attack attempted to discourage her assailant or even notify the police (Heer, 1968). Thus, cities have been compared to concentration camps, in which life is regimented and computerized and the individual is overwhelmed and lost in the masses, so that social contacts become impersonal and feelings of alienation, ranging from apathy and despondency to aggression and violence, result.

A study by Young, Willmott, and Whyte has shown, however, that a high population density has little harmful effect in areas of stable and homogeneous populations; rather, heterogeneous populations with recent arrivals are more adversely affected by high population densities. The consequences of migration are factors contributing to this finding: migrants have a higher rate of mental illness than non-migrants at their place of destination; and greater social disorganization, or anomie, is present among migrants. These factors increase the effect of high density and thereby its adverse aspects (Heer, 1968).

Past studies of mental illness and population density have shown mental illness rates to be higher near the center and more densely populated areas of cities than in the periphery. Using the concentric zone theory of city growth, studies have found that a steady decline in mental illness occurs from the center toward the periphery of the city. It is hypothesized that the characteristics of the population in the various zones is produced by the style of life within them, with higher densities inevitably having an effect on this style. One type of psychosis is schizophrenia, which consists of apathy and indifference, lack of contact with reality, disharmony between mood and thought, stereotyped attitudes, delusions, illusions, hallucinations, impaired judgment, lack of insight, lack of attention, defects of interest, negativism, and autistic thinking. Schizophrenia, like other forms of mental illness, decreases from the center to the periphery. Rates for paranoia, for example, are high near the center and low on the periphery of the city. Patterns of rates for hebephrenia are similar to those for paranoia. No exact pattern of rates for this type of schizophrenia exists, but many catatonic patients are from foreign-born slum areas. Indices of social disorganization, and therefore schizophrenia, include: stability as measured by home-ownership; mobility and per cent of lodgers; and foreign-born and Negro population (Faris and Dunham, 1960). These three factors are indirectly related to the population density of an area; thus the rates of schizophrenia are also indirectly related to population density.

Another type of psychosis is manic-depressive psychosis in which the patient is either extremely elated or extremely depressed. The rates for manic-depressive psychosis are random, with the highest rate in the central zone area and the other zones are approximately equal (Faris and Dunham, 1960).

Alcoholic psychosis, drug addiction, and general paralysis from a syphilitic infection of the brain, considered to be types of psychoses, have much higher rates near the center of the city than in the outlying areas (Faris and Dunham, 1960).

It is important to note that while many reasons exist for these patterns of mental illness, some of which are chance, poverty, statistical or methodological errors, and drift, the usually overcrowded conditions in the central city areas may also be a contributing factor. It would seem that the transmission of a standardized cultural view of the world requires the family, community and surroundings to be somewhat stable and consistent with a continuous stream of intimate social communication (Faris and Dunham, 1960). Many of these factors are missing in areas of high population density, as in the center of cities. Thus, it seems population density is a contributing factor in areas where the rate of mental illness is high.

The relationship which exists between overcrowding and stress seems to also exist between overcrowding and psychosomatic illness. Psychosomatic disorders are the result of the interplay between mind, the psyche, and body, the soma. Both physical and mental stressors affect psychosomatic disorders. Types of psychosomatic disease include: (1) hypochondria, (2) functional psychogenic disease, and (3) psychogenic organic disorders, which result in conditions of ulcers, asthma, and heart conditions (Levi, 1967).

Psychosomatic disorders exist because the body reacts with physical preparedness to a symbol of danger. Continual reactions in the form of preparing to fight or escape result in pressure and tension. Such prolonged stress may eventually lead to psychosomatic disorders (Levi, 1967). As in mental illness, the stressors precipitating psychosomatic disease are the results of many complex factors. The increasing stress in overcrowded conditions, however, must be considered as one such factor which at least contributes to psychosomatic diseases.

A very recent survey from the Department of Health, Education and Welfare on symptoms of psychological distress has refuted some of the findings of earlier studies. Twelve symptoms were studied, including: (1) nervous breakdown; (2) feelings of an impending nervous breakdown; (3) nervousness; (4) psychological inertia; (5) insomnia; (6) hand trembling; (7) nightmares; (8) perspiring hands; (9) fainting; (10) headaches; (11) dizziness; (12) heart palpitations. Investigated by use of a questionnaire, one general finding was that rates were lower in metropolitan areas and higher in other urban and low population areas. One explanation for this finding, without invalidating the hypothesis that greater population density increases the probability of both physical and psychological disorder, may be that population density is no longer greatest in the metropolitan areas themselves, but has shifted to other urban areas. A second finding of the study may help to explain the unexpected distribution of rates with regard to geographic area; the rates of these symptoms were higher among the lower educated groups and lower income groups (U. S. Department of

Health, Education and Welfare, 1970). These conditions exist in areas other than the more affluent metropolitan districts, and may have outweighed the influence of population density in this study. A thorough investigation of why these results occurred would be helpful in discovering if the long-standing observations of other studies should be modified or are still valid.

As aggression, frustration, and stress increase with increasing densities, so pathological behavior and deviance increase also. Crime, juvenile delinquency, and racial antagonisms rise due to numerical increase (Day and Day, 1964). Neuroses develop, and eccentric or abherrant forms of behavior follow. Dependency, divorce, desertion, and suicide are more prevalent in urban, crowded areas than in rural regions; similarly, riots, the hippie movement, and drug use have increased as the stress of overcrowding has increased. Deviant behavior such as this may be viewed as the effect of adapting to an overcrowded, urban environment (Ehrlich, 1969).

In an article entitled "The Sardine Syndrome" the claim is made that violence is essentially a response to overpopulation, and that by eliminating population stresses free, friendly, and peaceful societies would eventually result. Human aggression, which leads to deviant behavior including crime, riots, and war, is caused by the stress of overpopulation in the same way in which the overcrowding of monkeys, apes, and rats results in tension, violence, and attacks. An example of the deviance resulting from overcrowding is the increase in incidence of violent crime in Newcastle, England, as it became very densely populated: the most crowded third of the city produced five times as many offenses against persons and four times as many larcenies as in the least crowded third of the city (Weinraub, 1970). Therefore, deviant and pathological behavior, together with mental illness and psychosomatic disorders, may be viewed as the direct and indirect consequences of overcrowding.

Any solutions to overpopulation and overcrowding are hard to foresee. A temporary measure which can be taken, while the population continues to grow, to decrease overcrowding and population density is town planning. Redesigning large cities and planning for new ones is very important. The urban environment is an important framework for a majority of Americans since they reside in it. Town planning, defined as the community's ability to influence and build its own environment (Steigenga, 1964), must be able to provide full scope to society and to the human personality, or else the social strains and socio-pathological problems previously discussed will develop.

One of the most important factors that must be considered by town planners is the adjustment between spatial opportunity and social demands for open space if the physical environment of urban people is important. As stated by Edward Highbee, "the physical and mental health of the nation is related to its outdoor facilities for decent exercise and temporary relief from the common causes of tensions in a metropolitan world where most of the day is spent inside home, school, car, office, or shop" (Steigenga, 1964). Thus town planners such as Doxiadis develop configurations that will allow for continuous expansion without creating intolerable expansion around the static center (Toynbee, 1966); Frank Lloyd Wright plans for decentralization of the urban population in the Broad Acre City; and LeCorbusier concentrates the urban population in long linear bands (Steigenga, 1964). The major problem in dealing with the factor of open space is how to avoid too much concentration and not lose the open spaces by too much decentralization.

Other factors concerning the town planner which influence mental and social well-being include: (1) the living density in a dwelling; (2) the distribution and arrangement of rooms; (3) the disturbance by noise and smell; (4) the homogeneity or heterogeneity of the population; (5) the structure of recreation facilities; (6) the kind and length of time concerning means of transport; and (7) the conditions of privacy and contact (Strotzka, 1964). Town planning is, therefore, a very important area, one in which the use of the proper methods can minimize and control stress and overcrowding, at least to a certain degree.

A more permanent solution than town planning to the problems of overcrowding and overpopulation must necessarily be found, however. To escape overcrowding, some form of population control must develop. Since man's homeostatic control is not automatic, as it is in other animals, and since he has increased food productivity (Wynne-Edwards, 1968), population control is more difficult for humans than for animal species. Primitive societies reduced overpopulation by means of infanticide, human sacrifice, mutilation, head-hunting, cannibalism, and sexual taboos (Morris, 1969); modern man is both unwilling and unable to use such methods for population control. In the nineteenth century, Ireland regulated fertility by deferment of marriage and nonmarriage, while France employed contraceptive methods in controlling the population. In other western countries there was only partial control, and fertility changed very little as it was counterbalanced by high mortality (Spengler, 1969). Today, in the twentieth century, a recognition for the need to control numbers has evolved, and the IUD and the pill were developed as effective contraceptives. Motivation for their use, however, has been individual incentive and private conscience, and it has not been effective. A general will, based on a new ethic and ideal of family size, must develop before population growth will decline as the result of using contraceptives.

In order to establish within a country the general will to regulate population growth, parenthood must come to be considered more of a privilege than a right. Certain steps may be taken to induce population control: (1) establish a Federal Population Commission which would emphasize the fact that a rising population lowers the quality of life; (2) change tax laws to discourage population growth; (3) give instruction in birth control in public schools; (4) continue biomedical research in the area of population regulation; (5) make methods of birth control easily available; and (6) legalize abortion. The main problem in dealing with population control lies in the fact that any coercion in regulating reproduction destroys the quality life that one is attempting to preserve.

The psychological effects of overcrowding have been demonstrated, directly and indirectly, in the paper. Overcrowding has been shown to endanger the quality of life, both physically and psychologically. Although the United States is not suffering from severe overcrowding and overpopulation yet, population control must become a value before the stress of overcrowding becomes too great. A new ethic, in which the worth of each life is expressed in its fulfillment, must develop, so that life, in its fullest sense, can be experienced by all members of the society.

BIBLIOGRAPHY

Alsop, Stewart. 1970. Dr. Calhoun's horrible mousery. *Newsweek,* 78: 96.

Calhoun, John B. 1962. Population density and social pathology. *Sci. Amer.* 206: 139-148.

Carrighar, Sally. 1968. Wild heritage. *In* Louise B. Young (ed.) *Population in perspective.* New York, N.Y.: Oxford Univ. Press.

Day, Lincoln H., and Alice Taylor Day. 1964. *Too many Americans.* Boston, Mass.: Houghton Mifflin.

Ehrlich, Paul R. 1969. World population: is the battle lost? *The Reader's Digest,* 94: 137-140.

Faris Robert E. Lee, and H. Warren Dunham. 1960. *Mental disorders in urban areas.* New York, N.Y.: Hafner.

Heer, David. 1968. *Society and population.* Englewood Cliffs, N.J.: Prentice Hall.

Hoaglund, Hudson. 1968. Cybernetics of population control.. *In* Louise B. Young (ed.) *Population in perspective.* New York, N.Y.: Oxford Univ. Press.

Keith, L. B. 1963. *Wildlife's ten-year cycle.* Madison, Wis.: Univ. of Wisconsin Press.

Levi, Lennart. 1967. *Stress: sources, management and prevention.* New York, N.Y.: Liveright Pub.

Morris, Desmond. 1969. *The human zoo.* New York, N.Y.: McGraw-Hill.

The problem of pollution. 1970. *Life,* 68: 8-15.

Querido, Arie. 1964. Population problems and mental health. *In* Henry P. David (ed.) *Population and mental health.* New York, N.Y.: Springer Pub.

Ross, Edward Allsworth. 1927. *Standing room only?* New York, N.Y.: Century.

Spengler, Joseph. 1969. Population problem: in search of a solution. *Science,* 166: 1234-1238.

Steigenga, Willem. 1964. Urbanization and town planning. *In* Henry P. David (ed.) *Population and mental health.* New York, N.Y.: Springer Pub.

Strotzka, Hans. 1964. Town planning and mental health. *In* Henry P. David (ed.) *Population and mental health.* New York, N.Y.: Springer Pub.

Thiessen, D. D. and David A. Rodgers. 1961. Population density and endocrine function. *Psychological Bulletin,* 57: 441-451.

Toynbee, Arnold J. 1966. *Change and habit.* New York, N.Y.: Oxford Univ. Press.

U.S. Department of Health, Education, and Welfare. 1970. Selected symptoms of psychological distress. Rockville, Md.

Weinraub, Bernard. 1970. Two Britons discern a "Sardine Syndrome," linking recent violence to the pressure of overpopulation. *New York Times* (August 16), p. 53.

Wynne-Edwards, V. C. 1968. Population control in animals. *In* Louise B. Young (ed.) *Population in perspective.* New York, N.Y.: Oxford Univ. Press.

The Economics of Environmental Quality

Eugene A. Philipps

I. INTRODUCTION

Although ecology is basically a biological term, the concept of ecological equilibrium is clearly extensible to social systems of which economics is one part. The oldest and most basic forms of economic activity are food gathering and the provision of shelter, two activities over which man certainly has no monopoly. For example, consider the beaver, the wolf, the African baboon, the lion, and even the mouse, and the obvious parallels between man and other forms of life in these respects become apparent. It could be argued that, were it not for the destructive presence of man on this planet, an ecological equilibrium would be possible in the sense that a unique set of sizes of populations of all species would emerge in which each species finds that the level of population size of all other species is such that its own population will neither increase nor decrease. Sometimes equilibria exist for short periods of time; in most cases, however, disturbances are too profound and frequent to allow this. Although natural factors sometimes cause changes, the primary generator of ecological havoc seems to have been man himself who, among all the forms of life, is uniquely capable, for better or worse, of altering and controlling his habitat and along with it destroying the very delicate balance existing among its various elements. Mans' numbers, like those of other species, are *theoretically* limited by the means of subsistence, but science, technology, and man's singular capacity to comprehend the forces of nature have served to constantly delay the subsistence crisis. Some large nations, such as India and Indonesia and some smaller ones such as Haiti and the Dominican Republic, are engaged in a desperate footrace with the ever-present image of starvation. Others, like the United States, Canada, Australia and New Zealand are capable of supporting larger populations at higher consumption levels. Human beings, in other words, are not dispersed globally in proportion to the available means of subsistence. Sometimes wars have been fought in the mistaken belief that these imbalances could be corrected, but the wars usually accomplished

Written for this volume. Dr. Eugene A. Phillips is Professor of Economics at Moorhead State College, Moorhead, Minnesota.

nothing more than a shift in political boundaries or a redesignation of the nation or group which determines how the means of subsistence will be distributed.

Historically, natural disasters, lack of knowledge, high natural death rates contagious diseases and, to some degree, armed conflict have operated to check population growth. From the year 1 A.D. to about 1500 A.D. world population was fairly constant at about 300 million. By 1650 it had risen to 400 million but by 1950 to *3 billion.* Today, even the most conservative estimates project potential population at *6 billion* by the year 2000. Population growth has not been limited by the natural forces that control the sizes of other species. Barring the possibility that man will destroy himself by nuclear or biological warfare, what factors might contribute to a population equilibrium? Consider diagram #1.

Diagram 1

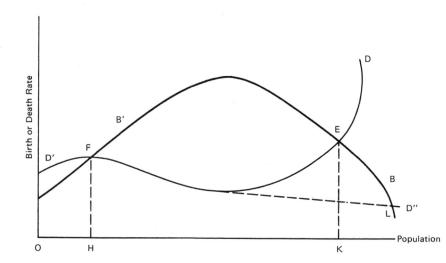

The solid lines D'D and B'B represent the death rate and the birth rate, respectively. The two rates are equal at F and E but only E is an equilibrium position because to the right of F the birth rate is above the death rate and population would grow until E is reached, beyond which D'D rises above B'B. If man's numbers were checked by the same natural forces as other species, point E might be reached but the past 100 years have been marked by a rapid fall in death rates (the dotted downward extention of D'') *which, even though birth rates have fallen or slowed down, has resulted in a tremendous acceleration in population growth.* (I will leave it to the reader to imagine what life would be like at point L.) Why is it then, we should ask, that man has allowed this growth to occur with the knowledge that such growth may be upsetting the ecological balance of his habitat through the senseless waste and destruction of his life-supporting resources? The answer is complex but some clue is to be found in the philosophies that have guided the course of human events since the middle ages.

II. HISTORICAL FORCES

A. Our European Heritage

It is not accidental that historical population growth shows a sharp upward acceleration around 1500 A.D. The Middle Ages were dominated by a synthesis of Aristotelian philosophy and Christian theology called "natural law" which was used as the basis for a rationalization of static social and economic relationships. Economics was not yet "scientific" but was bound up with ethical considerations. Trade, commerce, production, and lending motivated by a desire for profit were thought to violate both natural and divine laws. The spirit of the Middle Ages was, in many respects the antithesis of the view which was to prevail during the "liberal" revolution of the 18th century. During the Middle Ages population was fairly static due to frequent famine, low levels of agricultural technology, and outbreaks of contagious disease, but, perhaps most importantly, man was regarded as part of his environment, a species in equilibrium with his life-support systems. In retrospect this view of man in harmony with his surroundings (the Thomist interpretation of "natural law"), which identifies spirit with nature has great relevance for the present age.

Between 1500 and 1750 (roughly) powerful nation states began to emerge. Feudalism had declined as a form of social and economic organization and along with it some of the enormous influence of the Church. There were many reasons for this transition but one of the most important was the rapid introduction of new production techniques culminating in the so-called "Industrial Revolution." Many nations attempted to harness this increasing economic potential to enhance the power of the State which was rapidly replacing the feudal nobility and the Church as the object of citizens' allegiances. This practice has been called "Mercantilism" (by Adam Smith), less a philosophy than a set of guiding economic policies. "Mercantilist" writers tended to regard a growing population favorably for several reasons:

1. a large population ensured a steady supply of labor which tended to keep exports cheap (competitive) and ensure a nation's ability to obtain precious metals through its balance of international payments.

2. a plentiful supply of precious metals and manpower provided a safeguard against aggressive rival nations, and

3. a growing Colonial population engaged in producing raw materials for the decreasing cost, large-scale home industries provided a growing market for the outputs of these home industries.

During this period, however, two other very important developments were occuring. First, the emerging Christian notion of a transcendent God, removed from nature, served to remove spirit from nature and allow, in an ideological sense, for an easy exploitation of nature, which now became a separate substance spiritually irrelevant to man. Second, the "natural law" doctrine underwent a transformation and came to be used as a rationale for self-interest rather than a moral restraint upon self-interest, which it had been. John Locke, for example, identified nature with human appetites, and natural law was cited as the very reason why self-interest should be given free play. The historian R. H. Tawney has described the moral confusion of the common man during the sixteenth century as follows (Chalk, 1951):

> A century before he had practiced extortion and had been told it was wrong: for it was contrary to the law of God. A century later he was to practice it and be told he was right: for it was in accordance with the law of nature. In other words, it was the whole conception of social theory based ultimately on religion which was being discredited.

Mercantilist thought was in the process of gradual erosion when Adam Smith's famous *Inquiry into the Nature and Causes of the Wealth of Nations* appeared in 1776. By this time the Industrial Revolution was well underway and the interests of the State were giving way somewhat to the interests of individuals. Smith argued that the strength of a nation is to be found in the improved welfare of its people which in turn depends on its ability to raise per-capita income through the division of labor, greater specialization, and the generation of technological change. A system of "enlightened self-interest" with the free-wheeling capitalist-organizer at its hub seemed to him the most logical way to achieve prosperity. The *laissez faire* economy needs little guidance; it simply grows like a tree along with, it might be added, population and the exploitation of nature, and it grows better the lighter the hand of government.

In stark contrast to the new optimism of Smith stood two rather pessimistic writers, David Ricardo (1772-1823) and Thomas Malthus (1766-1834) whose ideas influenced economic thinking in the early part of the 19th Century. The Malthusian-Ricardian model reached dismal conclusions with respect to the future of mankind. Malthus, as we know, was concerned about rising population pressing dangerously on the means of subsistence. Ricardo developed an ingenious model at the core of which was the distribution of total national income under conditions of diminishing returns to land. By this he meant that as man resorted to farming inferior land (to increase his means of subsistence) the costs of growing food would rise, the landlords would become rich and, to the detriment of the industrialists who wanted low wages, the costs of feeding industrial workers (wages) would rise thus depressing profits and growth. The deck was stacked, so to speak, against the capitalists unless cheaper food could be imported to compete with the output of England's landowners.[1]

The ideas of these two writers formed the basis for a theory which suggested that any attempts by labor to raise wages or attempts by the poor to alleviate their condition by pushing for stronger "poor laws" (welfare measures) were doomed to failure. The only hope, Malthus argued, rested in the willingness of the poor to have fewer children. Wages and employment were thought to be determined by the size of a "fund" held by capitalists (accumulated profit); consequently, higher employment, lower wages, poverty, decline in labor force or, alternatively, higher wages, less employment, smaller profits, smaller wages fund, less capital accumulation, lower productivity, etc.

Extending the Ricardian structure, John Stuart Mill, writing in 1848 (Fusfeld, 1966), noted that increasing accumulation of capital might force the rate of return (profit) on investment so low (because capital was becoming less scarce relatively to labor) that all accumulation might cease. This "stationary state," as Mill called it, might not be so bad if society stopped growing at a point where its capital stock were sufficient to insure a pleasant level of living at which all basic economic needs were satisfied. Man would now be free to pursue other non-economic activities aimed at development of the cultural side of life.

In the 1870s three writers, all of different nationalities, independently developed ideas which were to lead to a reconstruction of economics.[2] The synthesis between the older ideas of Smith, Ricardo, and Mill, and the newer thinking of the 1870s is reflected in the work of Alfred Marshall who is perhaps the best known expositor of the "neo-classical" economics. Marshall argued that a system of free markets was the best way to maximize the welfare of each individual in society. If people are free to maximize their satisfactions (utility), the pattern of

---

[1]The infamous corn laws ("corn" meaning grain), which limited food imports, were finally repealed in 1846.

[2]The three individuals were William Jevons (English), Leon Walras (French), and Karl Menger (Austrian).

production would reflect this maximization and in this sense be welfare maximizing. Competition would push the "costs" of production (only the actual *money* costs, not costs of pollution, which were excluded from the calculus) to the lowest possible level. Arthur Pigou, Marshall's successor at Cambridge, began to take more notice of "social costs," the classic case being factory smoke.[3] Prior and subsequent to Marshall-Pigou, economists revealed an awareness of these "social costs" but virtually no attempts were made to include them in the calculation of society's "welfare." This can hardly be said to reflect the situation today. The influence of "Keynesian" economics (in the noncommunist world) in the past thirty years has diverted some attention from questions of efficiency and resource allocation in favor of greater stress on means to control aggregates such as total employment, total income, total consumption and that most sacred of all success indicators, the "rate of growth," but the literature of the past decades also reflects a revival of interest in distributive and allocative questions, particularly those involving pollution control costs. Although environmental questions have been discussed for the past 25 years with some sense of urgency in the heavily populated countries of Western Europe, serious discussion of the economic aspects of pollution, for example, have only recently begun to appear in this country. The reasons for this, I believe, are to be found in the uniqueness of the American experience, which will be discussed below

The United States

In the period of history prior to the Civil War our economic philosophy was characterized by a general adherence to the ideas embodied in the English classical tradition, most notably, belief in the sanctity of private property, individualism, competition, and "progress." However, two exceptions should be noted:

1. Americans never fully accepted the classical arguments for free international trade. From its very beginning (Alexander Hamilton's *Report on Manufactures,* 1791, for example) the United States relied on protective tariffs to develop its manufacturing industries. Our "unlimited" natural resources of timber, water, farm land, minerals and fuels would be developed by home industries.

2. The dismal conclusions reached by Ricardo-Malthus were not accepted simply because they "didn't apply" to a sparsely populated land of enormous size and resources.

On the eve of the Civil War (1860) the United States was a nation of

[3]Social costs are avoidable costs which can be shifted to third parties or the community at large in the process of pursuing private gain. See Karl Kapp (1967).

32 million people of whom 65 per cent were engaged in agriculture.[4] The "typical" American was foreign-born, independent, religious, and lived on the land providing the bulk of his basic needs himself. He was firmly committed to "individual enterprise" simply because there was no other kind of enterprise in which to believe under the circumstances. His activity was the mainstay of the economy and his markets, domestic and foreign, were expanding. His property was his to do with as he pleased except in instances where the doctrine of "eminent domain" was invoked for the greater public good.

The period 1865-1900 witnessed a remarkable revolution in American life.[5] Population grew rapidly, new cities appeared, old cities expanded, the transport and communications systems covered the nation, industry was growing at a rapid pace, agriculture was declining in relative importance, immigrants were pouring in from the densely-populated centers of Europe, but, perhaps most importantly, the public's attitude toward the system that spawned these developments was changing and these changing attitudes were being reflected in the writings of a new breed of economists who were less concerned with timeless theoretical models than with the historical forces creating changes and the social consequences of affluence. The new counter-current to unrestricted *laissez faire* is described in Fine, (1967), pp. 167-8):

> The opponents of the philosophy of *laissez faire* proposed in its stead the rival philosophy of the general welfare state. Whereas the advocates of *laissez faire* contended that the government could best advance the common weal by rendering itself as inconspicuous as possible and by permitting individuals to work out their own salvation . . . amid the free and unrestricted play of natural forces, the proponents of the general-welfare state argued — and this was the essence of the concept of the general-welfare state — that the state could best promote the general welfare by a positive exertion of its powers. They regarded the democratic state not as an evil force but as an instrument that the people could and should use to further their common interests, to ameliorate the conditions under which they lived and worked, and to provide for their health and safety and, to some extent, for their social and economic security. They wished to see the powers of government used both in the negative sense of restraining wrongdoing and in the positive sense of securing good, and they were inclined to believe that the repressive functions of the government would tend to diminish as time went on and that its positive, ameliorative

[4]In contrast, population was 275,000 in 1700, 1.2 million in 1750, 5.3 million in 1800, and 76 million by 1900. The percentage engaged in agriculture fell to 38 per cent by 1900 and by the 1970s to about 9 per cent.

[5]This period and its importance to contemporary American institutions and attitudes is thoroughly analyzed in Fine, 1967.

functions would increase. Although they were advocates of specific reforms for their own era, they did not, as a rule, conceive of the general-welfare state in terms of this or that function but, rather, took the position that the state must act whenever its action seemed likely to further the general well-being.

This spirit has been continuously reflected in legislation broadening the government's power to intervene in the economy when the public welfare is threatened. As a consequence of this steady retreat from unrestrained *laissez faire* and the chaos of "natural law," the American economy today is "mixed," that is, it functions through a blend of private and public (collective) decision making.

Another turning point occurred during the depression of 1929-33. A prolonged business contraction idled men and machines for what many thought to be unnecessary reasons. As a result, broad but weak legislation was passed in an attempt to stimulate growth and high employment. After World War II one of the most significant pieces of economic legislation in our history was passed, *The Employment Act of 1946,* which has been described as the "economic Magna Carta" of the United States. (Fishman, 1969) The Declaraction of Policy of that Act states:

... that it is the continuing policy and responsibility of the Federal Government to use all practical means ... to foster and promote ... conditions under which there will be offered useful employment opportunities ... for those able, willing, and seeking to work ... and to promote maximum employment, production, and purchasing power.

The Act specifies, however, that these ends are to be achieved by means which are consistent with the basic economic institutions of the United States. In the past 25 years under the *Employment Act* the United States has achieved a remarkable record of economic growth. Productivity and scientific advances have brought greater affluence to more and more people without a repetition of the serious levels of unemployment that marked earlier periods. Our postwar malady has been inflation, not widespread unemployment.[6]

It would appear, however, that some of our postwar affluence is more apparent than real, for in the trail of a growing Gross National Product is strewn the wreckage of our natural resources, the reconstitution and replacement of which will be incredibly difficult, if not impossible, to achieve. In addition, we may have set in motion some processes which threaten to seriously deteriorate the quality of life or else destroy it entirely if nothing is done. In the section that follows some of the basic

[6]This is not meant to imply that 6 per cent unemployed is satisfactory, but that it is preferable to 15 - 20 per cent (1932).

economic reasons for environmental deterioration and the implications of alternative economic methods of dealing with the problem will be examined in detail.

III. THE ENVIRONMENTAL CONSEQUENCES OF ECONOMIC GROWTH

As our economy becomes more sophisticated, the importance of machines, technology, and skilled manpower increases; that of unskilled labor declines. As our population grows it becomes socially imperative that more jobs be created, but the degrees of skill required in these new jobs become successively greater. "Two hands and a strong back" are no longer enough.[7] Unfortunately, the general upgrading in the education and skills necessary in today's economy do not keep pace with its demands. As a consequence, more and more people become "structurally" unemployed and even during relatively prosperous times many find jobs scarce. In keeping with its charge under the *Employment Act of 1946* our government has followed an "expansionist policy" designed to keep the economy (the G.N.P.) growing at a rate sufficient to absorb additional labor and to generate sufficient spending-power with which to absorb the increasing output of an expanded economy. If this line of reasoning appears somewhat circuitous, it is because it is. Indeed, it constitutes one of the root causes of our environmental problems and, therefore, warrants closer analysis.

The Gross National Product is the value of all goods and services produced in a country for a given period of time, usually one year. It consists of the values (at current market prices) of:

C_d – Goods and Services Consumed Domestically
  1. Goods
     a. durables (autos, appliances, etc.)
     b. non-durables (food, clothing, gasoline, etc.)
  2. Services (medical services, T-V, auto repairs, etc.)

I_d – Domestic Investment
  1. Plant and equipment spending by business
  2. Additions to inventories
  3. Construction (residential, office buildings)

G – Net Government Spending on Goods and Service
  1. Federal (military, postal service, courts, etc.)
  2. State (roads, schools, public services, etc.)
  3. Local (police, fire protection, road maintenance, etc.)

[7]For example between 1947 and 1966 total "blue collar" and farm employment actually declined by 600,000 while the total labor force grew by 15 million. In the same period "white collar" and service employment increased 17 million.

X — Goods and Services Exported to Foreign Countries

Having defined the components of GNP we can write, for any period of time,

$$GNP = C_d + I_d + G + X$$

When economists and politicans speak of "economic growth" it is the change in GNP from year to year of which they speak. The magnitude of these changes has erroneously come to be accepted by the general public as a measure of economic progress although it can be argued, as Kenneth Boulding has, that it should be renamed "Gross National Cost," (1970a).

The GNP is a misleading indicator because:

1. It includes some of the direct costs associated with its creation, depreciation of the capital stock, which means that some of the total investment consists of replacement of worn-out equipment.

2. It includes in the public sector (G) many items which never enter the market place — military expenditure, for example (about $80 billion currently).

3. Indirect costs such as commuting to and from work and pollution are included. In the act of producing, someone pollutes and someone cleans it up. The costs of the cleanup are counted as part of GNP.

4. It tells us nothing whatever about the "quality of life" and the extent to which the things produced contribute to improving it.

5. As a welfare indicator it is meaningless unless we know how it is distributed among the citizens of the nation.

6. It says absolutely nothing about the quality (style, durability, usefulness) of the goods produced. The costs of maintaining and repairing shoddy, short-lived goods will be included in future GNP as services and give the erroneous impression of growth.

7. It does not take into account the effects of increased resource use on the future cost of these resources (i.e. depletion of coal or oil reserves).

8. It includes only goods in the market and ignores completely household production.

9. It is a total figure and does not indicate per capita changes which are, after all, more important.

Much more fundamental than any of the nine observations made above (and more could be made) is that the GNP mentality "assumes that economic activity is a throughput, a linear process from the mine to the garbage dump." (Boulding, 1970 (a), p. 162).

Now if the GNP, for some of the reasons given above, is not an accurate measure of welfare or, more strongly, a transparent hoax, why is it of such great importance to policy makers and why is news of its ups and downs greeted with great concern by the national communications media? The answer lies in the fact that its size and growth are the main aggregate determinants of employment and it is full-employment to which our political and business decision-makers are dedicated.

The environmental significance of the relationships between GNP and employment is extremely important. Our economy is still basically "capitalistic" which means that most of the future decisions regarding the composition of economic growth (increases in GNP) will be privately made. If the bulk of the estimated increase of $400 billion in GNP required to insure high employment by 1980 consists of privately-produced and marketed goods, the strain on our resources and unpaid "social costs" of pollution will probably be greater than if the increased output consists mainly of services. Fortunately our economy is leaning more and more in the direction of services. In fact, we are the only society in history to have reached the point where more than 50 per cent of the GNP consists of services, the first "post-industrial" society as some writers observe. Further, it should not be concluded that high unpaid "social costs" and environmental destruction are monopolized in the private sector. The operations of the U.S. Army Corps of Engineers, government-financed studies of new pesticides and artificial fertilizers, policies of the Department of the Interior and the Atomic Energy Commission, not to mention hydrogen war, are examples of actual or potentially destructive activities by government.

The economic side of the environmental dilemma seems to be rooted in the growth requirements of the system. High growth must be maintained to provide employment but rising per capita income and population are necessary to provide outlets for the steadily increasing capacity of our industries which is spurred on by more investment in machinery, science and technology. But if we decide as a nation that social costs must be paid as a prerequisite to improving the quality of our habitat, some means must be found to redirect economic growth to serve this end.

An interesting parallel exists between the pollution problems of the United States and the Soviet Union. Both nations, with their opposite political and economic systems, emerge as the world's two leading polluters and neither, apparently, is currently capable of finding solutions through existing institutions. We have our Lake Erie; the Russians have a similar problem with their Lake Baikal. In the October 2nd, 1970 issue of *Science,* Professor Marshall Goldman pointed out that pollution is at least as serious in the Soviet Union as in the United States despite the assumption that "if all the factories in a society were state-owned, the state would insure that the broader interests of the general public would be protected." The assumption appears groundless, however, when we consider that both nations have institutionalized environmental mistakes in the name of Gross National Product which, apparently, also excludes "social costs" in the Soviet Union. The unique nature of "socialist" accounting (ironically) makes no allowances for "social costs," a reflection, no doubt, of the Soviet managers' preoccupation with meeting physical quotas.[8]

It has been said that one of the roles of government in our society today is "to set the rules of the game; to define the level at which competition takes place." If the rules are changed through the development of strict anti-pollution legislation, industries, organizations, and individuals will bear the costs of better environmental quality through reductions in their money incomes. Greater growth will undoubtedly occur in private investment, particularly in the development of low-pollution production systems and in the government sector. Federal, state, and local governments will find it necessary to raise taxes to finance anti-pollution efforts. This will result in lower private disposable incomes and, presumably, in a lower growth rate in the demand for consumer goods. Somewhat less obvious is the potential impact of rising production costs, which will now include social as well as private costs, on real incomes. Although average money incomes will increase, taxes will be much higher and, presumably, so will the costs of goods. The consumer may well be squeezed two ways. Hopefully, however, some of the technical and scientific ingenuity, which in the past has been so successful in providing us with an abundance of goods and services will be directed toward solutions of environmental problems. If history is a good indicator, there is some reason to be optimistic on this point.

One of the main tasks of economists, in addition to simply stating a problem, such as we did above, is to try to determine the most "efficient" way of achieving a given objective. On this point, such questions as "efficiency," the distribution of pollution-control costs, the non-economic benefits which will accrue to society, and the directional or "guidance" system to be employed in achieving our chosen goals have been ignored. In the following section these questions will be discussed. Our object will not be to find answers to all questions but rather to isolate the variables and relationships which must enter into the solutions.

---

[8]The apparent victory of the "Liberman reforms" since 1965 may serve to lessen the stress on physical output with more emphasis on rational cost calculations. For more information on this point see Helibronner, "Ecological Armageddon," pp. 269-85 in (12)

IV. ECONOMIC COSTS AND THE QUALITY OF LIFE

A. Social Costs

It has already been pointed out above that economists have long been aware of "social costs" of production but until the relatively recent upsurge of interest in environmental economics, discussion of such issues was confined to a body of economic knowledge called "welfare economics'"—or else such costs were regarded as accidental or minor. Social costs are avoidable costs which can be shifted to third parties or the community at large in the process of pursuing private gain. Such costs are "unpaid" in the sense that the full costs of production would be higher were social costs included. Producers are thus able to appropriate a larger share of the value of a product than they would otherwise be able to and consumers are able to obtain products at prices somewhat lower than they would have been able to had the producers been forced to pay the "full" costs of production. Generally, therefore, it may be said that our overall material level of living has been raised by an unwillingness to pay the full, zero or low pollution costs of production. The stockholders and consumers of the products of a certain firm, for example, may be located far from the polluted lake or stream whose loss or inconvenience is suffered by those persons living near them who now are denied recreation such as swimming, boating and fishing.

B. Distributional Effects

Economists are always concerned with the basic distributional effects of a policy—how the inclusion or lack of inclusion of social costs affects the real incomes of various groups in society.

1. Emission standards are imposed by the Federal Government on an industry, say steel. Compliance involves techniques and equipment which raise the average cost of a ton of steel but not necessarily by the same amount for each firm in the steel industry. Immediately the relative competitive position of all firms may change. If the steel firms are rational, they will attempt to pass on the entire cost increase to the consumer. But this may be difficult if domestic substitutes for steel are available from industries whose emission-compliance costs were not high in the first place or if steel imported from foreign countries with less restrictive pollution laws now becomes competitive. If, for one reason or another, "full cost" cannot be reflected in higher prices, the rewards of the factors of production employed in producing steel may be reduced. The profits and wages of all those involved in the production, distribution, and fabrication of steel may be adversely altered.

2. Emission standards are imposed on the products themselves, say, the automobile or the gas it burns. Here there is no doubt the full cost will be reflected in higher prices for the products. The privately owned automobile, which formerly was capable of ejecting harmful elements into the air breathed by all of us, will now become more expensive to operate due to the higher costs of lead-free gasoline and an effective exhaust system.

3. A plan is formulated to regenerate a body of water, say, Lake Michigan. It is impossible to identify precisely those who in the past have contributed to the situation or the extent to which an obvious polluter has contributed. The issue is a social, not a private, one and the costs would undoubtedly be paid out of taxes. But whose taxes? Those who live on Lake Michigan? Those who use it? Such questions are impossible to resolve with any great degree of equity. No doubt some of the tax monies expended could have been collected in California or Maine. A logical solution would seem to lie in sharing the burden — taxes collected in the adjacent states are matched in some way by federal funds.

4. A community is forced to comply with new emission standards for sewage. Here, it would seem, the possibility of real equity would be greatest. But this isn't necessarily true unless all are taxed in proportion to their volume of sewage. The costs of measuring individual sewage volume may be so prohibitively high that the community would be better off simply paying a higher pro-rated property tax or approving a new bond issue.

These four examples are meant to be illustrative, not exhaustive, because there are other even more perplexing questions to be answered, such as "how will the costs of policing standards be met?" The coming decade will see an enormous expenditure of public and private resources on pollution control and prevention. A great portion of the estimated $400 billion increase in GNP over the next 10 years, perhaps as much as 5 per cent, will be drawn off one way or another into projects designed to improve the environment. As is the case with any activity involving large sums of money, attempts will be made to cheat, and costly new bureaucracies will materialize to enforce compliance and prosecute offenders.

C. Pollution Control and Economic Efficiency.

The question of how to achieve a given result, say, reduction of certain emission to a safe or desirable level at the lowest possible cost is an important one for society. A number of alternatives are available.

1. *Direct Regulation* —The establishment of licenses, permits, compul

sory standards, zoning, etc., designed to prescribe precisely how a particular result is to be achieved.

2. *Payments*—This would involve direct government subsidies, forgiveness of property taxes, or accelerated depreciation allowances on pollution control equipment, payments for decreasing discharges, tax credits by the Federal Government, etc.

3. *Charges*—This includes schedules of charges or fees for discharges of certain pollutants, taxes on specific sources of pollution such as coal or the internal combustion engine.

The above alternatives apply mainly to private "pollution-control costs." Public pollution control costs involve such things as municipal garbage systems, sewage treatment plants and are best dealt with through techniques such as "cost-benefit" analysis.[9] "Pollution costs" refer to the costs of making already polluted water drinkable or reconstituting a body of water such as Lake Erie, both of which are "public" in nature.

Alternative #1 above is objectionable on the grounds that:

a. it may involve extensive bureaucratic meddling in the activities of an industry or firm.

b. the private operator faced with compliance with certain standards is in a better position to ascertain how, in his particular activity, the standards can be achieved most cheaply and, therefore, most efficiently. Government interference in a system like ours is a poorer incentive to a firm than minimization of cost.

c. it is rigid and inflexible and loses the advantages of decentralized decision making.

Alternative #2 is somewhat preferable to #1 because it allows polluters to choose the method of compliance. It also tends to distribute the costs between the firm and the public. Normal depreciation on pollution-control devices adds to the firm's costs and a portion of this, no doubt, will be reflected in higher prices to consumers (or lower profits). The merits of tax credits, direct payments, etc., have been debated at length by economists, but the point that should concern us here is that any of these techniques could be capable, with adequate policing, of achieving prescribed standards.

The merit of #3, direct charges for polluting, lies in the fact that each firm would be allowed to make its own adjustments to the extent and in the manner best suited to its situation. A unit tax on emissions of mercury, if sufficiently high, will encourage such practices, unless the firm is in a position to pass the whole tax on to the consumer. The tax

[9]This method of economic analysis is explained by Dales (1970, pp. 39-57).

proceeds, presumably, would be used to deal with the problem "externally," that is, through public action. However, *Resources For The Future,* a research organization supported by the *Ford Foundation* says that "an ounce of pollution prevention is worth a pound of cure." The ratio cited is 16 to 1—a dollar's worth of prevention (pollution-control cost) is worth $16 of cure (in pollution costs).

The above alternatives are by no means mutually exclusive. Undoubtedly there will be situations (the very dangerous ones perhaps) in which #1 is appropriate or in which #3 would be adequate (mere nuisances, for example). Another thing to bear in mind is that emission standards may change over time. What may be acceptable today may be catastrophic if allowed to continue. Also, there may be a certain "lumpiness" in pollution-control investment spending. For example, the current standard for mercury may be 0.5 parts per million but the technically-feasible alternatives may be 0.75 *or* 0.35. Needless to say, each situation will have to be considered in light of its fairness to the polluter and its impact on the health and well-being of the public.

V.   THE FUTURE

With the energy needs of the nation doubling every 10 years and the rate of increase in refuse estimated at about 4 per cent per year (almost exactly the same as the average yearly increase in GNP) it seems obvious that we are facing a painful choice between a continuation of "business as usual" and a drastic, if not radical, reorientation of our economic life. As a nation, we have proven in the past that when faced with a *visible* threat to our security we can reorient our economic life. We did so in World War II. What we are confronting today is a threat, less visible perhaps than a hostile foreign army, but nevertheless present and becoming more dangerously visible each day. The statistics of ecological catastrophe are uncomfortably familiar. An urban unit of one million people produces 500,00 tons of sewage, 2000 tons of solid waste and 1,000 tons of airborne particles every day. The introduction of this amount into our water and air has already affected marine life in rivers, lakes and the oceans, and affected the livelihood of those who earn their living from the water. In 1967 American mines discarded 100,000,000 tons of waste rock and tailings, and in the same year 20,000 automobiles were scrapped (joining from 40-50 million already on junkpiles). Every year America makes 50 billion cans, 30 billion bottles and jars most of which become, almost immediately, solid waste of which little is reclaimed (it isn't "economic"). Of the eight billion pounds of plastics we produce, only 10 per cent is reclaimed. Of the 1.75 million tons of rubber products produced each year only 15 per cent is reclaimed. Reclamation may not be privately profitable but, somehow, reclaim and recycle we must, no matter how high the costs.

Perhaps the most crucial question of all has yet to be answered conclusively. Associated with any desired level of environmental quality is a cost. There exists, at least in a theoretical sense, a trade-off between economic cost and environmental quality. But in making the choices there may well be a range of standards, differing in cost, which yield the same results. How does society identify these ranges, their costs, and their environmental payoffs? Answers can only be found through the coordinated efforts of physical life, and social scientists who, if they are ever to succeed in solving what may well be the most important problem facing man in the years to come—survival—must begin to more thoroughly understand one another's disciplines.

BIBLIOGRAPHY

Baratz, Morton. 1970. *The American business system in transition.* New York, N.Y.: Thomas Y. Cromwell.

Boulding, Kenneth. 1970(a). Fun and games with the Gross National Product. *In* Harold W. Helfrich, Jr. (ed.) *The environmental crisis.* New Haven, Conn.: Yale Univ. Press.

Boulding, Kenneth. 1970(b). *Economics as a science.* New York, N.Y.: McGraw-Hill.

Chalk, Alfred. 1951. Natural law and the rise of economic individualism in England. *Journal of Political Economy,* Vol. 59: 330-347.

Chamber of Commerce of the United States. 1966. World population: prospects and problems. Washington, D.C.

Cipolla, Carlo. 1967. *The economic history of world population.* Baltimore, Md.: Penguin Books.

Dales, J. H. 1970. *Pollution, property and prices.* Toronto, Canada: Univ. of Toronto Press

Fine, Sidney. 1967. *Laissez faire and the general welfare state.* Ann Arbor, Mich.: Univ. of Michigan Press.

Fishman, Betty G. and Leo. 1969. *Employment, unemployment and economic growth.* New York, N. Y.: Thomas Y. Cromwell.

Fusfeld, Daniel. 1966. *The age of the economist.* Glenview, Ill.: Scott, Foresman

Gray, Petter, and Shanti Tangri (eds.). 1970. *Economic development and population growth.* Lexington, Mass.: Raytheon.

Heilbronner, Robert L. 1970. *Between capitalism and socialism.* New York, N.Y.: Random House.

Kapp, Karl. 1967. Social cost of business enterprise. *In* Marshall Goldman (ed.) *Controlling pollution.* Englewood Cliffs, N.J.: Prentice Hall.

Mermelstein, David (ed.) 1970. *Economics: mainstream readings and radical critiques.* New York, N.Y.: Random House.

Romano, Richard and Melvin Leiman (ed.) 1970. *Views on capitalism.* Beverly Hills, Calif.: Glencoe Press.

Bio-Ethics
Reflections on Political Ecology

A. Khoshkish

We cannot command nature except by obeying her.

Francis Bacon, *Novum Organum*

I – PROGRESS, POPULATION AND PRODUCTIVITY

A. The Material

Man, by his own definition, is an animal living on the planet earth. He is an omnivorous mammifer who is adapted best to a savannah type of climate. Except for certain physiological adaptations such as a greater number of perspiration glands in warmer climates or fat deposits in colder weather which make him more resistant to certain tolerable climatic fluctuations (Coon, 1954), he would not have been able to survive in many parts of the earth. Yet man managed to explore and inhabit practically the entire surface of the planet, and this by artificial means, i.e., by unnatural processes. The natural process for a naked man in the Arctic would be to freeze to death and in the tropics to die of exposure.

Beyond gathering food and hunting, man used the skin and wool of his victims for warmth, domesticated animals, constructed shelters, and developed agriculture. Of course, the interference of man with nature for his survival has had its natural repercussions. Some species of animals are known to have been hunted to death, while deforestation and erosion of soil have turned arable lands into arid deserts and dried up rivers, as happened with the desert of Bahawalpur in northwestern India and the once mighty Hakra River flowing through it (Tinker, 1966).

Nature, however, kept man under control. Disease and famine managed to keep man within reasonable numbers. Man himself also gave a hand to nature by

© A. Khoshkish, 1970. This article was originally prepared as a discussion paper for groups concerned with ecological problems following the U.S. National Commission for UNESCO's National Conference on "Man and His Environment" in San Francisco in November, 1969. Dr. A. Khoshkish is Professor of Political Science at Moorhead State College, Moorhead, Minnesota.

indulging in self-extermination through wars. Malthus called these positive checks! The fittest under the circumstances, depending on the situation, survived. Man had few pretensions of harnessing nature and was conscious of its existence and its awe. The curve of world population growth by the year 1800 looked like this (President's Science Advisory Committee Report, 1968):

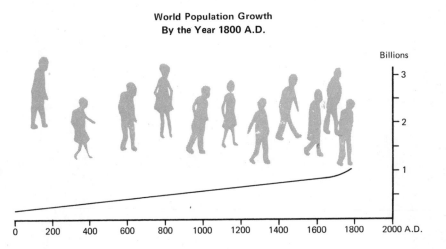

**World Population Growth
By the Year 1800 A.D.**

Then part of mankind started to overdraw nature's deposit. Science, technology, and medicine enabled man to explore and use nature as a tool for *progress.* "Progress towards what?" you may ask. We are in the habit of using this word as a goal in itself, as if it had a majesty of its own. In fact, in the last analysis progress boils down to the drive for ever better satisfaction of man's animal needs: to spare him from death as long as possible and lengthen his survival, to bring him comfort and spare him from hardship, to give him more leisure and satisfy his curiosity and his drives for amusement. The technological age made it possible for man to look for progress towards these ends through material well-being.

Before this age, beyond their material efforts limited by nature, the mass of men, be they kings or serfs, searched for the extension of their survival and comfort, and for answer to their curiosity, in metaphysics rather than physics. Alchemy and magic were more psychological supports than material help, while Heaven secured survival after death and solaced those who lacked material comfort in this life.

The European industrial revolution seemed to bring with it the promised land right on earth, at the beginning for the few, and more recently for the multitude. The curve of world's population growth then became like this (PSACR, 1968):

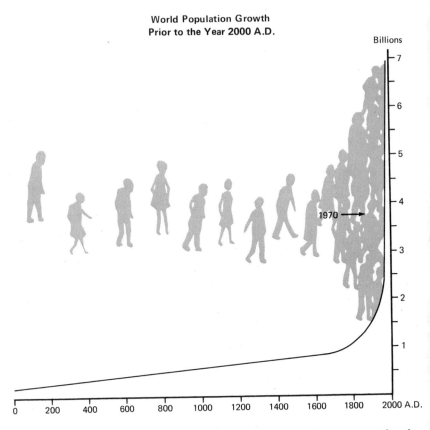

World Population Growth Prior to the Year 2000 A.D.

Nature seemed to be there for exploitation. Its generosity was considered as endless and its passivity the very salt of the earth. Viewed in this way, all progress needed was more men to exploit nature and to be exploited. So the growing population which was the consequence of progress was a welcome factor. Population meant more labor force, bigger markets, more profits—in short, more power! And power is of interest to politics! Progress was the thing. It was strived for and promised. Whether in the name of Adam Smith or Marx, the politician promised longer and healthier survival, better comfort and more leisure.

Through progress the boundaries seemed unlimited. And if injustices existed in the distribution of wealth today, they would be remedied tomorrow, be it through equal opportunity for all under competitive free enterprise or to each according to his needs under communism.

B. The Ethical

The revolutionary pace of industrialization and its social consequences brought into the forefront dimensions of ethical concern more related to the human conditions arising in the modern technological world. Whether under the banner of Christian charity or social justice, these ethics were to serve as vanguards against those aspects of human shortcomings, such as exploitation of other men, which were likely to be amplified in the process of progress and production.

The social pattern evolved parallel with scientific explorations and technological development. The patriarchal and corporative texture of the society changed into a paradoxical combination of egocentrism and ethnocentrism, individualism and nationalism; one giving more autonomy and fluidity to the units within the group; the other creating a framework for regimentation and integration. Both were instrumental to progress and production in their economic take off, and to power politics, internal and external. Even social philosophies like communism, which preached internationalism and put emphasis on the communal duties rather than individual rights and incentive, had to revert to patriotism and recognize the need for individual initiative and satisfaction in order to keep progress and production, at a certain stage, going.

Family, however, remained the basic cell of the society. It provided bases for control, supply and early socialization of the population. It also provided the appropriate store for basic social and moral values. After all, even though progress made longer life possible, it was through procreation and offspring that man could secure his continuation. And the political system promised a better future and better education for the coming generations. The Malthusian theory was discredited by the colossal possibilities technology and science could offer. Together with apple pie and the flag, motherhood became one of the American trinities, while the Soviet Union bestowed the title of Heroine of the Union to her productive mothers!

Matter seemed to dazzle the spirit. Religion, which has been the harbour of hope in times of intermittent abundance, was now giving place to machine and technology which promised perpetual affluence. Now on occasions of man-made catastrophes like war did gods become momentarily popular. The church, however, served the purpose of sanctifying the institutions like family and procreation which complemented the new ethics. In some instances its basic doctrine did clash with the new trends. The precept of renunciation did not quite fit in with the drive for material gain, and the concept of loving your neighbor was not quite in tune with profitable bargaining for cheap labor.

The church thus compromised between blessing the useful and overlooking the hypocritical. Some systems like the Soviets tried to dispense with the church altogether but encountered difficulties. They apparently did not believe in Dostoyevsky when he said that "man cannot bear to be without the miraculous, he will create new miracles of his own for himself and will worship deeds of sorcery and witchcraft, though he might be a hundred times over a rebel, heretic and infidel." (Dostoyevsky, 1880)

Speaking of miracles, however, progress did seem to present one worth worshipping, and material gain did become a goal for its own sake. In the words of Stewart Udall, the Gross National Product became the American Holy Grail.* The new divinity was of such a forceful impact that it succeeded where over two hundred years of colonization and Christian missionary work had failed. Moslems, Hindus, Buddhists, and Confucians in the developing countries were modifying and rejecting their convictions and traditions to embrace the gifts of western civilization in the name of progress. They were accepting the denomination of "developing"‡ in the technological and economic sense, relegating spiritual heritage to the background. After all, their goal, too, was longer and healthier life, more comfort, and better leisure. Heaven, Brahman, and Nirvana were good for times when you could not do better on this earth.

Indeed, for awhile progress through production seemed to be man's ultimate answer to his questions. Had mother earth been generous enough to give what man asked for and had she been indulgent enough to swallow whatever waste man threw into her, it seems that at some point man's voracity would have been satiated.

When economic development reaches the stage where attractive social motivations are offered to individuals, the curve of population growth levels off.* This reduction in population growth is also due to better education and socialization, teaching among other things the use of contraceptives (Notestein, Kirk** and Segel, 1963). Diversification of pastimes and entertainment is another factor, and finally, according to some biological theories, the protein-rich diet accompanying development reduces the briskness of movement of reproductive cells at a certain age and contributes to population control (Notestein, Kirk and Segel, 1963). It seemed, therefore, technologically feasible to close the gap between the rates of increase in food demand and food production in the developing countries, thus permitting them an economic take off theoretically

---

*Reported by L. W. Lane, Jr., to the U. S. National Commission Conference on "Man and His Environment" in San Francisco, November, 1969.

‡After being labelled "backward" and "underdeveloped."

**For an interesting conceptual approach to the problem see Joseph L. Spengler, Values and Fertility Analyais in *Demography* 1966, III, 1, pp. 109-130.

followed by levelling off of population growth on the basis of the criteria enumerated above.‡

II – PROGRESS, POLLUTION AND POVERTY

A. The Material

But then mother earth had a word to say. She called for attention. Not that nature counter-attacked. It is man's vision of struggle that makes him think that he is at war with nature: If he only could see that he is part of nature and that his birth, life and decay are natural processes within that context. At the Conference on Man and His Environment organized by the U.S. National Commission for UNESCO in San Francisco in November 1969, we were presented with a grim picture of this reality: Man has found out that pesticides such as DDT are deposited in the soil and in the water undissolved for long periods of time, and end up in animal bodies that he eats. The FDA has established an interim tolerance limit of five parts per million of DDT compounds in the eatable fish. Recently Jack mackerels taken in the Pacific Ocean near Los Angeles were found to contain 10 ppm of DDT. So were the Coho salmon taken in Lake Michigan. The brown pelicans which feed on marine fish have been wiped out of Louisiana because the pesticides in their food thinned the shell of their eggs to the point of not being hatchable (Risebrough, 1969). At the same time the pests for whom the pesticides and insecticides were originally fabricated are becoming more and more immune to them. In 1963 fifty times more DDT was required, as compared to 1961, to control insect pests in the cotton fields of Texas (Commoner, 1969). Very soon the fat American may no more go on a diet safely because the DDT deposit in his fat may poison him (Ehrlich, 1968).

‡The technological feasibility is, however, not a real possibility as demonstrated in the following table (Sanders and Ruttan, 1969).

Minnesota:

Estimated levels of population income, food demand, and food increase in the developing countries, in 1980 (1968 = 100)

Population	136
Per Capita Income	133⊕
Food Demand	157⊕
Historic Food Production	140
Probable Food Production	151
Technologically Feasible Food Production	160

⊕The discrepancy between the per capita income increase and food demand is due to the fact that the undernourished population will spend the greater parts of its earlier income increase in the purchase of additional foodstuff. As we shall see later, even if the technologically feasible food production could be materialized, other problems would arise.

The 10 to 15 per cent increase in the minute amount of carbon dioxide in the atmosphere since 1900 has caused surface temperatures to rise 0.2°C and the temperature in the stratosphere to decrease by some 2.0°C (Malone, 1969). In the United States we produced a yearly amount of 125 million tons of air pollutants, including some 65 million tons of carbon monoxide, 23 million tons of sulfur oxides, 8 million tons of nitrogen oxides (Waste Management and Control, 1966). The emission of SO_2 will increase by 75 per cent in 1980 and another 75 per cent by the year 2000 (Malone, 1969). As much as 100 million tons of oil enter the ocean through spillage or wastage every year, and accidents like the oil leakage off the Santa Barbara shore or the pollution of the English and French beaches by Torrey Canyon are likely to increase rather than decrease in the future (Risebrough, 1969).

The yearly production of solid waste in the United States alone amounts to 3.65 billion tons! This includes, for example, food (garbage), dirt (rubbish), paper, tin cans, plastic containers, abandoned cars and trucks, demolished concrete, paints, industrial scrap metals and chemicals, asbestos processing waste, blast furnace and smelting operation wastes, coal culm banks, and animal wastes produced in concentrated operations near urban areas (Eliassen, 1969).

If we try to eliminate these 3.65 billion tons of garbage, rubbish, and waste through our technology we will create additional problems. For example, technologically speaking, our sewage treatment has indeed advanced far enough to convert the noxious organic human waste into innocuous inorganic materials that could be disposed of in rivers and lakes. But then the addition to the water of excessive inorganic products, which are algal nutrients, results in algal overgrowth destroying in turn the self-purifying capability of the aquatic ecosystem (Commoner, 1969). This is what happened to such a massive ecosystem as Lake Erie where the harvest of pike fell from some seven million pounds in 1956 to 200 in 1963.

Suppose the some seven billion human beings who are expected to occupy the surface of this earth by the year 2000 reached the garbage producing capacity of the United States' present population. In that year alone the world would produce some 127.75 billion tons of garbage. That amounts to 250 tons per square kilometer of the surface of the earth—land and sea included. That would be a lot of garbage for a year.

This, of course, is a human calculation of what man defines as waste and "dirty." Looking at it from the point of view of nature, we can see how man has artificially complicated his life. Of the 3.65 billion tons yearly waste product of the United States, one single item, constituting over half of it (58 per cent) is agricultural waste, including mainly animal waste (43 per cent), notably produced in concentrated feedlots near urban areas (Eliassen, 1969). While man juggles with the problem of disposing of it, nature is deprived of this beneficial organic material which is the source of nitrates in soil and water, and the supplier of nitrogen to plants, and the animals that feed on them. Cattle which were originally grazing in the Midwest pastures and contributed to the natural recycling of the soil were moved to the feedlots near urban areas. The land was then used for intensive grain production with massive use of inorganic fertilizers which, due to their high quantity and nonabsorption by the soil, ended up in streams and lakes, increased algal growth, and created water pollution. In cases where the polluted river water is used as a source of water supply, this creates the danger of infantile diseases (Commoner, 1969).

In short, man's technology, after having damaged nature, is using it as a medium to turn against its own master. Man is no longer doing his share and in turn drawing his share from the ecosystem, but disrupting the recycling process of the whole nature and thereby threatening his very survival—the "ecological backlash."

There seem to be two dimensions to the problem. One, that there are natural limitations on man's use of his technological possibilities, and two, that there is not going to be enough room and food for the increase in population, mainly in the underdeveloped parts of the world. The two aspects of the problem were summed up in the following passages of Dr. Sterling Bunnell's paper presented to the conference.

> For example, if we attempt to postpone world famine by a crash program of feed production by any and all expedient applications of modern agricultural technology (especially synthetic fertilizers and persistent pesticides) we are apt, as Paul Ehrlich has wisely warned, to wreck the biosphere with chemical pollution; if we hope to easily replace fossil fuel power with nuclear power we exchange the problems of CO_2 and hydrocarbon pollution for pollution by the equally dangerous and more insidious biologically active radio-isotopes. If we try to extricate ourselves by conversion from fission to fusion power we may raise the tritium concentration of the world's water to a level fatal to our species. The critical mutation lead (if you are unfamiliar with this concept, consider it evidence of the inadequacy of your education to meet the requirements of survival) is uncertain before it is reached and there will be irresistible economic pressures to exceed any arbitrary limit in an overpopulating world hungry for power. Thus it seems that the problems of food production, power demands, industrialization, and waste disposal are not soluble in isolation, but only in conjunction with stabilizing population at levels which allow us to stay within the limits of environmental tolerance. A "breakthrough" on one problem (e.g. greatly increased food supply as by development of synthetic carbohydrates) could finish us off by allowing population increase to intensify other problems (e.g. pollution, oxygen balance, thermal balance, etc.).

B. The Ethical

As I drove to the airport under the hazy smoggy sky of San Francisco I had a lot of compassion for those crossing my way. I was looking into the other cars, seeing people living in the smog of the Bay Area and pondering the problems that were facing mankind.

As I flew out of San Francisco and over the vastness of the United States, I started wondering whether the problem was there, under the little hub of pollution covering the Bay Area, indeed, little it was compared to what is left of this great country. True, 60 per cent of the U. S. population lives in 1 per cent of its land. But could the some 77,000 persons per square mile of Manhattan Island not go and live away from the smog? After all, the population density of the United States as a whole was only 50.5 per square mile in 1960 (Heer, 1968).

The answer to the question was unfortunately negative. They cannot. It is like sending the cattle in the feedlots back to the Midwest pastures. It is not *profitable.* Like nature's cycles man creates for himself value systems which turn into a vicious circle. The more vicious they become, the harder it will be to break from them. Our industrial civilization has created its own system: that of progress, production, population, profit, and pollution. The system is not an exclusivity of the capitalistic free enterprise; the socialist and communist regimes enjoy it as well. It is that of the materialist approach to life. We pollute Lake Erie, the Soviets pollute Lake Baikal. One should produce, which is more profitable when there is concentration of manpower and market; and consequently, one way or the another, one pollutes. As we saw earlier, even if we try to treat the waste we get the ecological backlash.

Man, like Dr. Faust, has sold his soul to the devil of material progress.

In the optimistic frenzy of materialist drive it was believed that despite numbered bank accounts in Switzerland, despite tax loopholes, and despite helicopters going into flames, man could make so much out of mother earth that some day the leftovers of those who are good at competitive free enterprise or state capitalism, depending where they are, would finally bring to the rest of the lot those material gadgets which would qualify them as a "two car family," or whatever the criteria of prosperity may be at the time. It was believed that the spoils and the overflow of abundance would finally reach ghettos and make the urban crisis disappear, and that despite colonial concessions, the developed could return enough charity to the developing that he would be able to satisfy his hunger.

Had nature remained passive and unlimited the question would have been: was that the desirable end? We may hypothesize an isolated situation where a country like the United States (minus its racial components and out of the context of its poor neighbors) went for unlimited material well-being under free enterprise. Would it ever get there? Not unless it changed its basic terms of reference in the meantime, because the driving force of such a system is want. You have to keep running for it, and as long as you are running you haven't reached it, and if you stop running you will never get there! At some stage of material satiation such a society would have to stop and ask the question: so what?

Fortunately or unfortunately, depending on how you look at it, that hypothetical isolated utopia does not exist. In the hypothetical isolation and absence of stimulants we may have imagined the young indoctrinated to follow the path of the older generations, to cherish the same values, and to keep running a long time. In the context of the real world many come earlier to ask the question: so what? And understandably enough, most of them are from "two car families" and above! We are reaching the end of the blind alley. Resources are not unlimited and discrepancies, contradictions, deprivations, conflicts, and hypocrisies are immense.

Above all, our ethics and values are questionable. We are told to tell the truth (because the child who tells the truth is better controllable), and yet we may find in the behavior of our own parents that honesty does not always pay in the way of making a profit! We are taught rectitude but may find the very ones who preach it to be unctuous. We are taught to love our neighbor and see how that love of neighbor has become a material artifact of fund-collecting, while hates and jealousies are what make the competitive world go.

We are told that sex is dirty and that we should get married and raise a family (because that is still the best way of creating responsible citizens). But then we look around us and see our parents' sexual hangups, the near-to-pathologic sex commerce, unhappy unions, and lack of communication between parents and children, and we wonder whether the old institution corresponds to the new realities.

The surface is being polished; the dirt is creeping in. The ethical structure of our society is not only hypocritical, it has become, in its artificiality, masturbative and prophylactic! Not only is love dirty, but the body should not smell, the genital organs are a shame. We are denying nature its empire. The same way we take away the animal waste of the cattle, which nature appreciates, from the prairies of the Midwest and make them "dirt" in human terminology in the feedlots, the same way we are killing our sensual side and inhibiting our energies for the sake of aggressive profit-making! The use of four letter words by the younger generation is not only a revolt against the established hypocrisy, it is a means of shedding away the prophylactic culture. They are making acquaintance with their glands, bowels, and genital organs and their uninhibited functions. Incidentally, this revival of communion with the sensual side of man may help racial understanding between the young blacks and whites in the United States, as the latter start developing and appreciating the sensual side which the former have always enjoyed.

The problem is that the issues are so basic, the solutions so contrary to the established values, and the time for conversion so short that humanity finds itself in the prerevolutionary psychological conditions. Some pound the table of argument to the point of revolt, the others stick their heads in the sand for solution.

Those who revolt do so against the established values, but theirs is not necessarily a solution unless they are prepared to go all the way to the logical conclusion of their act. A revolt is not a cure in itself. It is the fever and the bursting of the abscess.

Thus, for example, the hippies are returning to nature. While their way of life is a reaction to the material and technological civilization, one wonders whether in the context of the surrounding technological society it can be a lasting culture and whether it can be an answer to the problem of population increase. It is likely that in the absence of a deep-rooted social and spiritual doctrine, second-generation hippies who will not have the personal experience of their parents about the materialistic civilization will succumb to its glittering polish. That is, if we assume that the first generation itself will not. The hippie experience has yet to stand the test of time. Many attempts at communal life with varying levels of organization have been made in the past, from the Brook Farm Institute to the Oneida Community, and they have not survived.

But suppose a movement for communal simple life and return to nature could create enough of a deep-rooted doctrine which enabled it to perpetuate itself and propagate its message. It will only be serving its purpose of man's salvation if, as indicated earlier, it is prepared to draw the logical conclusion of its raison d'etre, i.e., total renunciation of its surrounding techological facilities. No appeal to technology and medicine for better nourishment and health, letting nature regulate their number by famine and disease. Even appendicitis, not to speak of epidemics, can kill a lot of people.

Without such renunciation they are solving no problems. They are adding more. The Hutterites, following their simple communal existence have a 4.00 per cent birth rate, together with that of Cocos-Keeling Islands (4.2 per cent) the highest in the world (Eaton and Mayer, 1953; Sheps, 1965; Smith, 1960).

There are those on the other hand who foresee the solutions of man's problems through more of the same things. The more fantastic their forecasts are, the more they skip the phase of conversion and delude themselves in day-dreaming. Thus, they say, the day will come when we will live in artificial satellites, extract metals from sea water and ordinary rocks, stabilize world population at about three times its present number, but solve food and health problems by radical transformation of human nutritive habits and universal hygienic inspections. Unfortunately, they don't tell us how they are going to get us there. (Ellul, 1964). Even Ehrlich, who is making more transitional proposals to solve the problems of pollution and population (such as addition of sterilants to staple food or the water supply to keep the population from procreation) does recognize that they are socially unpalatable and politically unrealistic! (Ehrlich, 1968).

It is precisely the social, economic, ethical, and political stumbling blocks which cause some to revolt against the establishment and others to shut their minds about conversion and dream about the next scene, utopia. But they offer no real solutions, and the more we beat around the bush the more it becomes obvious that the key to the problems must be found within the ethical and social contexts which are held as taboos.

III – PROGRESS, PEACE AND PLENITUDE

For the great enemy of the truth is very often not the lie–deliberate, contrived and dishonest–but the myth–persistent, persuasive and unrealistic.*

Redefined, in brief, materially speaking, the problem that faces man is that on the one hand he is growing in number and on the other hand he cannot provide for the mass of humanity the comfort, energy and food that it will *want*. If he technically tries he will face the ecological backlash, and even if he succeeds he will face the spiritual question, "so what?" He has to limit himself in procreation and he must limit the satisfaction of his material wants. The proposition is whether instead of materially restraining himself he will not be better off if he reviews the values on the basis of which he first started on the course towards increase in population and material wants, and to see whether through an intellectual and spiritual re-examination of his basic values he can change his basic goals.

The assumption is that the desirable end is the happiness of man. If man restrained himself in procreation and satisfaction of his material needs despite the existence of want in him toward these ends he would be unhappy. But if he came to realize and convince himself that these are not desirable goals to start with, then man would find himself in the happy state of rationally and voluntarily not wanting them and finding them superficial and irrelevant.

I say "rationally and voluntarily" in order to distinguish between myth and indoctrination as against reality and will. It is in the latter context that we should look for the solution. A close look at some of our prevailing values will not only .show their anachronistic nature, but will reveal that despite the resistance and hostility of the bigots, a trend towards their critical analysis and change has already started. But the pace is slow and the attitude limited to a group of elites who because of other social motivations do not always confess their inclinations. They play the bourgeois game and pay lip service to the religious, political, and economic establishments.

The modern man should realize that the social motivations he has created for material satisfaction and bourgeois contentment have not only ceased to be sufficient for bringing happiness to man but are becoming detrimental to him.

*J. F. Kennedy, address to the Yale University Commencement, June 11, 1962.

A. Happiness and Knowledge as Values

When we look at some of the values which make the Western civilization go, such as hard work, individual enterprise, and material progress, we get the feeling that our materialistic approach to life somehow missed the Jeffersonian boat. Jefferson had a point when he paraphrased Locke and turned "life, liberty, and property" into "life, liberty, and the pursuit of happiness."

1. Less Temptation

Is there no better way of being happy than to procure more wealth and do better than others? Does competition really make man happy? Does it offer a means for satisfying wants or does it only provide the social incentive to produce more? Surely if progress and production as social norms could go on with no drawbacks, the artifact of competitive enterprise could make the individual a better tool for the perpetuation of those norms. But if they are going to end up in the pollution of man's body, soul, and environment is it not time to bring a halt to that frenzy?

For the consumer to start wanting less, the producer should want less. But who is the producer and who is the consumer? In 1952 only about 6.5 million, or 4 per cent of the Americans were shareholders, by the end of 1968 some 26.5 million, or 13 per cent of them held shares.*

Thus the logical extension of wanting less is really wanting less profit and what has become its ultimate manifestation, money. But capitalists are many. In order to reason with business we have to deal with its shareholders. It is the average shareholder, consumer, and producer, in other words, the public at large whom we have to reach and convince that wanting less is for his own good.

Of course under the present conditions of competitive free enterprise with little regulatory system of distribution we are not well justified to bring this messianic word to the some 26 million people in the United States who are below the poverty line.‡ The sermon should not be misused as yet another gimmick to make the poor render to Caesar what belongs to Caesar. The poor's want is a need, not a frivolous desire. True, it is difficult to draw a hard and fast line between what is needed and what is a superficial desire. But somewhere between the adequate amount of protein for healthy survival, or reasonable shelter on the one hand, and increased temptation to over-eat apples by the addition of artificial coloring, or insertion of a semi-nude in a new super car

---

*Data compiled by the New York Stock Exchange as of January 15, 1969.

‡Source, U. S. Bureau of the Census, 1967. See also Herman P. Miller, The Composition of the Poor, in Margaret S. Gordon (ed.), *Poverty in America,* San Francisco; Chandler Publishing Company, 1965. Notably Table 7 for statistics which, although pertaining to 1960, make a better point of poverty-stricken families.

(going 160 mph for highways mostly having limits of 70 mph) to make it irresistible on the other hand, a fairly clear line can be drawn.

We must make a new evaluation of the GNP of junk based on waste economy and conditioning of the consumer through publicity. Is the United States' GNP really comparable to that of Sweden or Germany when they produce a car to last, while the American producer makes a car to go to the junk yard? When most of the private houses in the United States are built to be torn down by the time their mortgages are paid, that is, if they have not been knocked down by a tornado or a hurricane? Not only is the production ephemeral, the consumer has been indoctrinated to want it that way.

The irony of it all is that the indoctrination of the whole population with the lure of materialistic well-being and profit-making has made the task of disentanglement a much more colossal job. Were we faced with a few capitalists, presumably well-educated and materially satiated, we would probably have less trouble demonstrating to them the imminent dangers of over-production and pollution resulting from their appetite for profit. Indeed, some come by themselves to realize that there is more to a man's life than the satisfaction of amassing wealth. Extremes such as David Owen in early 19th century England are few, but Kennedys, Rockefellers, Carnegies, or Fords have social ambitions beyond material profit. Of course, this tendency is also a short-cut direct to power.

But the system has become the peoples' golden calf. The middle-class shareholder buys shares to maximize his profit, not for doing charity. He does that elsewhere at his church or United Fund—adding to his prestige and status. He has the mentality of the common man with the "common" standards of our bourgeois civilization. He wants to be successful.

We have to get to him and tell him that he has fallen into a vicious circle. That where he is running to is nowhere and by accelerating he is only complicating life for himself and humanity. That the faster he runs the less he sees and appreciates what passes him by. It is an absurd thing to do, considering the fact that he is running nowhere. Time is short, we cannot wait for him to come to himself. The younger generation is awakening. But all those over thirty whom they don't trust are going to be around for a long time and will continue on the track set before them and in the process corrupt the young.

In short a crash adult education program to disentangle the people from obsolete myths and values is urgently needed. Granted, man has not been very successful in the past in bringing aesthetic, philosophic, and spiritual appreciation and taste to the level of the commons. But has that not been a question of lack of means to bring adequate education to all? Can the affluent society not make a try at it? There have been times of Buddhist, Judeo-Christian, and Islamic piety when societies lived in relative harmony with themselves and nature. Should man be made reasonable only by the fear of God and heaven? Is there not a possibility that man may rationally limit the use of his material wealth with moderation, distribute it better, and make little waste? Can he not come to use his intellectual and spiritual capacities and his reason to the maximum?

The hope for some success in this direction exists in the fact that as things go, the growing number of those who live in the congested smoggy concrete jungles may come to see a point in it. It will be easier to convince a New Yorker than a rural villager that he should restrain himself in the use of his car and go for a public transportation system which will be providing facilities for all and therefore will be better distributive, more efficient, and less wasteful.

For this we will have to reverse the trend of present-day salesmanship publicity. Indeed we may have to fight it. Man should not be enticed to long for bigger, faster, and flashier cars with four-barrel exhaust pipes. He should be made conscious that every time he pushes on the pedal and creates more carbon monoxide, he is committing an unethical act—if not a crime—considering the statistics which show the increase of lung and skin diseases due to smog. If air and water are common property, it does not mean that man is at liberty to throw his garbage into them. Every time he does so, whether as an individual or as a manufacturer, he is transgressing the rights of the others who breathe, drink, and use these common properties The driver should be encouraged to hike whenever he can. It will be good for both his own well-being and his appreciation of his social and natural environment. He should be made to use public transportation which, if he did, would permit its improvement and bring him more in contact with his fellow men.

Along the same lines people should be taught that it is unethical to induce a man to consume more than necessary and to buy what he does not need. That it is unethical to make goods of low quality which could be made better and longer-lasting. That it is equally unethical to replace utilities before they cease to be useful and thus create more junk. That products should not keep changing their form and fashion, creating more temptations. That even if it may be economically not *profitable,* wastes such as scrap iron, paper, glass, etc., should be used to avoid pollution. Many European countries with limited resources have been doing that.

I do realize that all this means less consumption, less production, less profit, and less employment. Reduction in the first three items is the desired end. As for the last item, the assumption is that a total examination of man's goals and values will permit him to realize that in a less competitive and more reasonable society there are better possibilities of social justice and redistribution, permitting all to do their share and satisfy their needs. I do realize the difficulty of bringing about such a drastic change in a civilization so totally deluded in materialistic interests and profit-making that it can hardly find judges for its high court who have not indulged in profitable transactions (Fortas and Haynsworth) and its government has to lift its law on harmful products (cyclamates) and stop pursuing its action against fraudulent banking (numbered bank accounts) under pressures from appropriate lobbies.

In the present psychological state of modern man it is in a way easier to make him take sterilants in his water and staple food as Ehrlich suggests than to do away with his profit (Ehrlich, 1968). Sterilants affect his body which is already full of stimulants, tranquilizers lead, DDT, radiation, etc. What is being suggested here is to lighten his pocket. That hurts. But like the constipated child who has to take his Milk of Magnesia sooner or later, the modern man will have to take the laxative, better sooner than later.

Where is he going to start? Obviously what it all boils down to is a massive eye-opening program. The only problem is that it will need the help of those whom it is eventually going to *demystify*. But the issue is not as hopeless as it appears because of the seriousness and reality of the hazards involved in not undertaking it.

The conservationist movements may start a campaign similar to the one undertaken by the Cancer Society against the cigarette industry. Congress ended up passing laws against the cigarette industry and curtailing its advertisement. Are the exhaust pipes and what is connected to them or the artificial food coloring not equally noxious for human organisms? In fact, there are more laws than one thinks against abuses by the industry. But very often they are dead letters, not implemented or not properly enforced.

The campaign should in the first place, be directed against commercial advertisement and toward intellectual education of the masses. It will eventually make the politician aware of the problem and make him adhere to it when he sees the possibility of support from an awakened public. Ideally, legislative action should ban publicity and advertisement for commercial purposes, and create incentive for redirecting funds thus liberated to foundations which would make them available to mass media for the development of educational and recreative programs under the supervision of scientific, cultural, and educational institutions.

Depending on the response from business and industry, laws can be made more or less categoric. There are, no doubt, obstacles in the way of such a project. Only a few years ago the FCC faced the strong opposition of the House Interstate and Foreign Commerce Committee for wanting to impose on the industry its own standards for advertisement on the TV and the radio.

But what is suggested here is really nothing spectacular. The TV and radio programs of many countries in Europe did not have commercials on them until recently. Now they are trying the American way. The trend could have been in the other direction. Of course, in many of the European countries the TV and the radio stations are under governmental control. In the U. S. they are in the hands of business. Can we not liberate them for awhile and see what cultural institutions and higher learning can do to them?

2. More Learning

The scientists should be recruited to co-operate actively in such a campaign. They should also re-evaluate their role and responsibilities within the society. They should be reminded that in the earlier days, material application of research was only an incidental part of the scientific drive. The scientist was learning for the sake of learning, although some became so involved in their drive for knowledge that they sometimes overlooked the side effects and undesirable consequences of their research and discoveries. As the tools of scientific research became more expensive with progress, and as those after profit and power found out about the practical uses of science for their own ends, business and government flaunted the facilities they could offer to the scientist and ended up buying his services. The regrets of J. R. Oppenheimer for having unleashed the nuclear power are well known.

In the process, the gap between different branches of science widened. The industrialist in search of profit would immediately opt for the use of technology in the automation of his enterprise or the manufacture of a new product invented by the physicist or the chemist. The works of a political scientist or psychologist pointing to the adverse social effects of the new technology could find no immediate hot buyers. Those interested in the social problems are either social scientists without means for actions, or philanthropists with limited means. The government agencies, in state controlled economies, often behave like the capitalist industrialist, and, in the free enterprise societies, lag behind in dealing with social problems and cope with them only when they become acute or when they help in reelections. The example of water and air pollution in the United States and other industrialized countries is significant.

The scientists are today in a position to act. They should first of all become conscious of their solidarity in their ultimate goal: that of simple and yet immense happiness in learning. They should develop further interdisciplinary consultative mechanisms among the physical, natural, and social sciences enabling them to have a more global approach to the effects and consequences of their scientific advancements. Those who are concerned about the adverse effects of technology and environmental deterioration can help in the establishment of this dialogue between the scientists free from governmental and business patronage. Ways and means should be examined for the control of the indiscriminate use and abuse of scientific discoveries by business and government. They should assert the rights of the scientists to control the application of their knowledge. Finally, scientists should play a capital role in awakening public interest in the appreciation of knowledge and the joys of learning as an end in itself.

Imagine investing all the money business is spending in publicity for educational purposes. Not only would it stop the creation of new wants, new products, and new pollutants, but it would create such a variety of means of learning that knowledge could be made attractive to the most unmotivated and unsophisticated individual.

Man does want to learn. Unfortunately in our materialist and bourgeois civilization the common man is oriented to learn for a material purpose, not to learn for learning's own sake. His drive for learning is then satisfied by superficialities and gossip; and thus being limited, exploited for political and economic purposes.

Imagine the day when men can spend their time learning creative art, music, painting and dancing. When they can study oceanography and astronomy, history and anthropology, savor their knowledge of flowers and animals, plains and mountains. When the man you meet will tell you about the interpretation of the prehistoric paintings of Altamira and you can tell him about the latest pictures of animal life in the deep seas. When the man you meet will no longer limit his early questions to whether you have a family and children and how much money you make: Clearly he is the product of our materialistic civilization. These are the same questions the banker asks you in order to give you credit. He does not care whether you are an honest man or not, and, under the circumstances, he is right. If you are a product of this civilization, the best way of checking on your honesty and responsibility is to see whether you have surrounded yourself with the commodities, wife, children and other belongings, which make you materially responsible and respectable. The Wall Street offices were surprised recently to find their hippie messengers more reliable than their usual bourgeois employees.

The time has come for industrialized society to realize that man is not the tool of technology, but the latter at the service of man. Man and nature are the ends. With our means for material satisfaction, let us try the contemplative happiness dear to Aristotle and Jefferson.

B. The End of the Bourgeois Family

But so far what we have discussed has been aimed at reducing the material wants of man and thus curtailing consumption, production, and therefore the ill of pollution. Whether we have at the same time advanced any solution to the problem of population is not apparent. The modern educated man may prefer his sausages without artificial coloring and delight in the study and admiration of ancient Egyptian obelisks. Why should he stop making children? For that we have to revert back to our original proposition for the critical reexamination of our values and see whether they correspond to our modern realities. The educational programs should not only aim at the appeasement of the material wants, but question the social myths and values surrounding them.

1. Procreation

"It is the nature of every man to love life and hate death, to think of his relatives and look after his wife and children. Only when a man is moved by higher principles is this not so," said Ssu-ma Ch'ien.

The higher animal that man is, according to his findings, controls his behavior more by socialization than by instincts. Thus he should be able to justify his acts and institutions socially. Should he want children? Ehrlich, by adding sterilants to staple food and water supply, wants to make of children a scarce commodity (Ehrlich, 1968). I suggest making man aware, through education, that the reasons for which he wanted children no longer exist and therefore he should no longer desire begetting them and be happy not having them. He should realize that today children are only a heavy social responsibility.

Why did man want children in the first place?* In the social context, the child corresponded to an economic tool in rural areas and early industrial societies. It was also considered as a support for old age. In developed countries, these roles of children are replaced and can be further replaced by social phenomena such as social security and mobile manpower. A survey in Japan shows that while in 1950 more than 55 per cent of those interviewed answered definitely yes to the question as to whether they expected to be supported by their children in their old age, only 27 per cent gave an affirmative answer in 1961 (Freeman, 1968). Incidentally, Japan is one of the nations which has had a descending population growth rate.

In the days when man had little amusement and his entertainment was not diversified, one may well imagine the source of joy the children were. Girls who played with dolls made of cloth rejoiced to change diapers of real babies. Today their early dolls speak, wet, and walk. Nothing is left for them to imagine. And as a young married couple was saying, children would interfere with their social activities, travel, and television watching! If only we could make the contents of these events more meaningful.

Man also saw in children his own continuation after death. But in our fast-moving world, even before their teens children no longer identify with the world their parents have lived in and parents cannot recognize their own image in their progeniture. And then before maturity is reached, children fly away to become often far away acquaintances in the long life which normally awaits aging parents these days.

---

*Maybe we should record here the currently prevailing socio-psychological and biological thesis according to which women's maternal drive is due to socialization rather than instinct. We should therefore search for the cause of the drive for procreation in the social context.

Then what is left of the drive for making children? Well, people do not know for sure, but feel they should make them. It is above all the indoctrination received from the parents, which may have been justified in the past when factors reviewed above were still valid, but are no longer. People should be made to understand that it is most irresponsible to inculcate the younger generations with the drive to get involved in marriage and procreation.

No doubt there is much pleasure in holding a child in the arms, caressing its fluffy hands, looking into its big innocent eyes, seeing it smile and mimic. But one should be made aware of all the accompanying troubles and responsibilities. Just because people can engage in sexual intercourse does not make them good parents and educators. They may pass on to new generations the shortcomings of their own character and personality. Much of the generation gap the parents are complaining about is precisely due to the inefficient, permissive, anomic, and double standard education they have provided for their children.

On the birth of a child, then, the parents should be presented with censure and condolences. Congratulations should go to them if on his 20th birthday their child is well-educated and the parents have managed to keep the lines of communication and understanding open with him!

Should, however, couples beget children while recognizing their incapacity to give them proper education and care, they should see to it that adequate arrangements are made (which they could make on a communal basis near their home base) for the competent men and women with pedagogic inclinations, know-how, and feelings to be entrusted with the care of the children at an early age. This again will not be a spectacular innovation in our proposed campaign but simply will aim at making the masses conscious of what is in reality taking place but is obscured and slowed by deep-rooted obsolete and hypocritical attitudes.

Parents equate happiness and success with getting married and having children, or men or women want to have a child—as if a child were a toy; and fathers and mothers declare that they want to take care of their children themselves—as if the children were their exclusive property; forgetting that society lives with their children longer than they do!*

The politician running for election who displays his wife and numerous children on the podium as a factor of persuasion is a doubtful candidate. If his children are well brought up he must be regarded as a selfish man not fit for public office, even if he had a good record of public achievements, because one should wonder how much better he would have done for the people had he not fiddled with his family! If his children are well brought up because he had

---

*For other views on these topics see Albert Rosenfeld, *The Second Genesis*, Englewood Cliffs: Prentice Hall, 1969.

entrusted their care to competent educators, he has no merit. And finally if his children are not well brought up he is obviously an irresponsible person.*

2. Matrimony

Then what of marriage and family, when the incentive of making children is reduced? Traditionally, the family has been the basic social unit for the division of labor. The man used to gain the livelihood outside while the wife had a full-time job making the fire, cooking, washing, sweeping, mending, and looking after the children; and of course, satisfying her husband's sexual appetite—sometimes enjoying it herself too. In most societies, due to the inferior social status of the women this position was equated to a long term exclusive prostitution in exchange for protection and upkeep.

All these premises of the institution of marriage have become irrelevant. The electrical appliances do better and much quicker cooking, washing, and sweeping than the ablest housewife doing them by hand. Besides, the younger generation of females are not very good at mending and make a point of it, too! They have gained social equality and do their share of economic division of labor outside the house. On the other hand they come more and more to emphasize that if socially equal they are physiologically different — "Vive la petite difference," said Madame Paul-Boncour. So they ask for their share of orgasms, too, which tends to make sexual relationships not so exclusive after all. Newspapers recently reported liberalization of laws to this effect in Sweden.

Then why marriage, you may ask. Indeed why? For companionship? But does companionship need to be sealed by a contract and consecrated by the Lohengrin nuptial march! Can people, or rather, should people, not simply live together? They will thus daily reaffirm "to love and to cherish" and the hypocritical and ridiculous repetition of "till death do us part" will be avoided for re-wedding divorcees! Marriage should not be the business contract it is. It should in essence sanctify a dimension of love which does not correspond to the reality of the institution we have made of it for the satisfaction of our material purposes.

In a diversified society, where males and females who are attracted to each other may be of different environments, of different educational, ethnic, and religious backgrounds, and may have occupational specializations pulling them apart, would it not be wiser to leave companionship to the free laws of attraction and personal compatibility? You may be surprised, we may well have many more harmonious, long-lasting unions.

For the close of the 1960s, the AP Newsfeature writer, Sid Moody, reported

---

*Maybe he should be allowed a maximum of two children. The knowledge of the children's behavior is important for a man who holds public office. He can, by observing the growth of the children, find out how much of childishness remains in man through the ages, hidden under the veneer of old age and respectability.

Amitae Etzioni's concern about the danger that the new generation of college girls and boys after living together, avoiding thus the boys' living in fraternities and going to whore houses—which he found wholesome and approved of—may end up not wanting to found families. This, he said is dangerous because family and authority are the basic factors for social order. But doesn't he see that it is precisely the kind of social order we can no longer afford?! The social order which produces more, among other things, people, pollution, and unsatisfied individuals, and whose authority is in the hands of the producing machine which imposes itself on the ignorant masses softened to submit because they have a family to feed and a respectable status to maintain, and because they run and salivate for what the social order has conditioned them to run and salivate for.

Should the future social order not rely instead on responsible and educated individuals who have cultivated the wisdom of limited wants, and boundless contemplative, spiritual, and aesthetic joys? Anarchy has two meanings, one is the more popular understanding of it as a state of chaos, the other the highest degree of individual's consciousness of his social role and responsibility to an extent which makes external control and authority meaningless. Has the time not come to try it? The time is too short to go for anything less than man's ultimate dreams. This seems the only realistic way!

C. Nation Among Nations

But who is going to try it? The western affluent society? Then what will become of the 800 million Chinese, the 400 million Indians, and those millions who, under the banner of Marxism, have set the goal of surpassing the United States in material production.

So far I have tried, I hope with some success, to combat hypocritical values and situations. At this stage stepping on a few more toes will make no difference. So let us examine some of the international dimensions of the problem.

A program of the nature proposed above will aim at a more educated public, a more distributive, economy, and enlightened human beings who will be less aggressive as a nation on the international plane.

The United States or for that matter any developed country will not be able to envisage such a situation unless it has sufficient grounds to believe that this policy is the general trend of all developed countries.

There must also be reasonable hopes that the developing countries have overcome their inferiority complex of wanting to get in the same critical situation in which the developed countries find themselves. They should be prepared to modify their national Weltanschauung and to adopt a policy of growth which will not create in their population the frenzy for excessive material goals, but will blend with it contemplative, aesthetic, and philosophic dimensions. This proposition may be easier for the Eastern people than for the West because of already existing deep-rooted traditional premises. Like the western traditions, however, theirs should be purged of superstitions and obsolete myths. It is unfortunate that in the East, too, spiritual values are dying in the face of glittering material incentives.

As one follows meetings, committees, and conferences on pollution and population, one distinguishes between the two opposing concerns of the haves and the have-nots. Even when a conference is a national gathering, the particular concern of the category involved is discernible. The haves are really afraid of population. "They are going to come and get us," one seems to read in the back of their minds: the Visigoths plundering Rome, the hordes of Attila and Chengis Khan galloping across the European plains, the Turks charging the walls of Constantinople.

The have-nots are thirsty for material comfort and power. They seem to think, "They don't want us to get there," and their thought invokes the spectre of colonial days. A close look at the U. N. debates on the subject will provide revealing samples of the hidden motives. These concerns cut across the ideological frontiers. The Soviets want to get "there" and at the same time are afraid that "they" will come and get them.

The madness of competitive enterprise has become an international ill. How can those fighting the construction of SST not realize that the United States cannot renounce such means of transportation when others have it? That is the only way to stay ahead, to remain vigilant and defend the national interests. The others think the same way, both the haves and the have-nots, each holding to their respective weapons and, in the process, committing suicide. The technologically advanced are going at it full speed for total pollution. The underdeveloped, especially the competitive ones, are holding to their ultimate weapon: the masses, to starvation (Pearson, 1969).

According to the latest information, the Soviets are dotting their Chinese frontier with missiles, and, last August, nominated General Vladimir-Tolubko, missile expert, to head the Far Eastern Military district, while the Chinese Militia, estimated at some 200 million, are digging individual fall-out shelters on the other side of the border (L'Express, 1969). The eventuality of such a confrontation which will drag the whole of humanity into disaster may seem absurd. But has man not committed more absurdities than reasonable deeds? Only this time we are more numerous and we have more destructive toys at our disposal.

Then should the developed countries not feed the hungry before "dematerialization?" Had there been a possibility of success, it could have been considered. True, if the United States cultivated all its arable lands to the maximum, she would be able to fill in the world food shortage in the 1970s and even have a surplus. That is to say, by extensive use of energy, pesticides, and fertilizers, turning her lands into vulnerable reservoirs of chemicals and its waters into algae soup! Yet at the present rate of world population growth, the battle will be lost sometime around 1980. Besides its not being realistic, this kind of concessional help risks damage to the aided country's agricultural development by killing local incentive (Pearson, 1969).

Let us, then, face the fact that the world, divided as it is between the haves and the have-nots and along ideological lines, with its limited food producing capacity and its growing population, has a problem. A serious problem of survival. As things stand the problems can be solved only at the price of great sufferings, sacrifices and compromises. Unfortunately, at the international level, the egocentric and ethnocentric tendencies of man are more accentuated and the means available for curing them inadequate. It is easier in the national context to make a campaign to persuade those who are struggling in the smog against social injustice and anachronic social structures near to their skin to take a second look at their values and institutions. It is more difficult to make the fat, developed nation to feel what chronic hunger feels like, or to make a deprived nation realize the emptiness of material prosperity in a dog-eat-dog smoggy world. It has to get to their skin before they feel it, and by then it will be too late.

At the international level, means of persuasion are limited and the anachronistic concept of sovereignty supreme. Under such circumstances, achieving the strict minimum for man's survival will be the greatest feat of mankind in the coming decades. Sad as it is, it will be proving immense naivete to recommend that nations turn their tanks into tractors.

The recent Pearson report makes a whole range of recommendations for the minimum degree of co-operation needed in way of development (Pearson, 1969). Let us hope that by the time of the U. N. Conference on Man and His Environment in Stockholm in 1972, the developed donors of technical assistance will have pledged themselves and started implementing the recommendations of the Pearson Commission to bring their resource transfers to developing countries to a minimum of one per cent, and their official development assistance to a level for the net disbursements of 0.70 per cent of their GNP by 1975.

Let us also hope that by 1972, the developing countries will be in a position to take the responsibilities that go along with sovereignty and independence and will pledge themselves not to require foreign concessional food aids by 1975, except in cases of natural catastrophies. Such a proposition seems to be in line with the actual trend in many developing countries and could be achieved by all if they directed their national efforts to the rational use of their agricultural resources. Hoping that it will be brought about more by better management and improved agricultural techniques, such as extensive farming and choice of superior seeds, than by excessive use of chemical fertilizers and pesticides.

A policy of this nature will also have to bring about the purge mentioned earlier of the superstitions and obsolete traditional myths and practices which are constituting social and economic stumbling blocks particular to those societies. Here again the role of a mass national educational campaign becomes obvious.

We have to recognize however that a special effort is needed on the part of the United States to do her share, even in this limited international program. In 1968, the U. S. official development assistance constituted only 0.38 per cent of the GNP (Pearson, 1969 - Table 7-3). Further, a substantial amount of U. S. aid to developing countries has been in food aid (31 per cent of the U. S. aid commitments in 1967). This is due to the fact that the U. S. food aid to developing countries ever since 1954 has at the same time served as a self-help to regulate the national food production surplus (another materialistic dimension of this culture).

So if by 1975 the developing countries are to stop asking for concessional food aid, and if the United States is to reach the minimum target of resource transfer and official development assistance of 1 and 0.70 per cent of her GNP respectively, the campaigners against pollution should include foreign aid in their mass education program.

They should also take into consideration the broader international problems briefly referred to earlier and realize that, for example, an international conference such as the one planned for 1972 in Stockholm on pollution and population will not be a realistic undertaking if it does not have the 800 million Chinese represented, or does not link its topic directly to the questions of disarmament and development.

IV – EPILOGUE

It may sound a curious proposition to the conservationist to be asked to look into our material, ethical, social, and international values and problems in order to save the trees, flowers, and animals he cherishes. But that is where I think he should start. And he had better start quickly, because the alternatives will not, I am afraid, be to his liking.

At the one extreme is the very serious threat, considering the idiocy of mankind, of a nuclear war. Its protagonists should, by the way, be made aware that it will not be a short one. With the miseries, hates and deprived masses that it will leave behind, man will get involved in a long and savage war degrading him to the stone ages on top of the ashes and blown around by the radiated air.

At the other extreme is the technologically perfect world which is no longer in the realm of science fiction but a reality awaiting us around the year 2000, that is, if we ever get there. If we did, we would no longer be we! After the Beckwith/Shapiro recent scientific achievement at Harvard of isolating the single gene, it will soon be possible for man to manipulate genes to produce the ideal "man." Or shall we say the ideal "being"? Man's ideal being. And that creature will not look like man at all. We are already planning ahead. The prototype is not yet ready but some ideas are crystalizing.

For example, according to Nobel Prize winner physicist, Charles H. Townes, man should be smaller and lighter, and according to Dr. D. Recaldin of London University, he should have chlorophyll under his skin in order to perform photosynthesis like plants. He will be green?! Then why not have wings too? And why should we see only in front of us? Why not have compound eyes? We will nearly succeed being bees, green bees! Maybe this is the way bees started on the road to beehood! We must also consider the fact that we will also be able to grow children *in vitro,* and not just any child. We will use congelated ovum and sperm of selected men and women who have passed away and whose superiority we can objectively determine on the basis of their deeds (Ellul, 1964; Rosenfeld, 1969). Man will feed on synthetic food and acquire knowledge through electronic messages directly transmitted to his nervous system. Obviously man's social problems will be solved by proper arrangement of the genes and the electronic messages so that everybody will be performing his social role satisfactorily and with satisfaction. These are not phrases taken from Huxley's *Brave New World.* Besides, Huxley's dream is rather simplistic compared to what science has in reserve for us. Charles H. Townes and Herman Muller are Nobel Prize winners!

Jules Verne and H. G. Wells predicted man's adventure in the space. We did it. How are we not to get to the Brave New World?

> God is dead! God remains dead! And we killed him! ... What lustrums, what sacred games shall we have to devise? Is not the magnitude of this deed too great for us? Shall we not ourselves have to become Gods, merely to seem worthy of it? There never was a higher history than any history hitherto!" — Here the madman was silent and looked again at his hearers: they also were silent and looked at him in surprise. At last he threw his lantern on the ground, so that it broke in pieces and was extinguished. "I come too early," he then said; "I am not yet at the right time. This prodigious event is still on its way, and is traveling — it has not yet reached men's ears. Lightening and thunder need time, the light of the stars needs time, deeds need time, even áfter they are done, to be seen and heard. This deed is as yet further from them than the furthest star, — *and yet they have done it!* (Nietzche, 1882)

BIBLIOGRAPHY

Bunnell, S. 1969. The idea of ecology and awareness. Paper presented to the U.S. National Commission Conference on Man and His Environment, San Francisco.

Coon, S. S. 1954. Climate and race. *In* H. Shopley (ed.) *Climatic change,* pp. 13-34 Cambridge, Mass.: Harvard Univ. Press.

Commoner, B. 1969. The ecological facts of life. Paper presented to the Conference on Man and His Environment, San Francisco.

Dostoyevsky, F. 1880. *The Brothers Karamazov.* Trans. by Constance Garnett. New York, N.Y.: Modern Library.

Eaton, J. W., and A. J. Mayer. 1953. The social biology of a very high fertility among the Hutterites. *Human Biology* XXV: 206-263.

Ehrlich, P. R. 1968. Population, food and environment: is the battle lost. *Texas Quarterly.*

Eliassen, R. 1969. Solid waste management. Report prepared for the Office of Science and Technology, Executive Office of the President, Washington, D.C.

Ellul, J. 1964. *The technological society.* Trans. by John Wilkinson, New York, N.Y.: Knopf.

Freeman, R. 1968. The high fertility of the less developed nations. *In* D. M. Heer (ed.) *Readings on population,* p. 165. Englewood Cliffs, N.J.: Prentice Hall.

Heer, D. M. 1968. *Society and population* Englewood Cliffs, N.J.: Prentice Hall. pp. 13-14 et seq.

L'Express, Paris, No. 964, December, 1969.

Malone, T. F. 1969. The atmosphere. Paper presented to Conference on Man and His Environment, San Francisco.

Miller, H. P. 1965. The composition of the poor. *In* Margaret S. Gordon (ed.) *Poverty in America.* San Francisco, Calif.: Chandler, Co.

Nietzche, F. 1882. *The joyful wisdom, (La Gaya Scienza),* Book III, para. 125. Trans. by Thomas Common, *In* Oscar Levy (ed.), *The Complete Works of Friedrich Nietzche,* (1909-11. Reprinted 1964) New York, N.Y.: Russell and Russell, Vol 10, p. 169.

Notestein, F. W., D. Kirk, and S. Segel. 1963. The problems of population control. *In* Philip M. Hauser (ed.) *The population dilemma,* p. 127. Englewood Cliffs, N.J.: Prentice Hall.

Pearson, L. B. 1969. Partners in development, Report of the Commission on International Development, presented to IBRD, New York, N.Y.: Praeger.

President's Science Advisory Committee Report on the World Food Problems — Agency for Internal Development, Washington, D.C., 1968.

Risebrough, R. W. 1969. The sea: should we now write it off as the future garbage pit? Paper presented to the Conference on Man and His Environment, San Francisco.

Rosenfeld, A. 1969. *The second genesis.* Englewood Cliffs, N.J.: Prentice Hall.

Sanders, J. H., and V. W. Ruttan. 1969. Another look at the world food problem. *In Minnesota Agricultural Economics.* Minneapolis, Minn.: Univ. of Minn. Press, No. 515.

Sheps, M. C. 1965. An analysis of reproductive patterns in an American isolate. *Population Studies* XIV, No. 1: 65-80.

Smith, T. E. 1960. The Cocos-Keeling Islands: a demographic laboratory. *Population Studies* XIV, No. 2: 94-130.

Spengler, J. J. 1960. Values and fertility analysis. *Demography* III, 1: 109-130.

Ssu-Ma, Ch'ien. Letter to Jen An. *In Records of the Grand Historian of China.* Trans. from the Shih Chi by Burton Watson, 1961. New York, N.Y.: Columbia Univ. Press.

Tinker, H. 1966. *South Asia, a short history,* pp. 37-38. New York, N.Y.: Praeger.

Townes, C. H., and D. Recaldin. 1969. Man revised. *Sciences.* New York Academy of Sciences.

Waste Management and Control, National Academy of Sciences — National Research Council, Pub. 1400. Washington, D.C., 1966.

Life Style Adjustments and Implications

Introduction

Articles in the previous sections have basically presented ecological implications related to man's degradation of the environment through overpopulation and life style demands. Commencing with this section, the articles differ from the majority of ecological books in that environmental opinions are presented in an interdisciplinary approach as they question our life styles. Contributions from various disciplines tend to remove the "blinders" of a particular specialization. Specialization, by itself, is not at fault; however, specialization without regard for the total impact on society or the environment is at fault. Our present world needs responsible citizens in all walks of life who specialize in one area yet understand and appreciate its relationship to a harmonious, life-sustaining environment.

Man's compatibility with the natural system is a living ethic which inescapably involves stewardship, changes in social attitudes, behavioral modifications, and adjustments in our value system. In order for man to realize the implications of his domineering attitude, basic concepts must be challenged and investigated from various approaches. For this reason this section will be offensive to some and a revelation to others, but hopefully, it will cause everyone to think about his role in life on the finite earth that ultimately sets the limits of man.

Sacred Cows in Our Society

Donald R. Scoby

Is the United States a civilized, modern country? While most Americans enjoy a well-balanced diet, we often look at underdeveloped countries like India and have trouble understanding why the people there have a particular "life style." In the country of India the cow is a sacred animal. Even though people may be starving to death, beef is not eaten because of the holiness of the animal. Indians provide "old cow homes" while their brothers starve to death. Ignorance? Superstition? To our western way of thinking, perhaps. But do we have sacred cows in our society?

For our purposes, let us define a sociological sacred cow as something a society refuses to give up, even at the cost of death. Most of the sacred cows that we harbor are either related to social attitudes or to technology.

Family size is one sacred cow in our society. For the most part, we tend to uphold the large family and deplore the small. Historically speaking, it was once practical to have a large family. But as our agrarian society became more urban, the economic argument for having many children became weak. It is estimated that the cost of raising one person in our society is $30,000—not taking into consideration the cost of a college education. True, the birth rate is on the decline, but as of yet it has not come down far enough to coincide with the death rate.

It does not take a sociologist or a biologist to see the signs of overpopulation and related pollution in our society. A person can feel aspects of these pressures as he drives through a ghetto in a metropolitan area. These pressures are also very obvious on highways. Americans will spend a warm Sunday afternoon at the beach relaxing, then will spend three hours developing ulcers in seventy-some miles of bumper-to-bumper traffic on the way home. Have you stood in line at a supermarket or been involved in the increased pressures placed on leisure time facilities? More obvious signs of too many people.

Let's try to relate these examples to our society and see the signs of additional sacred cows. To begin with, let's define the word progress. Our first source of help is Webster. He defines progress as: (1) a movement forward; (2)

Address presented at the meeting of the Fargo-Moorhead Zero Population Group, Chapter #71, October 12, 1970.

growing or getting ahead; (3) a journeying forward; (4) gradual betterment; progressive development or evolution of mankind as a process. Every one of these definitions refers to a road to betterment. Is progress a sacred cow in our society?

The recent rise in crime rate—is this a progressive feature of our society? Environmental deterioration of our air, water, and land—is this a progressive feature? The relation of chemicals to our bodies; the increase of cancer and the possible increase in "natural deaths"—this is progress? Psychosis and neurosis on the increase—is this a progressive feature? Are these progressive features, or are they in fact a type of regression? Perhaps this country needs to think of progress in terms of educational television, reading, the better enjoyment of nature; learning to live within the limits of nature. Perhaps this is a more progressive attitude towards progress.

Americans seem to have an obsession about equating progress with industrial growth and with the almighty gross national product. It's rather interesting to note that the state of Oregon is the first state in the union to actually discourage new people and new industry from coming into the state. Their advertisements are not the typical travel brochure type; they lay emphasis on the fact that they have 300 days of bad weather. Likewise, an equipment plant in North Dakota puts out an advertising brochure that in effect says that "bad winters are good because they keep out the riff-raff." Quite a switch from the average Chamber of Commerce attitude which stresses for North Dakota "delightful summers and invigorating winters."

Many small cities across the nation have launched programs designed to attract new industry into their community. What would it mean to a town of 50,000 to receive new industry and 1,000 workers? To some it would mean 1000 new workers and 2,600 new family members. It would mean at least 980 new cars. It would mean $9 million in bank accounts. But to some people—namely the middle class people who are aware of our sacred cows—it would mean 980 new pollutants. People encouraging industry might argue that 3,600 new people would be a shot in the arm to the economy of the town. But here is another aspect of this particular sacred cow: new people would bring in additional capital to the already wealthy businessman, but would bring only more crowded conditions and higher taxes to the average middle class citizen. To the middle class taxpayer, new industry with more people would result in the necessity of wider streets to accomodate more cars. Hence, it would mean more taxes for all economic classes. However, Mr. Middle Class's income will not graduate in the same ratio as that of the big businessman. In fact, he will lose potential buying power. New industry and new people would also require a bigger landfill—still more taxes. So new industry brings money to the hands of an elite few, and takes money away from the middle class citizen. A group of Midwest educators recently remarked that soon only the rich and the poor will be able to send their children to college. The poor because of the fact that our society is geared to send them, and the rich because they have the money. The middle class, supporting the rest, will not have the funds, according to the educators, to send their children to college.

What is the solution? We obviously cannot feasibly say: "People stay away." Americans must, instead, concentrate on stabilizing population and on making adjustments to the problems resulting from overpopulation. For example, the cost of an industrial product should reflect its total cost (at most the "true least cost") to the environment, and the consumer must be willing to pay this cost. There should definitely be stricter fines for environmental non-conformity, in every portion of the nation. At the present time, our country has designed certain fines to make industrial corporations pay for their pollution. Some large corporations pay a tribute price for their daily dumping of debris into waters. The fine is so small that it would be as if a citizen would phone a neighbor and say, "John Doe, here is a penny. Now I'm going to load up my week's garbage and dump it in your living room. The penny will cover the costs." New heavy fines will have to be set up for companies negligent in conserving their debris. Laws must be passed now. If we are serious about environmental problems, companies can perhaps look forward in the year 1975 to paying 1/365 of their annual gross for each day's violations, which means that for every day they would continue to pollute, the company will lose two days' income. Money speaks, and chances are good that the rivers and air would be clean in a relatively short time. And as we discuss the fines for the polluting companies, we must remember that a basic responsibility also rests on the shoulders of the demanding consumers. We buy the products; then we ask for a new, improved version of them. Better that we should be willing to pay more for the product and hence save our waters and air from becoming industrial garbage pails.

Under present circumstances, a scientist has to receive a research grant in order to examine a polluting company. He must buy costly equipment, which enables another equipment manufacturing company to raise the gross national product another $2-3 million. After the scientist discovers that the first company is indeed polluting, another company must be established—the cleaner-upper company. These additional companies, rather than ending pollution, cause their own pollution and drain the natural resources while boosting the gross national product. It would seem a bit more logical and practical to say, "Look, companies, we have a problem. Why don't you treat the sewage before dumping it back into the river? Ditto for the air." The companies would then argue that it would cost more, and they would be correct. Again, the demanding consumer should be willing to pay this total cost when he pays for the product.

Saturday Review ran a letter to the editor some time ago from a man relating a story about his father. The story ran something like this: My father told me this a long time ago when, after driving the horse and buggy, we switched to a car ... he said, "When I drove a buggy with one horse, all I had to do was put in one bag of oats and I had a pile of manure. When I drove a buggy with two horses, I supplied two bags of oats and had two piles of manure. Now you guys have 360 horse-power and so you'll end up with 360 piles of manure." The basic pollution concept is not difficult: if the amount of power is increased, the amount of pollution is in turn increased.

Power-generated leisure time is another sacred cow in our society. Americans seem to be suffering from a power syndrome; we have to have something powerful underneath us before we can "seemingly" enjoy nature. Motorboats, dune-buggies, motorcycles, snowmobiles—the list is endless. Although the automobile is termed a "necessity" in our country at the present time, it also serves as a form of entertainment for many people. This is costly fun—65 per cent of air pollution is caused by automobile exhaust fumes. At the present time, our solution seems to be to simply plug something in the exhaust pipe to end pollution instead of cutting down on the size of the engine. Of the possibilities, the latter is the more sensible. We must learn to conserve power sources and natural resources for the future. Other people speak of correcting the exhaust fume problem in terms of incorporating electrical power. But electricity is not penny-cheap—most of the electrical power comes from non-renewable resources, namely coal and oil. More electrical power would demand additional nuclear power plants, which also would tax our environment. We must learn to accept the fact that in order to best conserve our resources, we are going to have to be willing to live with less—and that includes less power. Unfortunately, as of yet no type of power comes from thin air. All power costs something in terms of the environment. Perhaps electrical power from an isolated and an environmentally approved plant is part of a solution. But it is not the ultimate answer; consumption rates must be changed from encouraging a wasteful attitude to one of conserving what we have. Therefore, the ultimate answer is to learn to do with less. Should a city of more than 50,000 people outlaw the car? People frown on this drastic measure, but mass transportation is the best solution for cities above a certain size. Perhaps city planners should outlaw cars over 30 horse-power and devise a transportation system of mini-buses. The five minutes spent waiting for a ride would be less than the current thirty minutes spent waiting for a traffic jam to clear. City planners should emphasize the downtown shopping areas, which are better served by a public transportation system, rather than the sprawling suburban shopping centers whose existence depends on the automobile. Nationwide, Americans could travel by trains and rapid transit systems. Engineers could devise a mono-rail system in the spaces between the lanes of inter-state highways. Perhaps lake planning commissions should outlaw motorboats with motors bigger than 5 horse-power This sounds far-fetched, perhaps, but not as far-fetched as an environment hostile to man.

Today many scientists are suggesting that automobile manufacturers design cars with materials that could easily be recycled into new cars. Perhaps, again, this would cost the consumer a bit more, but we need to conserve the natural resources. Whatever method is devised (either fees added to license tags or factory costs), it should be on a "size of car" basis and not "straight across the board." This country can no longer afford to take up land with car junk-yards.

Another sacred cow, especially relevant to largely rural areas, is maintaining a "horse and buggy ideology while unquestioningly accepting modern technology." In rural areas of the Midwest, towns were established when the railroads came in. Towns were staked out approximately every eight to fifteen miles. This was feasible for hauling grain; eight miles was a good day's distance for a team of horses pulling a wagon of grain. In a sense, we are now suffering from this former practicality. Since the establishment of these small towns, man has developed trucks that go 60 miles per hour. Basically, man has accepted the technology to produce more, and one man can now do more work. With better equipment, he can farm more land. A form of pollution? Perhaps not; however, a farmer with a large family does not need all the children to maintain the farm. The children, therefore, go to college, get a good job, and move to Los Angeles and New York to contribute to the cities' pollution problem.

People often offer trite answers. A supposedly well-educated politician seriously suggested that our country's crowded condition could be alleviated by redistributing people. But we must learn to equate people with resources. People need room in which to live, but they also need water, natural resources, and air. For instance, the state of Montana, for all its wide open spaces and big sky, cannot support 1,000 people per square mile. It's not made that way. People must be balanced with the resources necessary to support them.

What is the solution to this horse and buggy technology problem? There are two basic alternatives. We could revamp county government to work with our modern technology. In other words, if we want to accept the technology and all its implications, we must be willing to change the archaic structure of the rural community. The other choice, which I prefer, is to do a complete about-face and encourage the rural community to return to small farms, thus encouraging the small town. One of the two choices should be made. It is up to us to decide which is preferable. However, we cannot drift toward the large farm, with the resulting smaller population to support the small town, and at the same time insist that small towns and an archaic political structure be maintained.

Inevitably we must come to the conclusion that perhaps some forms of technology are unnecessary. We must sit down and carefully study products and their effects on the environment. We must plan to fit man into the natural environment, rather than assume that man is above and dominant over nature.

A fat sacred cow in our society is a general ecological credibility bias. For example, people comment on so-called "scare tactics" used by ecologists. While ecological data may be very scientific, obvious and accurate, some people will rationalize their environmental immorality by calling these ecological claims and warnings "scare tactics." They say that scientists are wrong in going around acting like professional crepe-hangers, spreading "doom" wherever they go. These same people, however, will maintain that if the industrial-military complex changes to the "true" cost economic principle, the country would suffer an economic disaster. Isn't this statement also a type of scare tactic? Weighing very carefully all factors involving the future of man, I feel the environmental depression we are now in is far greater than the consequences of any economic depression we could ever face. Some people claim that if questionable man-made chemicals were banned, the nation would suffer a disaster. This is another scare tactic. We have not always had these chemicals, and crops grew. Farmers had to go out and hoe a little but crops still grew. Basically, I know that man has lived *without* all the chemicals we are dumping into our environment, but I am not at all confident that our offspring can live *with* them.

Insurance death adjustment rates indicate that an older person (say 65 years old) has experienced a slight drop in potential longevity. This drop in conjunction with one of the theories surrounding "natural" death — a cell accumulates metabolic poisons (i.e. Hg, Pb, other metabolites from man-made chemicals) until the cell can no longer tolerate the interference and dies — leads to the following hypothesis: the number of "natural deaths" will increase and will be a result of the thousands of persistant and unknown chemicals made and used in large quantities. Is this another "scare tactic," or is it something that makes sense and suggests a challenge to existing life styles?

We need scientists who will accept their complete social responsibilities. A recent report told of two Washington, D.C., climatologists who reported that if all fossil fuel in this country were burned, the present oxygen level would come down to 20.8 per cent. This level would not be harmful to man. In basic chemistry, one learns that any action causes a reaction. Matter cannot be totally destroyed; there will be an output someplace. What the two climatologists failed to report is that the burned oxygen in question would turn into two things — carbon dioxide and water. The carbon dioxide level would increase 3-5 fold, which has the potential to be an ecological disaster as far as present plant and animal life is concerned. Will it do man any good to theoretically be able to breathe if he is already dead?

And there are more examples of a credibility bias. One report stated that the chemical 2,4,5-T was found not to be dangerous to the environment, a rebuttal of an earlier report. Clues pointed to the fact that the scientist who made these findings worked for Dow Chemical Company. Whether his report was accurate or not, his association with one of the main distributors of 2,4,5-T does not add to his credibility. We must accept what is called the burden of proof. In our western Judeo-Christian heritage, we assume that a man is innocent until proven guilty. While this is fine as far as man is concerned, it should not be the ethic when dealing with man-made chemicals. We have passed this ethic on to the military-industrial complex, and in turn our environment has been damaged. There are over 500,000 chemicals developed by man, and we know the environmental effects of only about 10 per cent of these. The others should be guilty until it has been proven beyond a reasonable doubt that they will do no harm to the environment. We should have a Federal Inspection Bureau (above briberies, lobbies, etc.) to research and pass judgement on these. This "burden of proof" should not fall on to the shoulders of the consumers, but rather to the companies making the chemicals. And, once more, the consumer must be willing to pay the reflected costs of proving the chemicals to be innocent of environmental deterioration.

In summary, there is much to be done. We harbor many sacred cows — family size, the definition of progress, power syndromes, a horse and buggy ideology in a technological age, and a big credibility bias.

Solutions will be hard to come by. We must incorporate honest people to research every aspect of American life and, as "muck raker" Ralph Nader suggests, practice what they preach. We must question and challenge the sacred cows, including sacred cows associated with the legal rights of industry and the military. We must declare war on selfishness and greed and come to realize that if our world is worth saving, we are going to have to make a few sacrifices. We must recognize "scare tactics" on both sides of the question as well as the growing increase of eco-pornography and then decide, through self-education, which is the most logical.

Do you have to be an ecologist or biologist to help? No! But you must learn to be an environmental realist. This includes responsibility. This form of consciousness must hit home to every person.

An old man, a veteran of World War I, sat at a curb, watching a parade. As the American flag passed by he started talking about the shape of the world and the various "rabble-rousers" in our society. He said something like, "I think that all those people who don't think we should be in Viet Nam should get out. And that goes for those people always screaming about pollution. If they don't like it, they can just get out. Love it or leave it." During the time this man sat talking, he smoked four cigarettes, all of which he threw into the street, along with his empty cigarette pack. This man loves the flag but does not care for the country. We need citizens who see the whole picture, including the environment. Whether people are Democrats or Republicans, liberals or conservatives, the time has come to say, as far as environment goes, "America — change it or lose it."

The Christian's Role in the Problems of Contemporary Human Ecology

J. Frank Cassel

The Christian's role in the problems of contemporary human ecology is that he caused them all (White 1967). White, arguing on the basis of Genesis 1:28, claims we have all too well obeyed the command to subdue and have dominion over the earth. In his paper, obviously designed to get Christians "up tight," White (1967:1207) concludes, "Hence, we shall continue to have a worsening ecologic crisis until we reject the Christian axiom that nature has no reason for existence save to serve man." What has given White the idea that the blame for our ecological crisis can be laid at the feet of Christians and Jews? While he may not exegete the Scriptures too well or be too accurate in his summary of Christian doctrine, he *is* a keen observer and an accurate reporter of the modern scene. What credit can we take, *as Christians,* for conserving and protecting God's world, or for giving consistent leadership in stemming the rush of materialism which has accompanied our fantastic technological progress? White (1967:1207) is convinced that "Since the roots of our trouble are so largely religious, *the remedy must also be essentially religious, whether we call it that or not.*" The purpose of our deliberations is to examine the ecologic crisis to determine its nature and to delineate, if possible, remedial action.

Wright (1970) in his recent answer to White points out that the roots of the crisis probably lie in the nature of the species, *Homo sapiens,* rather than in his theology. The destruction of an aspen grove by a newly constructed dam can scarcely be blamed on or even be said to "have its roots" in the beaver's religion. By the same token, however, if the causes of environmental deterioration are not distinctly religious neither are the remedies necessarily or uniquely Christian. In other words, in determining the "Christian's role" in helping to solve our problems, we simply may be determining the role of T. C. Mits (the celebrated man in the street). On the other hand, our good news to T. C. Mits is that his full role in this world can be realized only through Jesus Christ. His role in ecology is not likely to be an exception.

Presented as part of the Second Scientific Symposium at Dordt College, Sioux Center, Iowa, October 23, 1970 and published in *The Christian in Science: Dordt College Christian Scientific Symposium* (copies available from Dr. Aaldert Mennega, Chairman, Department of Biology, Dordt College, Sioux Center, Iowa). Dr. J. Frank Cassel is Professor of Zoology at North Dakota State University, Fargo, North Dakota.

During the years when biologists of my emphasis were out of style while molecularly oriented biologists reigned supreme, people used to respond to my saying that I was an ecologist by a blankish stare, asking, "What's that?" It's nice to be back in style, and to be able to say proudly, "I'm an ecologist!" because now people's faces light up with a knowing, "Oh!" What disturbs me, however, is that despite the emphasis on ecology in the press and in current general journals, I get the feeling the average person really hasn't gained a great deal more understanding of ecology than he had ten years ago. Though now much more alert and knowledgeable about the problems of our environment, T. C. Mits has a poor understanding of the ecological principles upon which the sound decisions so important to our future existence must be made. May we review some basic ecological concepts, applying them to our everyday problems? If by doing this I raise more questions than I suggest answers, at least I will have furnished a basis for further discussion.

Ecology is the study of the interrelationships of plants and animals in their environment. In this context we will treat man as one of the species of animals intricately related to his physical environment and to the organisms in it—plants, other animal species and other men. Seeing ourselves as part of the environment helps us approach and understand many of our environmental problems in their total context. Although the individual organism is the only unit capable of responding to the complex stimuli which make up its immediate surroundings, the ecologist, a typical probablistic scientist, works also with groups and with multivariant systems. He is often a bit confused when he tries to distinguish in his thinking those facts which he has learned by considering groups of facts about individuals, and those he has learned by studying actual groups of organisms in nature. If you can enter into this confusion with me, let me try to describe some of the ideas which help us think about the environment.

POPULATION ECOLOGY

Organisms seldom occur in isolation in nature. All the organisms of the same species occurring in the same area are known as a *population*. Populations have certain group properties. The most obvious of these is numbers or *density*, usually expressed in terms of number per unit area. In bisexual populations the *sex ratio* is important to our understanding the reproductive potential of the group. The *age distribution* of the members of the population is also important. An animal population can produce no more offspring during a breeding season than the number of young one reproducing female is able to have, times the number of reproducing females in the population. Also, the number of individuals which can be added to the population in a year depends upon how often each female conceives that year. The whitetailed deer, as an example, usually have a sex ratio of about 1:1. Females can usually not conceive until their second year. Mating once a year, in the fall, a healthy female will probably bear two fawns. Therefore, even under the most favorable conditions, a population of White-tailed Deer cannot double itself in one year. Contrast with this the potential of field mice which also have populations with an approximately equal distribution of males and females. Females can be sexually mature at three to four weeks of age, they can bear as many as ten young and average five to six per litter, and one female was known to bear seventeen litters in one year! Not only can one female produce 80 to 100 young per year, but it doesn't take long for the half of her offspring which are females to begin making their own contribution to the population, so that, if all lived one pair of field mice alone could account for over 1800 mice in one year!

Fortunately the *reproductive potential* of populations is seldom realized because of the many factors in the environment which tend to limit the number of individuals which can survive through the year. Lack of food may impair the health of the breeding females so that they do not bear as many young per mating and may not mate as often. Among other influences, adverse climatic conditions, predators and disease reduce numbers. A given habitat may be able to support only a fraction of the number able to be produced, thus causing extreme intraspecific competition of various kinds. Some species can respond to stresses by moving out of the area of stress, but in most cases only a limited number survive. In humans, the realized *natality* during the year is expressed as the birth rate. The number succumbing *(mortality)* during the year is the death rate. Studies of many populations of organisms suggest that most populations have established a dynamic level of density in their particular environment. This density fluctuates from year to year only within certain limits which permit the continued existence of the species but does not damage the habitat. *Optimum density* usually reflects what the habitat is able to support. These ideas are often expressed as a simple formula:

RP (reproductive potential) minus ER (environmental
resistance) equals CC (carrying capacity).

Since the reproductive potential of any species is basically determined by genetics, man can manipulate populations only by increasing or decreasing the environmental resistance. Agriculturalists work continually at reducing ER so that by realizing more of the reproductive potential they can harvest bigger crops or raise more livestock. They till the soil, fertilize, use pesticides, or furnish food and water in abundance. Game and fish managers work toward the same ends but more subtly and usually less successfully. Doctors tend to do the same thing, and their success is measured by our ever-increasing population density. Our national birth rate is going down, but until more people die in one year than are born in that year *our population will continue to increase.*

Environmental resistance is made up of a number of complex *limiting factors* which do not necessarily act in concert, but rather back up one another so that at one time one may be limiting and at another time some other one will be. For example, when the food is insufficient to sustain the population, it may be limiting; but if food is abundant the lack of nesting areas can control the number of individuals or pairs which can survive in a certain area. Availability of nesting sites may also govern how the organisms are dispersed or arranged in their habitat and how much aggression is exhibited between individuals. On the other hand, the innate tendency of some individuals to prefer to be close to others of their kind, that is to form *aggregations*, may also exert a control on the density of that population.

COMMUNITY ECOLOGY

Few populations in nature could long exist without numerous other populations being present to provide food, shelter, and other necessities of life. In fact, populations survive best it seems in groups or *communities*. We can identify a deciduous forest and predict that in eastern United States, among others, populations of White-footed Mice, Red-backed Mice, Grey Squirrels, Chipmunks, Red-eyed Vireos, Ovenbirds, and Wood Pewees will be found there. Or if native grasses are found in healthy abundance on our plains, it's a pretty good sign that domestic grasses will do well there also. In fact the distribution of biotic communities reflects differences in the physical environment such as climatic tendencies or types of soil or terrain or levels of pollution. One neither looks for tundra in an Arizona desert nor for Horned Toads at the Arctic Circle, nor for trout in a sewage lagoon.

Most of us think of nature in terms of communities, of how certain groups of populations impinge upon us or how we can impinge upon them. Seldom are you satisfied to have a lawn of blue grass only and no trees or flowers or vegetables in your yard. Seldom does a single fisherman go alone to a lake to fish for a particular species of fish. Even then that species is there in fishable abundance only because of the complex community relationships in the lake. Seldom, too, do control measures aimed at one species affect only that particular species.

ECOSYSTEM ECOLOGY

Many of these relationships can be understood in terms of *food chains*, a series of populations eating and being eaten. The many food chains are linked together in a *web of life* which is intricate and often delicately balanced. The energy of the sun is captured and stored by photosynthesizing green plants in the form of carbohydrates, fats, and proteins. The amount accummulated during a year, or the rate of production is called *productivity*. We think of plants as being *producers* and of animals as being *consumers*. Those feeding directly on plants (the herbivores) are primary consumers and those feeding on other animals (carnivores) are secondary consumers. Omnivores, such as man, operate at both levels. Some organisms serve to break down the dead organic matter so that it can be recycled in the system. These are *decomposers.*

Energy enters the community from the sun. Some is dissipated as heat, some utilized, and some stored by plants. Some of this stored energy is passed on to animals, and some to decomposers. At each of these *trophic levels* some energy is stored, some passed on, and some dissipated or lost to the system. The ecosystem is an open system through which energy flows to power metabolism, activity, and reproduction. Being an open system, the entropy obtaining throughout the system is reversed by the energy being constantly introduced so that, in most cases, the system builds up tremendous energy reserves. We heat and light our houses and drive our cars on reserves deposited long ago, preserved today in coal beds and oil fields. From fossil fuels and running water (also sun-powered) we obtain the power necessary to our highly advanced technology.

CONSERVATION AND A STANDARD OF LIVING

White seems intrigued with an idea he credits to St. Francis of a "democracy of all creatures." But I think most of us would be unwilling to practice such a philosophy in mosquito season. So, I venture, would White, even though he states (White 1967:1207) that "the present increasing disruption of the global environment is the product of a dynamic technology and science.... Their growth cannot be understood historically apart from distinctive attitudes toward nature which are deeply grounded in Christian dogma." Whatever has been going on, White seems to be saying, that's what Christians are doing.

As Elder (1971) points out in another paper in this symposium, this is an age of technology. Developing technology depends upon an expanding use of natural resources. Some resources can be rapidly and continually produced, are *renewable.* Some cannot—are *non-renewable.* Although White and others are quite rightly concerned with how and for what reasons we produce and exploit our resources, the use of these resources is a well-established way of life. Most of us in the establishment are disgustingly complacent in this way of life—at least that's the way my own offspring see it. A great deal of our motivation to activity from day to day and certainly most of our economic stability both personal and national is natural resource oriented.

Many of the current reports of concern seem to me to carry an "either-or," all or none, implication that reflects misunderstanding of basic conservation principles. Conservation means WISE USE! When we discuss the Christian's role in ecologic problems, we are trying to gain wisdom not to question the right to use natural resources. Man is by nature a manipulator of nature—an ecological *superdominant.* Let me illustrate.

I have always been interested in nature study and eagerly observed and collected specimens from each new place I visited. During World War II, I was stationed for a while in New Orleans. I had a great time collecting amphibians and reptiles. I was intrigued by the bayous and cypress swamps. When sent to the Southwest Pacific, I looked forward to seeing some real jungle. In New Guinea I was disappointed, for I found little or no jungle to match that around New Orleans. One day one of my officers consoled me with, "When the army moves in they move the jungle out." And that is exactly the role of man in his environment—he alters and controls it to his own ends, for his own comfort and convenience. This is civilization—our advance over the cave man. What then is our problem? Is it not in deciding just what is "comfort and convenience" and who should have it? And for how long?

Allen (1959) suggests that our standard of living, which is what we're really talking about, is a factor of our natural resources, of how many people need to use them and of our cultural level. He expresses this idea with the formula:

$$\frac{\text{Resources x Culture}}{\text{Number of People}} = \text{Living Standard}$$

Either a decrease in natural resources or an increase in population will lower the standard of living unless cultural advance keeps pace. Thus far in North America it has. Many doubt that technological advance can continue indefinitely, particularly since our mineral and fossil fuel resources are not renewable. It seems likely also that there is some inherent upper limit to the productivity possible for each species of food organism.

ECOLOGICAL DECISION MAKING

In eastern North Dakota, we who are concerned about conservation have been campaigning against a dam which the Army Corps of Engineers has proposed to build on the Sheyenne River near Kindred, North Dakota. Every so often, I think the report says on an average of once in ten years, West Fargo is subject to damaging floods. This dam, although not stopping such floods, will lessen their likelihood and thus cut their potential damage in half. The Corps now estimates the cost of such a dam at $20 million. The site proposed for the dam will have the permanent pool of the dam flooding several hundred acres of native deciduous forest, a habitat quite rare in North Dakota. As they do in all such reports, the Corps supports their proposal by reporting the cost of the damage flooding has caused in the past, and stacking that, plus the cost they estimate for the dam, against an estimate of the value of the damage which will be prevented over the life of the dam plus the benefits which will be derived from the addition of this water resource to eastern North Dakota. Such a *cost-benefit* estimate is often stated as a ratio, and illustrates what many feel is the soundest basis upon which to make ecological judgements.

We all tend to make decisions this way—will what we or others get out of a particular project be worth the time, effort, and money put into it? It's a neat and discrete way of looking at things which call for priority decisions. But, as you can see, while past property damage from flooding is a fairly easy datum to obtain, the value of the increased fertility of the farm land due to flooding, and the value of the benefits derived from a deciduous forest, from which prime timber has already been harvested, but which is an excellent wildlife and recreational area, and the value of potential benefits of a large body of water in southeastern North Dakota are a bit harder to come by. How do *you* value the benefit *you* will derive from the dollars *you* contribute to the building of a $20 million plus dam in southeastern North Dakota? I personally am annoyed by most people who deliberately build their houses or businesses in an area of potential flooding and then expect me to help pay to protect their property from flood damage. Wow! My wife says my attitude is unchristian. Is it?

What is the dollar value to you personally of the following:

A smooth, four-lane, limited access highway

A section (640 A) of ripe wheat waving in a July breeze

A lazy stream winding through a verdant woods

A sunset

In all seriousness, this is the nitty-gritty of ecodecisions. This is the kind of starting place which must be established before we can communicate.

CONTEMPORARY PROBLEMS

I have tried, I hope not too tediously, to lay a scientific background so that you can understand the context of our ecological crisis. But what *are* the areas critical to you and me? Some would argue, with much justification, that only one problem exists, and that the rest are simply facets or subproblems of this one prime cause:

POPULATION

Because more babies are born each day than there are people dying, the density of our human populations continues to increase at an alarming rate. We've termed it a *population explosion*. I sometimes feel that some eco-extremists would be most happy if we simply wiped out the human race thus solving in one fell swoop all problems of human ecology. On the other hand, this is what *is* going to happen *naturally* if we do not seriously apply our best technological know-how and intellectual potential to discovering and applying means of preventing it. Many are now suggesting, however, that the most pressing contemporary problem is really not either know-how, or environmental resources, or even population but simply the motivation for applying what we already know. Dr. George Harrar (1970), president of the Rockefeller Foundation, has enunciated this problem in the current issue of CATALYST in a paper entitled, "Ecological Crisis Demands New Ethic of Responsibility." "The first principle of the new ethic would be that man must control his own fertility." Someone has pointed out in relation to Genesis 1:28 that we have already abundantly fulfilled the command to "multiply and replenish" and that now it's high time to get on with "have dominion over" in a responsible way.

As I see it, our problems practically fall into two or three main categories: *Population Control, Resource Technology,* and, perhaps, *Environmental Deterioration,* which is really part of the other two. I am convinced, however, that population control, short of war or some other type of mass execution, is a relatively long-range solution. Technological advance takes time, too. Serious environmental deterioration is going on right now and must be stopped immediately.

ENVIRONMENTAL DETERIORATION

The intensity of man's effect upon his environment is relative to his population density. Some major factors degrading our environment are pollution (including the use of pesticides), intensification of agriculture, industrialization, urbanization, transportation, and recreation. The ultimate mitigation of the effects of these factors will not eliminate the factors. This perhaps is why I'm disturbed by solutions couched in "either-or," all or none, terms. No matter how serious our pollution problems become, "eliminating toilets" is not a possible solution.

Pollution can be thought of in at least five aspects.

1. *Air pollution* is becoming increasingly serious. From dust storms on the Dakota plains, through smog in industrial areas, to atomic fallout most sources of air pollution are man-made or man-caused. *Mephitis mephitis* (the skunk) is our only real competitor, and much of his contribution could probably be said to be "man-caused." Reduction of pollution will depend upon recognition of the problem and application of technology, largely already available, to prevent the pollutants from entering the air. The fume control attachments on your new car is an example of one such application for which you are now paying. Growing opposition to SST's is based not only on unwillingness to pay the cost but also because of the unpredictable effects of pollution of the space and because of the noise down here.

2. *Water pollution* has long been recognized as an environmental evil, but only recently have we begun to understand the many subtle ways aquatic ecosystems can be altered. When I first studied this subject, I learned that a rapidly flowing stream could purify itself in one hundred yards if the sun was shining. The distance increased considerably if the sun was not shining but aeration in and of itself would eventually do the job. In this restricted view,

"purify" refers only to assuring the elimination of pathogenic organisms. (We were concerned with mineral wastes too, but that was another question. Concern in this area increases with the widespread use of non-biodegradable detergents, etc.) We now know that some of our greatest water quality problems are caused by organic wastes which alter the whole energy cycle of the aquatic ecosystem. Runoff from feed lots can be controlled, although some of the farmers in this area are questioning whether they can apply the technology necessary to meet suggested standards in Minnesota and still compete economically with farmers operating in southern Iowa (Way, 1970). (Note news report – *Minneapolis Tribune*, 30 IX 70) Cost-Benefit again! Are *you* concerned enough about the economic status of the Minnesota farmer or about pollution to subsidize his operation? Or do you say to him, "Tough! Raise wheat, or walleyes, or something more appropriate to Minnesota." In my opinion, we Christians tend to be very ambivalent in our approach to such socioeconomic-political problems, making our judgements on other than ethical, moral, or even Christian bases. I personally see no Biblical basis for not suggesting that the Minnesota farmer change his method of livelihood—it just happens to be un-American. Perhaps some of you support the thesis that that in itself makes it un-Christian.

Although runoff from feed lots can be controlled and purified technologically, runoff from fertilized fields changes the nutrient base of the drainage water, while containing also residues of any pesticides utilized in the field. Mitigation of these effects probably must depend upon the use pattern of the substances.

We have made some progress in establishing standards of water purity. Most stages currently include restrictions on thermal pollution in their codes of pure water standards, because introducing water at a temperature differing markedly from that of the natural water can alter the ecosystem. The maintenance of water quality on a day-to-day basis is difficult not only because of the difficulty of regulating the introduction of pollutants, but also because prevailing climatic conditions can accentuate our problems. This fall the Red River at Fargo-Moorhead reached a low flow-rate comparable to that experienced in the droughts of the thirties. Lowering the volume of the water without lowering the nutrient and oxygen needs of the ecosystem supported by this water, puts demands on the system it is unable to meet. The result was a complete depletion of the oxygen with consequent suffocation of fish and depletion of other aerobic organisms.

Noxious substances, being introduced into a stream at a constant rate, occur in a much higher concentration in the system at periods of low volume and slow flow than when higher volume combined with faster flow provides rapid dilution. Standards, therefore, must be carefully drawn, because when they are set in the form of a code, there is a tendency toward minimum compliance by those affected.

3. *Soil pollution* is of relatively recent concern. Residues of fertilizers and pesticides, as well as the altering of the nature or rate of natural processes, such as percolation of moisture or the leaching of minerals, serve to change the soil ecosystem.

4. *Biotic pollution* is introducing unnatural substances into populations of organisms. Clorinated hydrocarbons (the base of many so-called hard pesticides), for instance, can be metabolically stored by some animals, either being built up to detrimental concentrations within the system of the individual organism or passed on along the food chain in geometrically increasing doses. The recent extinction of the magnificent Peregrine Falcon in eastern North America is an example of the result. Such inhumane practices must cease! So we outlawed DDT and its relatives. The Christian's role as a law-abiding citizen seems obvious.

But one minute, please! Have you fallen into a currently prevalent propoganda trap? Have you been subject to *mind pollution?* We've said DDT is bad. We've outlawed it not because it didn't do the technological job it was designed to do, but because it did it too well and was not discriminating enough about it. But Minnesota, for example, is also concerned about losing its elms. Dutch Elm Disease is caused by a fungus transmitted by a beetle. DDT destroys and controls the population growth of this beetle. To date we have discovered no other pesticide as effective or as economical in this control. But with the use of DDT being illegal because, among other things, it kills robins, we are faced with another "cost-benefit" decision. "Are you willing to give up elm trees so you can have robins?" Is there a Biblical principle which will help me make this decision? Don't misunderstand me. I'm not advocating renewed indiscriminant use of DDT. But I am suggesting careful consideration of the whole picture so that our solutions do not leave us with yet greater problems. While speeding up our search for adequate substitute controls, we must still exert effective holding action while we wait.

5. *Genetic pollution,* while of relatively recent concern, may prove more serious than some of the other types. The gene frequencies resulting from selective pressures of degraded environment could leave us with populations unable to reverse their evolutionary trends sufficiently to readapt to improved habitats. Genes can also be altered by radiation.

Intensification of agriculture puts ever greater stress upon the land. The necessary, repeated applications of fertilizer must be carefully monitored to maintain the proper nutrient balance in the soil. Constant tilling tends to change the character of soil, as does subjecting the land to irrigation. Irrigation increases the problems of leaching and runoff. Runoff carries nutrients and pesticide residues from the land to the water as noted in our discussion of pollution.

Moreover, economic pressures force a farmer to look for as much space as possible to utilize for crops and thus he looks to the extra area he can get by draining his wetlands. Besides, he thinks, good drainage will reduce the danger of flooding in his own field, at least. If he allows his cattle to graze in his woodlot he can take a little pressure off his pasture as well as add two or three more head to his herd. We can no longer expect the land owner to subsidize our sport and recreation. We must provide him with at least as much income from "raising" ducks on his wetlands or squirrels and rabbits in his woodlot as he would realize by utilizing them for crop production. That's the import of the recently passed Water Bank Bill. There *are* areas of progress in solving some of our problems.

The question calling for decision here is, do we want more ducks or more wheat? In days of over-production and crop curtailment, the answer seems obvious to most of us. But as our population density increases, and we need more food we may need to reverse the priorities.

Industrialization, in addition to increasing pollution, also puts continually increasing demands on our resources, particularly the non-renewable ones. Providing the mineral raw materials and power necessary to keep up with manufacturing technology alone has led to the rape of acres of surface and subsurface deposits leaving great scars on the face of the earth. How necessary are some of the non-degradable gadgets which add pizzazz to our daily life?

The least we can do is to recycle our resources. You can act today to improve the quality of Sioux Center's environment by refusing to buy products in non-returnable bottles or in aluminum cans. But what shall we do with our old cars?

Urbanization and its accompanying *suburban sprawl* is consuming more and more land. For many years, environmentalists have been concerned about the space necessary to support our expanding population. But we have answered this concern by building *up* as well as out. As we build *up*, however, we begin to concentrate portions of the population to such densities that we multiply the difficulties both in bringing goods and services in and in carrying waste products away. We have also increased the potential of disease transmission and of psychological stresses. Many public health dangers as well as some of its advantages are products of our cities.

Transportaion affects the environment by greatly accelerating the dispersal of exhaust substances and by constantly reducing our population due to increasing our mortality rate. In addition, fantastic amounts of land are dedicated to right-of-ways. Studies we (Cassel and Oetting 1970) are carrying out at North Dakota State University indicate that right-of-ways can provide productive habitats not otherwise available to wildlife. For example, 26 miles of Interstate Highway 94 in east-central North Dakota has produced an average of 90 broods of ducks for the past three seasons, and management in the form of restricted mowing seems to be effective in increasing the quality of the environment as measured by an increased productivity of ducks.

Recreation also contributes to environmental deterioration. I suppose opinion is mixed as to whether the great slashes through the forests near Aspen,

Colorado and near most other ski resorts is deterioration or improvement of the habitat of man. Lake surfaces roiled by the wakes of motorboats increase wave action and hence erosion of the lake shore. One of my colleagues is much disturbed about the increase in heat radiation and the reduction of oxygen contribution to air caused when a Tartan Turf replaces sod in a football stadium or baseball field.

THE CHRISTIAN'S ROLE

My catalogue of problems and examples could go on, but may we return once more to Dr. White's indictment. *Why,* amid fabulous technology and extraordinary intellectual reserves, does man find himself in an ecological crisis at all? We have long known the imperative of conservation—and that "wise use" means treating our resources in such a way that our grandchildren will have as much or more of the resource as we do. *Why,* as things get worse, is a drastic cure so long in coming? Because, I think, most of us are acting with more concern for ourselves than for our grandchildren. The economic squeeze is real, but intensified by our wanting more and more "advantages of civilization." In addition, when farmers cry that they have to pollute if they wish to compete, and factories employing many people threaten to close down because they can't afford to install adequate waste disposal facilities (and thus a person's job is on the line), the tendency to self-preservation becomes paramount for many of us. Are you willing to pay the price?

Certainly we should not be paying farmers *not* to raise wheat when people in India are starving. But wheat shipped to India rots or is destroyed by rats on the dock because India lacks facilities or funds or motivation to get it where it can feed the hungry. It would be less expensive to bring the starving people here rather than send the food there! We have the potential of supporting a much higher population density than we now have, if—we are willing to *reduce our standard of living!* Recall the formula I introduced earlier. If we reduce our resources consumption, we will reduce our standard of living. If we increase our population numbers, we reduce our standard of living. If we share our resources, we reduce our standard of living. Are *you* willing to have your standard of living lowered so that all other peoples of the world can have the same standards as we? I have an idea if the citizens of the United States were willing to really share, we'd drastically reduce the threat of war. But we can't even bring ourselves to opt for equality and equal opportunity within our own country. In my opinion, the only law that will order things on our campuses and in our ghettos is the law of love which makes men equal — equal in the sight of both man and God.

The basic problem of contemporary human ecology is *selfishness* — and selfishness is in. The wages of sin is death. The biotic world is dying!

Life—and hope—and love is in Christ Jesus. "Not that we loved Him, but that He loved us and gave Himself as a sacrifice for our sin." ". . . and that great secret is this, *Christ in you.*" You know that. You testify that you know it because you're experiencing it. And so am I!

Then why does my stomach get tied in knots when I think of what life would be like if we really brought in 100,000,000 peasants from India and distributed them in the space available in North Dakota, South Dakota, Minnesota, Iowa, and elsewhere?

You may be ready to fulfill your role as a Christian in alleviating the problems of contemporary human ecology—but I'm not sure I am.

BIBLIOGRAPHY

Allen, D. L. 1959. Resources, people, and space: a critique of the 24th North American Wildlife Conference. 24th *N. Amer. Wildl. Conf. Trans.,* 531-538.

Cassel, J. F. and R. B. Oetting. 1970. Ecological considerations may favor reducing mowing. *Public Works* 10(6):95-97.

Elder, E. K. 1971. The Christian and modern technology. Proceedings of the Second Scientific Symposium, October 23, 1970, Dordt College, Sioux Center, Iowa.

Harrar, George. 1970. Ecological crisis demands new ethic of responsibility. *Catalyst* 1(2):22-24.

Way, Ron. 1970. Feedlot proposal protested. *The Minneapolis Tribune* 104(129): 1&4

White, Lynn, Jr. 1967. The historical roots of our ecological crisis. *Science* 155:1203-1207.

Wright, Richard. 1970. Responsibility for the ecological crisis. *Bioscience* 20:851-853.

Too Little, Too Late

W. Russell Harris

A revealing set of facts reports that world population doubled between the years 1600 and 1800, and again between 1800 and 1900, still again between 1900 and 1960, and will easily have doubled yet again between 1960 and 2000.

Before the year 2000, we are assured, three people will stand in the United States where two stand today. Lake Erie by 1980 will become a miasmal swamp. Lake Michigan will be filled with water not fit to drink, and good for swimming only in selected areas. All of our rivers except parts of swift flowing streams in national parks will be running sewers.

The rest of the world, especially in South Asia and Africa will be in ever more dire straits of life from a combination of overcrowding and inadequately controlled use of resources.

We are awakening to an ecological crisis that is emerging under labels such as pollution, Man and Environment, and population explosion. Although every part of our existence and quality of life is being affected by these events, I feel the basis of the problem is rooted in the rapid growth of world population. As one writer has phrased it, "To put one's finger on the one problem facing mankind which overrides all others is simple. Unless we solve the population problem we can forget about the rest."

The glaring evidences of the problem show up in mass starvation and sickness resulting from malnutrition. There seems to be no way to avoid mass starvation in India, China, Indonesia, Mexico, and Egypt as well as other parts of the world. Tension and stress resulting from crowded and dehumanizing urban living take their toll. Increased industrialization and waste, which are related to overpopulation and the way in which we choose to live, are threatening to our environment. Even if we could feed ourselves, we may not be able to survive. We poison the air we breathe, the food we eat and the water we drink. In effect, we poison ourselves. We cannot do anything about these problems without doing something about the overpopulation problem.

The so-called ecological prophets of doom have been virtually ignored by the public, politicians, industry and the church. Frederick Elder said, "By the end of

Written for this volume. W. Russell Harris is Pastor of Faith United Methodist Church at Fargo, North Dakota.

the next thirty years, when crowded agitated man will long for solitude, when a necessary sameness of environment will bring aesthetic devastation to a peak, mankind will hear the announcement of judgement with new ears." It is difficult to gain a hearing from man who has manipulated his environment, successfully enegaged in interplanetary travel, and is now ready for whatever comes. We somehow have the feeling we can work through any problem regardless of how incredible it is. I have that faith and hope in man, but I feel the time to begin working on the incredible population problem is now and not thirty years from now. I personally doubt that much creative and imaginative change will happen without man taking far more seriously his role as a creation of God who has assigned man in the role of steward over that creation.

MAN IS RELATED TO ENVIRONMENT

Ecology is the science of interrelationships of organisms with their environment. Modern Biblical study is based on the principles of interrelationship. God created the earth and its environment just as surely as he created man. A Christian cannot base his ecological conscience on a concern of a poor environment that is detrimental to man. The Christian must be concerned about man's interrelationship with his environment. He then feels a responsibility toward it not only because his survival depends upon it, but also, because environment has an inherent right to survive for the sake of itself. What right have we to reshape the landscape and interbalance of the natural order just because it seems more suitable to our needs? Too often we run into the feeling that God has given us the brains to create the technology to subdue the earth. Man creates a mind-set which implies he can handle any problem that comes along, and he therefore does not become too concerned about neglecting the basic interrelations and dependencies of man and his environment. It is what William Kuhns calls the "subjugation mind-set." Rather than consider the consequences of our manipulating of the environment upon the total creation, we seem to operate with the feeling that God put us here and he will take care of us. If this attitude is to change it will require a change in our subjugation mind-set. Perhaps we should not be asking the question, what shall we do? The question may be better phrased, what shall I not do?

In contrast to the popular progressive view, restraint is the clarion call for today and the near future. We are now in a time when we may have to recognize that a trillion dollar gross product may not be in the best interests of man and his environment. Now is the time to recognize that God owns the earth; man is a tenant upon it; man is making a mess of the property and a time of judgement is at hand.

God must be viewed as the unity of the systems of the world, including the natural systems. When the systems are violated, especially the natural system, the violator confronts the power of God. The violator is out of bounds. As man goes on to violate the natural systems he is on the threshold of being hurt and even killed. We are facing what some writers are calling an "eco-catastrophe" brought on by man's violating the unity or interrelationships of the systems. The only hope of avoiding the catastrophe is for man to reorder his value systems and restrain his life style of living. Possibly after famine has visited often, when crowded agitated man will long for space and solitude, when aesthetic devastation of the environment reaches a peak, we will "hear the announcement of the judgement with new ears." Maybe then we will realize the importance of the unity of the systems, and the danger of overpopulation to our existence. It may then become clear that uncensored freedom and progress have become pathways to destruction.

A Biblical statement informs us, "The fear of the Lord is the beginning of wisdom." In the end wisdom on the part of man is his relation to the rest of creation. The elements of unity and harmony are the only basis for a satisfactory interrelationship. This places man in the position of a humble, reverent and restrained spirit. Such a spirit is the only one that is of value to both nature and man.

POPULATION MUST BE CONTROLLED

If there is to be harmony between man and nature; if the future is to be a hopeful state of life rather than a time of horror, we must find ways to bring the birth rate and the death rate of the world's population into balance.

How is population best controlled? By mass starvation, political chaos, disease, natural tragedy or population planning? No one accepts starvation, political chaos, disease, or natural tragedy as conceivable ways to reduce the birth rate. We are looking for a reasonable and rational method which is family planning.

We are aware of the undesirable consequences of uncontrolled population growth. We are convinced there is an interrelationship between man and his environment. The success of this interrelationship depends upon our ability to bring about needed and significant changes in our attitude toward population control. We have to recognize the truth of what Malthus wrote in 1798 in his *Essay on the Principle of Population.* "The power of population is indefinitely greater than the power in the earth to produce subsistence for men." We are now at this place in our history. There is no question but what population growth must be controlled.

The birth rate can be decreased by a number of methods. Science has helped bring on the population problem by giving us the tools for maintaining good health. Science has also provided us with tools for reducing the birth rate. Each of the following methods is effective.

1. Mechanical contraceptives.
2. Birth control pills.
3. The intrauterine insert.
4. Sterilization.

The problem with these methods is that by using them some human life does not come into being. The question is, which child shall *not* be conceived so that other children already living can have a fruitful life? This appears to be a tough decision to make. The decision is further complicated by religious teachers who would have us believe it is not the place of man to play God in determining who will and who will not be born. This position does not align itself with the premise that there must be a balance between the numbers of people the environment can sustain, and the number of people who are making demands upon the environment. When the numbers of people exceed the ability of the environment to support them, a quality of life is then sacrificed. I feel each child brought into the world has a right to be fed, clothed, housed, medically cared for, and supported by at least a minimal education. We simply cannot offer these rights to each child born in an overcrowded world. I think God has shown us the wisdom and the methods of controlling our population, and I feel this is done best through family planning.

God said to "be fruitful and multiply." He also said "replenish the earth." Replenishment means bringing back to fullness and completeness. It implies the balancing of man's numbers and his needs with the world and its resources. It means controlling the population.

Therefore, I feel it is theologically sound to say that man has a responsibility to use scientific methods to control the population of the world. It is not a problem of playing God with life in deciding who is to be born. It is a question of deciding the nature of the quality of life that can be offered to living people. Leroy Augustein, author of the book *Come, Let Us Play God,* told of the following experience. While attending an international conference on population explosion, a Protestant really raised havoc with the Catholics for obstructing progress. A priest then arose to defend the actions of his religion as follows. "All too often you Protestants are extremely arrogant. Thirty years ago we couldn't have held a conference on this topic. You Protestants appear to have moved more rapidly than we Catholics from this extremely rigid position. You appear to be fifteen years ahead of us. Give us time to examine our consciences."

At this point a genteel lady from India could restrain herself no longer and arose and said, "Sir, if you ask us for fifteen years you cannot have it. In my country, fifteen years from now, at our present rate of growth we will have 200 million new mouths to feed." There is an urgency about our need to accept our responsibility for population control.

I do not take the ethical and moral implications of scientific birth control lightly. We are a unity of systems and cannot root our moral and ethical decisions on a platform of self determination. The priest and all others who want to go slow on scientific birth control, must consider the fact that we are in community with men everywhere. Procreative behaviour is not an inherent right that cannot be balanced by the right of others. If it is going to remain our right at all it must be limited for the good of the community. "Family planning is not designed to destroy families. On the contrary, it is designed to save them." (Robert S. McNamara)

The population explosion is our largest and most worrisome problem. If we handle it badly there is no need for us to worry about the others. If man is to come of age and do his part in restoring balance and order to the divine systems, he must ask the question, under what conditions should human life be conceived? This is the only positive approach available to man to reconcile man and his environment.

I have intentionally avoided the suggestion of abortion as a method of population control. I say this because I accept the scientific methods previously listed as adequate methods of population control. I reiterate the statement that each child has certain inalienable rights by virtue of being born into society. These include adequate food, clothing, shelter, education and other necessities of life. But most of all a child has a right to be wanted. In such instances where an unwanted pregnancy occurs, I feel the parents should have the legal right to obtain an abortion upon demand. The question of the viability of the fetus is a futile one. It is simply assumed that the already born have a claim to life that is greater than that of the fetus.

CONSUMPTION LEVELS MUST BE RESTRAINED

Another side of the population problem is the rapidly rising human consumption of resources which contributes to the drastic upsetting of the balance of nature. There is no way in which we can speed up the biological or geological cycles to accommodate the crowded world of people. The speed with which we use up this planet's "copper, chromium, tin, bauxite and a score of other minerals in scattering them about Vietnam in the form of bullets, airplanes, and military equipment while wantonly destroying timber and all forms of life in that country, or the less destructive manner in which we commit our cement into myriads of ribbon trailing across the body of the nation" (Edward Shuck), is a good example of how carelessly we waste and loot our resources. We're chewing our environment to bits without thought of today or tomorrow.

Our demands for the affluent life style create a breakdown in natural balances. We rapidly transform our environment into forms of matter which we cannot consume, use, or recycle. The current psychology of man is to demand more excellent comfort items, and greater consumption levels. There is apparently no thought of the waste for which we do not have any realistic use. Nor does there seem to be a compelling concern for the pollution created in maintaining our consumption level.

Our prior thesis is that God must be viewed as the unity of the system of the world, and man in his greed is the violator. Man in his selfish desire for an ever more affluent life is creating a breakdown of the unity of the systems. For unity to be restored man will have to alter his values. Man will have to repudiate his traditional concepts of success and must make more than a mechanical or chemical response. Restored unity will come as economic growth as the standard of success is repudiated. It will require an altered educational system which can develop public attitudes capable of accepting revolutionary and early changes in our political theories and goals.

If consumption levels are to be arrested, man's appetites and desired must be altered. Former Secretary of Interior, Stewart Udall wrote, "America today stands poised on a pinnacle of wealth and power, yet we live in a land of vanishing beauty, of increasing ugliness, of shrinking open space, and of an overall environment that is diminished daily by pollution, noise and blight." Have we lost the capacity to foresee that our way of life is destroying the earth? Man and the ecosystems are inseparable. As we destroy the environment in our pursuit of affluent living, we destroy ourselves.

I BELIEVE

I believe there is a basic orderliness and unity in the way things interact throughout the universe. I believe God is to be viewed as the unity of the universe. As there is orderliness in the atom, our genes or in the mind, I believe there must be an orderliness in the way we humans treat each other and our environs. In early times we had a God of fire, a God of the hunt, a God of war, a God of love and so forth. Man was left at the mercy of the gods with the feeling he could do little or nothing for himself. This attitude slowly changed, and I agree with Dietrich Bonhoeffer that "man has come of age." Man is in a position where he can do something about the population problem. He can restore orderliness by controlling population growth. He can restore ecological balance by restraining his comsumption levels. God requires of us a human and responsible choice in every matter of moral decision including such grave matters as birth and death. The future is open. It depends upon us. Too little and too late are bitter words.

"All that is necessary for evil to triumph is that good men and women do nothing in time." The time is very short. We had better get busy today!

A Better World for the Children

George Wald

Throughout his history man has been engaged in an unending struggle to know. That is epitomized in science. Science is the systematic attempt to understand all reality. That covers a wide province: not only such simple things as stones falling and the structure of the atomic nucleus, but such more complex things as poets writing sonnets. All those things are part of one universe of reality; and science tries to understand them all. We are far from doing that yet, and we may never understand some of those more complex things; but we'll keep on trying.

As an attempt to understand, to know, science is altogether good, as our culture interprets the good. There can be no bad science. Any other view would be a plea for ignorance. There can be nothing wrong with science that ignorance can fix.

There is an altogether different kind of enterprise, the application of science for useful ends, technology. I have just said that science is altogether good, but I would not dream of saying that of technology. Technology is for use; and in a properly conducted society every enterprise in technology, new or old, has constantly to be judged in terms of that society's needs, goals and aspirations.

Sometimes I have tried asking scientists—most of my friends are scientists—I've tried asking them: Should one do everything one can? (The strange thing is that one is just beginning to think about that; it was a very strange question a few years ago.) The answer, of course, is: no. Of course not; one should do what it seems good to you to do, and useful to you to do. So, to summarize my feeling about this—*know* all you can, but do only what you think is good and useful to do.

Who is to make those decisions? Not scientists. Knowledge is one thing, and wisdom another, and wisdom is a much scarcer commodity. Nor the engineers and technicians engaged in this kind of enterprise. There is nothing so horrifying, destructive, or repulsive, that someone, somewhere, does not see his entire place in life, his aspirations, his status, wrapped up in that thing.

Reprinted by permission of Science and Public Affairs, the Bulletin of the Atomic Scientists. Copyright © May, 1969, by the Educational Foundation for Nuclear Science. Dr. George Wald is Professor of Biology at Harvard University, Cambridge, Massachusetts, and Nobel Laureate in Medicine and Physiology.

And not only the engineers who are making very complex destructive weapons. All kinds of people. To give you an example: I read a treatise on the population explosion, a symposium. One of the most distinguished demographers there was saying: What's all the worry about? Why are people shouting about a population explosion at this level? He had figured out that this earth can support a population of 40 billion people. Of course, as he pointed out, they wouldn't be eating *meat*—there would be no place for cows in a world like that (40 billion people). And as he described this, you saw he was just hungry for a chance to show that, given that opportunity, he could keep 40 billion people alive on the surface of the earth.

MAN-MADE MEN

I have a colleague at Harvard in psychology (he's a good friend). One day he said to me, with his face just shining, "Give us the specifications, and we'll make the men." I'm afraid I was a little rude, and my first reply was, "Not if I can shoot you first." That seemed to irritate him.

So who is to make those decisions? I think you listen to all those people, you listen very carefully; you want to hear everything the experts say, everything the industrialists have to say, everything the politicians have to say, everything all the "interested parties" have to say, whatever the source of their interest. But then it's we, all of us, who have to make up our minds.

I think my only quarrel with Dr. DuBridge's description of this process is that (if I heard him correctly) he put all those decisions at the production end. And I want to tell you where I think they belong. I think they must finally rest not with any of those who have anything to do, in any way, with the production. I think they have to rest with those of us who have to live with the products.

ORGANIC DESIGN AND DEMOCRACY

It's easy for me to hold a patriotic speech: America's my home. Not my business, my home. And I love it. I think we have the finest kind of government there is. It's called "democracy," a great thing.

I am a biologist. You see, there are two kinds of design in the world: technological design, and organic, or biological design. Technological design writes the specifications and then tries to produce the thing. That isn't the way biological design is produced. That isn't the kind of process that has produced all living things. And the simplest of living things is more complex, and works better, than the most complicated of all machines. Now, the process that made us, and made all living things, is a sort of technological design in reverse. You just keep trying, producing variations, and then trying them out. The things that work well are retained, and the things that don't work so well are eliminated. And that's democracy.

Democracy is the political equivalent of natural selection—the driving force of evolution. It's the kind of government that has built into it the capacity to evolve. And the most precious thing in it, the indispensable element, is its open-endedness. Being open-ended, it can always change.

We've got the best kind of government there is. I didn't say the best government, I said the best *kind* of government. And the best thing about that is, if we can keep it that way, we can change it. And the best thing about that is, not only might we get something better next time, but it makes the present government try a little harder.

My only trouble with democracy is trying to get it. It has given us a rough time lately. In my opinion, that last Presidential campaign, the campaigns that led up to the Convention, and all the rest of it, were all pretty frustrating. Some of you may know that there was a Convention in Chicago.

HARD TRUTHS

I think that we've had a hard time lately, but we're learning some rather hard truths. One of those truths is that bureaucracies are interchangeable. Another of those truths: money and political power are interchangeable. A third such truth: general staffs are interchangeable.

Our own Joint Chiefs of Staff, just the day before yesterday, changed the position on ABMs that it had held for many years; and the New York Times explained that the Joint Chiefs of Staff may be wrong, but they're always unanimous. That's what the New York Times said. Some reporters had dug out that there had been some possible dissensions behind the votes; but when those reporters asked why it was that the Joint Chiefs of Staff had changed their positions, they declined to discuss it.

Since all these things are interchangeable, may I say, as a patriotic American (because that's what I am), that nothing in the world today resembles the United States so greatly as the USSR. You know where I last heard that statement? From a great Russian physicist named Sakharov, the man who made their (so they say) hydrogen bomb. That's what he had to say; and he thought perhaps the time had come for us to get together, we've come to resemble each other so closely. There are differences, important differences. I wonder what's keeping Sakharov alive. I couldn't be talking this way in Russia. There are important differences. Let's try to keep our end of it the way it is.

I think that's the way it is with technology. New technology mustn't be accepted as an aspect of fate. The primary question isn't whether someone can make some money out of it; the primary question is whether we, society, the American people, the people who have to live with it, want it, find use for it. It's a wonderful thing when we can find a use for it. And it is we who have to decide.

THE LORDS OF THE EARTH

I had a curious thought about all of this the other day. I'd like to say it to you. You know, about 200 million years ago we had the age of reptiles on this planet. Dinosaurs were the lords of the earth. They looked pretty good, those dinosaurs. They were big, powerful. They were well-armed. Some of them had horns. Some of them had very big teeth. They were well-proteced. They had thick skins, and some of them armor plate. They looked pretty fine. And they were the lords of the earth.

But back in the woods, hiding in the corners, there were little, naked, tender, defenseless creatures, the first mammals. Those things didn't have anything else, very much, but they did have one thing: rather larger brains for their size. A dinosaur has an awfully small brain. The proportion of brain to brawn in a dinosaur is very, very low. The mammals were doing better in that regard. And after a while, the age of reptiles gave way to the age of mammals. And there were no more dinosaurs.

Those mammals flourished on the earth, and about two million years ago, they gave rise to men. A man is a beautiful thing. Think of him best without his clothes. A man is a beautiful thing. And, he's got that big, beautiful brain. You take a man, standing on his two feet, or walking, moving smoothly, all under control. He's something you could love. But put him in a car! ... Now the proportion of brain to brawn has gone down a lot. A man in a car is hard to love. And he's dangerous roaring through the streets, making a stink.

Cars, men in cars—you know, we talk of them as cars, though there's a man, at least one, in every car. Men in cars kill about 50 thousand Americans per year. That's more Americans than have yet been lost in the entire Vietnam war. But we take it as an aspect of fate, and bear with it. It's just as though a pretty good-sized war were going on all the time. But it's not a war, it's just men in motorcars. And the point is, it's a matter of great pride to use; it's part of that wealth that Professor Blackett talked to us about. An American man controls an enormous amount of power, amount of machinery.

MORE BRAWN THAN BRAINS

While we weren't watching, we've become dinosaurs again. There's just that brain that was beautiful and adequate for the naked man, but there's no more brain than that, and look at all the power. We've become dinosaurs again. The proportion of brain to brawn is going down with explosive speed. I'm picking my words, perhaps carefully. And this time, we have no competitors to do it better. No, this time it's going to be a do-it-yourself extinction. And we've got power enough to drag all the rest of life along with us.

There's another thing about mammals. Mammals brought a new thing to life—infinitely precious, it means everything to us: mammals take care of their young. The dinosaur just laid its egg out of doors and went away and left it. That's the way it used to be with all the other creatures—fish, amphibia, reptiles— but not mammals. Mammals carry their young as embryos, for long months; and then after they bear them, they nurse them for many months more. That term "mammals," that's the nursing. And then the young are cubs, and play in sun, and the mother and father watch them, bring them food, take care of them and teach them how best to live.

I think that that's where we're failing. I don't think that we're taking very good care of our young. I don't think we've prepared a very good world for them. And neither do they.

You who are young, you've got a secret weapon. It's your parents. And in a time that's grown so discouraging that some of us are a little desperate about it, the one thought that cheers me up is that almost everybody is a parent. Those sub-contractors, the bankers, the politicians, generals, admirals, almost all of them have kids. I'll tell you another thing, deeply mysterious: wherever there's a kid, there's almost always a mother. It is sometimes alleged that only American boys have mothers. That's an exaggeration. They all have mothers, all over the world. Chinese kids have mothers, Russian kids have mothers, I think even Viet Cong kids have mothers. So there are a lot of mothers.

MEDIEVAL INDULGENCES

I've been in some strange conversations since that talk on March 4, some very curious ones. I've had some of those before. The ordinary course of my life doesn't throw me together very much—I wish it did more—with big industrialists, bankers, and generals, and so on. But once in a great while, it happens. And then sometimes I have that curious conversation—it turns out we don't agree on everything. And then, a strange number of times, that person tells me about his kid in the Peace Corps. And you know, he says it proudly—I don't know what he says to the kid—I just know what he says to me. He says it proudly. It sounds to me like the modern American equivalent of the purchase of medieval indulgences. You make a pile of money in one way or another, but there's that kid in the Peace Corps. Let St. Peter look at *him*.

I had a curious conversation just the other day with a man who's a writer on Electronic News. He told me he'd been at MIT and heard that speech, and he kept saying, over and over in his conversation over the telephone, "You know, there's a lot that you said that I agree with personally, but of course, professionally I'm on the other side." And all the time this kept coming up: there's something in what you say, personally, but professionally, I'm on the other side. It's the compartmented life: personally a parent; but professionally, sometimes in a business that one worries about as a parent.

I'd like to say something to all those people. I have a message for all the defense contractors and subcontractors, and the people working for them, and the generals and the admirals, and all the rest of them. That message is: Clear it with the kids. If you haven't kids of your own to clear it with, clear it with the other people's kids. If you can clear it with them, if they'll buy it, I buy it too.

Well, that's what our problem is, I think. We have to make a better world for our children. But when I talk this way, people say: Oh, that's all very well, it puts you on the side of the angels. But for heaven's sake, have you got a plan? Tell us what to do. Have you got a program?

OUR NORTH VIETNAMESE

So, in some of these conversations, they say: How do we get out of Vietnam, for example? Ladies and gentlemen, please don't think I'm frivolous. I've thought about little else for a long, long time. I'll tell you where I come out. I'll tell you how I think we get out of Vietnam. *In ships.* And I'd offer one of those ships to those generals who've been running Vietnam for us. I wouldn't bring them here; I'd bring them to Paris and give them to de Gaulle.

I hope you know, and I hope all Americans know but let me say it again (because perhaps you don't), that almost every one of those generals who have been running South Vietnam is a North Vietnamese. You all know that Ky boasted about it lately; he wanted to lead the troops to reconquer his country. His country is North Vietnam. They are our North Vietnamese. But I'll tell you something else about them; every one of them fought on the French side in the Vietnamese revolution. Did you know that? That's the way it is. And when Americans wonder a little about why the great masses of South Vietnamese people aren't clearly enthusiastic about their leaders, this gives one the hint.

Do I have a program? Yes, I have a program. I'll tell you what it is, very simply. Again, please don't think me frivolous. You may think me naive, sentimental, academic; you just find yourselves some practical alternatives. This is my program: A better life for children. As our children go, so goes America. As all children go, so goes humanity. When we have made a better world for children, we will have the best world for grown-ups too.

You may think that's an impractical program. It's just as practical as can be. It's the most practical one I know. Are ABMs good for children? You tell me. Are nuclear weapons good for children? Are supersonic transports good for children? Is a big army good for children? Are more cars on the roads good for children? You tell me. But are good schools good for children? Good food, clean air, pure water, are those things good for children? Decent housing, open spaces, grass—who can eat grass?—trees, running streams, are they good for children?

A better world for children. But there are too many children—far too many children. We need to have fewer children. But not to cut down their numbers with war, famine, poverty, disease, turn loose the Four Horsemen of the Apocalypse on them. We can do better than that. No, to get fewer children, we'll need birth control; legalized, and much safer and more convenient abortion; and whatever other sensible procedures can be devised.

So that's my program. Let no man have a political philosophy that won't go on a button; and this one will go on a button: "A better world for fewer children." That's my program for us, for America, and for all mankind.

How I Got Radicalized:
The Making of an Agitator for Zero

John Fischer

To my astonishment, the political convictions that I had cherished for most
of my life have suddenly deserted me. Like my children, these were convictions I
loved dearly and had nurtured at considerable expense. When last seen they
were—like all of us—somewhat battered by the events of the last decade, but
they looked durable enough to last out my time. So I was disconcerted when I
found that somehow, during the past winter, they sort of melted away, without
my consent and while I was looking somewhere else.

Their place has been usurped by a new set of convictions so radical that they
alarm me. If the opposite kind of thing had happened, I would have felt a little
melancholy but not surprised, since people traditionally grow more conservative
as they get older. But to discover that one has suddenly turned into a militant
subversive is downright embarrassing; at times I wonder whether it signals the
onset of second childhood.

Except that I seem to be a lot more radical than the children. Those SDS
youngsters who go around breaking windows and clubbing policemen now merely
depress me with their frivolous irrelevance. So do most other varieties of New
Leftists, such as the Women's Liberation movement; if some dire accident
should, God forbid, throw one of those ladies into my clutches, she can be sure
of instant liberation. I am equally out of tune with those old fogies, the
Communists. The differences between capitalism and Communism no longer
seem to me worth fighting about, or even arguing, since they are both wrong and
beside the point. Or so it seems to me, since the New Vision hit me on my own
small road to Damascus.

Let me make it plain that none of this was my doing. I feel as Charles Darwin
must have felt during the last leg of his voyage on the Beagle. When he embarked
he had been a conventional (if slightly lackadaisical) Christian, who took the
literal truth of Genesis for granted. He had been raised in that faith, as I was
raised a Brass Collar democrat, and had no thought of forsaking it. Only
gradually, while he examined fossil shellfish high in the Andes and measured the
growth of coral deposits and the bills of Galapagos finches, did he begin to

doubt that the earth and all its inhabitants had been created in six days of October, 4004 B.C., according to the pious calculations of Archbishop James Ussher. By the time he got back to England, he found himself a reluctant evolutionist, soon to be damned as a heretic and underminer of the Established Church. This was not his fault. It was the fault of those damned finches.

Recently I too have been looking at finches, so to speak, although mine are mostly statistical and not nearly as pretty as Darwin's. His gave him a hint about the way the earth's creatures came into being; mine, to my terror, seem to hint at the way they may go out. While I am by no means an uncritical admirer of the human race, I have become rather fond of it, and would hate to see it disappear. Finding ways to save it—if we are not too late already—now strikes me as the political issue which takes precedence over all others.

One of the events which led to my conversion was my unexpected appointment to a committee set up by Governor John Dempsey of Connecticut to work out an environmental policy for our state. Now I had been fretting for quite a while about what is happening to our environment—who hasn't?—but until the work of the committee forced me into systematic study, I had not realized that my political convictions were in danger. Then after looking at certain hairy facts for a few months, I found myself convinced that the Democratic party, and most of our institutions of government, and even the American Way of Life are no damned good. In their present forms, at least, they will have to go. Either that, or everybody goes—and sooner than we think.

To begin with, look at the American Way of Life. Its essence is a belief in growth. Every Chamber of Commerce is bent on making its Podunk grow into the Biggest Little City in the country. Wall Street is dedicated to its search for growth stocks, so that Xerox has become the American ideal—superseding George Washington, who expressed *his* faith in growth by speculating in land. Each year Detroit prays for a bigger car market. Businessmen spend their lives in pursuit of an annual increase in sales, assets, and net profits. All housewives—except for a few slatterns without ambition—yearn for bigger houses, bigger cars, and bigger salary checks. The one national goal that everybody agrees on is an ever-growing Gross National Product. Our modern priesthood—the economists who reassure us that our mystic impulses are moral and holy—recently announced that the GNP would reach a trillion dollars early in this decade. I don't really understand what a trillion is, but when I read the news I rejoiced, along with everybody else. Surely that means that we were in sight of ending poverty, for the first time in human history, so that nobody would ever again need to go hungry or live in a slum.

Now I know better. In these past months I have come to understand that a zooming Gross National Product leads not to salvation, but to suicide. So does a continuing growth in population, highway mileage, kilowatts, plane travel, steel tonnage, or anything else you care to name.

The most important lesson of my life—learned shamefully late—was that nonstop growth just isn't possible, for Americans or anybody else. For we live in what I've learned to recognize as a tight ecological system: a smallish planet with a strictly limited supply of everything, including air, water, and places to dump sewage. There is no conceivable way in which it can be made bigger. If Homo sapiens insists on constant growth, within this system's inelastic walls, something has to pop, or smother. Already the United States is an overpopulated country: not so hopelessly overcrowded as Japan or India, of course, but well beyond the limits which would make a good life attainable for everybody. Stewart Udall, former Secretary of Interior and now a practicing ecologist, has estimated that the optimum population for America would be about 100 million, or half of our present numbers. And unless we do something drastic and fast, we can expect another 100 million within the next thirty years.

So our prime national goal, I am now convinced, should be to reach Zero Growth Rate as soon as possible. Zero growth in people, in GNP, and in our consumption of everything. That is the only hope of attaining a stable ecology: that is, of halting the deterioration of the environment on which our lives depend.

This of course is a profoundly subversive notion. It runs squarely against the grain of both capitalism and the American dream. It is equally subversive of Communism, since the Communists are just as hooked on the idea of perpetual growth as any American businessman. Indeed, when Khrushchev was top man in the Kremlin, he proclaimed that 1970 would be the year in which the Russians would surpass the United States in output of goods. They didn't make it: a fact for which their future generations may be grateful, because their environment is just as fragile as ours, and as easily damaged by headlong expansion. If you think the Hudson River and Lake Erie are unique examples of pollution, take a look at the Volga and Lake Baikal.

No political party, here or abroad, has yet considered adopting Zero Growth Rate as the chief plank in its platform. Neither has any politician dared to speak out loud about what "protection of the environment" really means—although practically all of them seem to have realized, all of a sudden, that it is becoming an issue they can't ignore. So far, most of them have tried to handle it with gingerly platitudes, while keeping their eyes tightly closed to the implications of what they say. In his January State of the Union message, for instance, President Nixon made the customary noises about pollution; but he never even mentioned the population explosion, and he specifically denied that there is any "fundamental contradiction between economic growth and the quality of life." He sounded about as convincing as a doctor telling a cancer patient not to worry about the growth of his tumor.

The Democrats are no better. I have not heard any of them demanding a halt to all immigration, or a steeply progressive income tax on each child beyond two, or an annual bounty to every woman between the ages of fifteen and forty-five who gets through the year without becoming pregnant. Neither Ted Sorensen nor any of the other Kennedy henchmen has yet suggested that a politician with a big family is a space-hog and a hypocrite, unworthy of public trust. No Democrat, to my knowledge, has ever endorsed the views of Dr. René Dubos of Rockefeller University, one of the truly wise men of our time. In an editorial in the November 14, 1969, issue of *Science* he predicted that in order to survive, "mankind will have to develop what might be called a steady state ... a nearly closed system" in which most materials from tin cans to sewage would be "recycled instead of discarded." His conclusion—that a viable future depends on the creation of "social and economic systems different from the ones in which we live today"—apparently is too radical for any politician I know.

Consequently I feel a little lonesome in my newfound political convictions. The only organization which seems to share them is a tiny one, founded only a few months ago: Zero Population Growth, Inc., with headquarters at 367 State Street, Los Altos, California 94022. Yet I have a hunch that I may not be lonesome for long. Among college students a concern with ecology has become, almost overnight, nearly as popular as sideburns. On many campuses it seems to be succeeding civil rights and Vietnam as The Movement. For example, when the University of Oregon announced last January a new course, "Can Man Survive?" it drew six thousand students, the biggest class in the university's history. They had to meet in the basketball court because no classroom would hold them.

Who knows? Maybe we agitators for Zero may yet turn out to be the wave of the future.

At the same time I was losing my faith in the virtues of growth, I began to doubt two other articles of the American credo.

One of them is the belief that technology can fix anything. Like most of us, I had always taken it for granted that any problem could be solved if we just applied enough science, money, and good old American know-how. Is the world's population outrunning its food supply? Well, then, let's put the laboratories to work inventing high-yield strains of rice and wheat, better fertilizers, ways to harvest seaweed, hydroponic methods for growing food without soil. If the air is becoming unbreathable, surely the technologists can find ways to clean it up. If our transportation system is a national disgrace, all we have to do is call in the miracle men who built a shuttle service to the moon; certainly they should be able to figure out some way to get a train from New York to New Haven on time.

I was in East Haddam, Connecticut, looking at an atomic power plant, when I began to suspect that technology might not be the answer after all. While I can't go along with the young Luddites who have decided that science is evil and that all inventions since the wheel ought to be destroyed, I am persuaded that technology is a servant of only limited usefulness, and highly unreliable. When it does solve a problem, it often creates two new ones—and their side effects are usually hard to foresee.

One of the things that brought me to East Haddam was curiosity about the automobile. Since the gasoline engine is the main polluter of the air, maybe it should be replaced with some kind of electric motor? That of course would require an immense increase in our production of electric power, in order to recharge ten million batteries every night. Where would it come from? Virtually all waterpower sites already are in use. More coal- and oil-fired power stations don't sound like a good idea, since they too pour smoke into the atmosphere—and coal mining already has ruined countless streams and hundred of thousands of acres of irreplaceable land. Atomic power, then?

At first glance, the East Haddam plant, which is fairly typical of the new technology, looked encouraging. It is not as painful an eyesore as coal-burning stations, and not a wisp of smoke was in sight. When I began to ask questions, however, the company's public-relations man admitted that there are a few little problems. For one thing, the plant's innards are cooled with water pumped out of the Connecticut River. When it flows back in, this water raises the river's temperature by about twenty degrees, for a considerable distance. Apparently this has not yet done any serious damage to the shad, the only fish kept under careful surveillance; but its effect on other fish and algae, fish eggs, micro-organisms, and the general ecology of the river is substantial though still unmeasured.

It would be possible, though expensive, for the company to build cooling towers, where the water would trickle over a series of baffles before returning to the river. In the process it would lose its heat to the atmosphere. But this, in turn, threatens climatic changes, such as banks of artificial fog rolling eastward over Long Island Sound, and serious wastage of water through evaporation from a river system where water already is in precarious supply. Moreover, neither this process nor any other now known would eliminate the slight, but not neglibible, radiation which every atomic plant throws off, nor the remote but still omnipresent chance of a nuclear accident which could take thousands of lives. The building of an additional twenty plants along the banks of the Connecti-cut—which some estimates call for, in order to meet future demand for electricity—would be a clear invitation to an ecological disaster.

In the end I began to suspect that there is no harmless way to meet the demands for power of a rising population, with rising living standards—much less for a new herd of millions of electric cars. Every additional kilowatt levies some tax upon the environment, in one form or another. The Fourth Law of Thermodynamics seems to be: "There is no free lunch."

Every time you look at one of the marvels of modern technology, you find a by-product—unintended, unpredictable, and often lethal. Since World War II, American agriculture has performed miracles of increasing production. One result was that we were able for years to send a shipload of free wheat every day to India, saving millions from starvation. The by-products were: (1) a steady rise in India's population; (2) the poisoning of our streams and lakes with insecticides and chemical fertilizers; (3) the forced migration of some ten million people from the countryside to city slums, as agriculture became so efficient it no longer needed their labor.

Again, the jet plane is an unquestionable convenience, capable of whisking a New Yorker, say, to either the French Riviera or Southern California in a tenth of the time he could travel by ship or car, and at lower cost. But when he reaches his destination, the passenger finds the beaches coated with oil (intended to fuel planes, if it hadn't spilled) and the air thick with smog (thanks in good part to the jets, each of which spews out as much hydrocarbon as ten thousand automobiles).

Moreover, technology works best on things nobody really needs, such as collecting moon rocks or building supersonic transport planes. Whenever we try to apply it to something serious, it usually falls on its face.

An obvious case in point is the railroads. We already have the technology to build fast, comfortable passenger trains. Such trains are, in fact, already in operation in Japan, Italy, and a few other countries. Experimental samples—the Metroliners and Turbotrains—also are running with spectacular success between Washington and Boston. If we had enough of them to handle commuter and middle-distance traffic throughout the country, we could stop building the highways and airports which disfigure our countryside, reduce the number of automobiles contaminating the air, and solve many problems of urban congestion. But so far we have not been able to apply the relatively simple technology needed to accomplish these aims, because some tough political decisions have to be made before we can unleash the scientists and engineers. We would have to divert to the railroads many of the billions in subsidy which we now lavish on highways and air routes. We would have to get rid of our present railway management—in general, the most incompetent in American industry— and retire the doddering old codgers of the Railway Brotherhoods who make such a mess out of running our trains. This might mean public ownership of a good many rail lines. It certainly would mean all-out war with the unions, the auto and aviation industries, and the highway lobby. It would mean ruthless application of the No Growth principle to roads, cars, and planes, while we make sensible use instead of something we already have: some 20,000 miles of railways.

All this requires political action, of the most radical kind. Until our Great Slob Society is willing to take it, technology is helpless.

My final apostasy from the American Creed was loss of faith in private property. I am now persuaded that there no longer is such a thing as truly private property, at least in land. That was a luxury we could afford only when the continent was sparsely settled. Today the use a man makes of his land cannot be left to his private decision alone, since eventually it is bound to affect everybody else. This conclusion I reached in anguish, since I own a tiny patch of land and value its privacy above anything money can buy.

What radicalized me on this score was the Department of Agriculture and Dr. Ian McHarg. From those dull volumes of statistics which the Department publishes from time to time, I discovered that usable land is fast becoming a scarce resource—and that we are wasting it with an almost criminal lack of foresight. Every year, more than a million acres of farm and forest land is being eaten up by highways, airports, reservoirs, and real-estate developers. The best, too, in most cases, since the rich, flat bottom lands are the most tempting to developers.

Since America is, for the moment, producing a surplus of many crops, this destruction of farmland has not yet caused much public alarm. But some day, not too far off, the rising curve of population and the falling curve of food-growing land inevitably are going to intersect. That is the day when we may begin to understand what hunger means.

Long before that, however, we may be gasping for breath. For green plants are our only source of oxygen. They also are the great purifiers of the atmosphere, since in the process of photosynthesis they absorb carbon dioxide—an assignment which gets harder every day, as our chimneys and exhaust pipes spew out ever-bigger tonnage of carbon gases. This is a function not only of trees and grass, but also of the tiny microorganisms in the sea. Indeed, its phytoplankton produces some 70 per cent of all the oxygen on which life depends. These are delicate little creatures, easily killed by the sewage, chemicals, and oil wastes which already are contaminating every ocean in the world. Nobody knows when the scale will tip: when there are no longer enough green growing things to preserve the finely balanced mixture of gases in the atmosphere, by absorbing carbon dioxide and generating oxygen. All we know is that man is pressing down hard on the lethal end of the scale.

The Survivable Society, if we are able to construct it, will no longer permit a farmer to convert his meadow into a parking lot any time he likes. He will have to understand that his quick profit may, quite literally, take the bread out of his grandchildren's mouths, and the oxygen from their lungs. For the same reasons, housing developments will not be located where they suit the whim of a real-estate speculator or even the convenience of the residents. They will have to go on those few carefully chosen sites where they will do the least damage to the landscape, and to the life-giving greenery which it supports.

This is one of the lessons taught by Ian McHarg in his extraordinary book, *Design With Nature,* recently published by Natural History Press. Alas, its price, $19.95, will keep it from reaching the people who need it most. It ought to be excerpted into a pocket-size volume—entitled, perhaps, "The Thoughts of McHarg"—and distributed free in every school and supermarket.

The current excitement about the environment will not come to much, I am afraid, unless it radicalizes millions of Americans. The conservative ideas put forth by President Nixon—spending a few billion for sewage-treatment plants and abatement of air pollution—will not even begin to create the Survivable Society. That can be brought about only by radical political action—radical enough to change the whole structure of government, the economy, and our national goals.

How the Survivable State will work is something I cannot guess; its design is a job for the coming generation of political scientists. The racial vision can, however, give us a glimpse of what it might look like. It will measure every new law, every dollar of investment by a cardinal yardstick: Will this help us accomplish a zero rate of growth and a stabilized environment? It will be skeptical of technology, including those inventions which purport to help clean up our earthly mess. Accordingly it will have an Anti-Patent Office, which will forbid the use of any technological discovery until the Office figures out fairly precisely what its side effects might be. (If they can't be foreseen, then the invention goes into deep freeze.) The use of land, water, and air will not be left to private decision, since their preservation will be recognized as a public trust. The landlord whose incinerator smokes will be pilloried; the tanker skipper who flushes his oil tanks at sea will be hanged at the nearest yardarm for the capital crime of oxygen destruction. On the other hand, the gardener will stand at the top of the social hierarchy, and the citizen who razes a supermarket and plants its acreage in trees will be proclaimed a Hero of the Republic. I won't live to see the day, of course, but I hope somebody will.

Indian Ecology

John F. Bryde

One of the sharpest differences between the Indian and non-Indian's attitudes toward the human part of the total environment is seen in the manner in which an Indian will address a gathering of people even when it is made up largely of strangers. Whereas the non-Indian will typically begin his address by greeting those present with the words, "Ladies and gentlemen," the Indian will begin by saying, "My Relatives," or "My brothers and sisters.";The phrase "My relatives" is not just a polite form of address, but reflects a basic attitude toward people in that the Indian sees all people as related.

The Indian value of Adjustment to Nature is "part" of Indian Wisdom in action. That "part" of the Indian value of Good Advice from Indian Wisdom was the "part" in which the Indian sees all things, including man, as related. Beyond strict blood relationships, all men have a deeper metaphysical relationship that makes everyone truly related. Toward all men, then, the Indian wants to act as relatives should act: they get along with and help one another out. Just as one should not compete with or try to get on top of his relatives, so should everyone deal with one another. Just as relatives are part of a larger body, the larger family of men, and parts don't work against the whole but with the whole, so should all men work together, getting along with one another and helping one another out.

One of the most remarkable similarities running throughout all the Indian people is this quiet but firm mental set of getting along with others. The Indian has a built-in sensitivity and responsiveness to the feelings of others that the average non-Indian doesn't have. In his social relationship with others, the Indian is a natural example of John Henry Newman's definition of a gentleman as one who would not deliberately cause another pain. There is a gentleness, a quietness and unobtrusiveness in the Indian personality that compels him to get along with others which many non-Indians sometimes label as shyness. The non-Indian's attitude toward the human area of the total environment is a competitive attitude which, although he will be "polite" and gentlemanly, underlies his

Reprinted with the permission of John F. Bryde from *Modern Indians.* Dr. John F. Bryde is associated with the Institute of Indian Studies, University of South Dakota, Vermillion, South Dakota.

actions and motivation like an invisible basement. Far from being shyness or bashfulness, this Indian quiet, soft spoken manner of dealing with people derives from the Indian world view as seeing all things, including men, as related, as well as from historical experiences in the past in which the Indian people lived most of their lives among relatives.

In order to understand Indian behavior, one cannot emphasize too much the necessity of realizing that the Indian, from his world view, is actively aware of himself as a living *part* of all of nature, which we call the total environment. Each part of total nature, the inanimate and animate, is active and alive and each active part, including himself, influences all of the other parts and consequently the living whole. Since the active, living whole is greater than any individual active living part, then it is up to the individual living part to *adjust itself* to the whole. The offending or upsetting of one little individual part could cause that offended part to upset another with a subsequent "domino effect" upsetting the whole; hence, one must be as sensitive to and adjust himself to each tiny individual part as we would be to the whole mysterious, holy total. Rather than adjust things (including people) to him, as the non-Indian is inclined to do, the Indian is aware that he, as the one responsible for keeping the balance among all things (including men) must adjust himself to them.

This harmony and balance with inanimate nature, springing from his reverent awareness of his being a part of this holy total, compels the Indian to rearrange nature just enough to get along. When it is cold, he rearranges it just enough to keep warm. When it is hot, he rearranges it just enough to keep cool. When he needs clothing or food, he rearranges it just enough to have bodily covering and remove his hunger. The more typical non-Indian attitude is to conquer nature as much as possible. Nature is something unfeeling, to be used, mined, rearranged and receive from man whatever new ordering of it man arbitrarily decides. Whereas the non-Indian seeks to control and predict nature, making for an emphasis on the future, the only control the Indian utilizes is within *himself;* it is from here that the harmony and balance is kept. Since the only time one can exercise this inner control in order to keep the balance is *now,* the emphasis on meaningful living is on the *now.* One can't control himself tomorrow in order to keep the balance; one can do it only now in order to keep the balance.

This responsibility to the now for exercising this desirable harmony coupled with the actual historical experience of the day to day struggle for survival brought a double emphasis to bear on responding to the *now* as a proper mode of human behavior. Life was so harsh and death always so imminent that simply to survive was the goal of their existence. As a fugue in their litany of petitions runs the constant prayer, "That the people may live." As each new day dawned and the sun moved across today's sky, they enjoyed it to the full because they had survived. The goal of existence had been achieved, therefore adjust to it and enjoy it now. Thus it was that from their world view of being aware of themselves as a part of the whole which is responsible *now* for the harmony of the whole as well as from their historical experience of enjoying the now of survival, there developed the mental set of getting along with everything, including men, *now* as the proper manner in which to live and relate to one's total environment.

To this day, the total contentment enjoyed by the Indian people in a simple gathering of friends and relatives for companionship and a good meal is unsurpassed by any other group of people.

It is almost common knowledge that historical incidents in the past of a people can develop attitudes which endure even after the original historical experiences have passed. Among the Indian people the almost universally common experience of living out their lives among relatives, namely, the extended family, gave rise to the attitude that everyone is related and, if there were no immediately obvious blood lines, then the mental set was there that there ought to be such blood lines.

In the old days, Indian peoples lived in small groups of people, all of whom were related by blood, marriage or adoption. When an Indian child was born, whether in a tipi, hogan or a cave in a cliff, the members of his immediate family, mother, father, brothers, and sisters, were not confined within the walls of his tipi or hogan, as are the members of the immediate family of the typical non-Indian child born today. The members of his family were all the people in the village.

As the Indian child grew and structured his world, he did not call one woman "mother" exclusively. For instance, among the Sioux, all the sisters on his mother's side were called mother also. The point to realize is that this was not just a courtesy relationship term but was a term meaning a true motherly function. These "aunt-mothers" as the non-Indian would call them, had all the responsibilities and privileges that the biological mother had. They trained the child, rewarded him, punished him, even nursed him if able and the occasion warranted it. In such circumstances, with so many mothers taking care of him, it could take several years for the child to sort out his real biological mother. With two, three or four mothers to love as he grew up, such a child had a greater sense of security and his emotions were more diffuse than a child whose security was founded in one mother. Consequently, if such a child lost his real biological mother, his sorrow was less keen than that of a child with just one mother.

On the side of the child's father, all of his father's brothers were not called uncle but father. Again, this was not just a courtesy title but a functional title. All of these fathers had the full privileges and responsibilities of the biological father. They trained the child, rewarded him and punished him when needed. Here again it might take the child several years to figure out his real biological father. With so many fathers to take care of him he had a larger base for security and again his emotions were more diffuse. If he lost his real biological father, his sorrow would be less keen than one who had just one father in whom he had invested all his filial love.

As for the aunts all the father's sisters were called aunts in the non-Indian sense, and all of the mother's brothers were called uncle in the non-Indian sense. An Indian child also grew up with a large number of functional brothers and sisters beyond his immediate biological family. For a male, all of the cousins, male and female on his father's side were called brothers and sisters. For a female all of the cousins, male and female, on the mother's side were called brothers and sisters. The term cousin was applied, for a male, to all of the cousins on his mother's side and, for a female, to all of the cousins on her father's side. The point is that all of the persons called cousins by the non-Indian, but called brothers and sisters by the Indian child had the same relationships and responsibilities that real biological brothers and sisters had. This made for many functional brothers and sisters.

Among the Dakotas or Sioux, there are twelve different words for cousin. Before the proper term can be used, it must be first determined whether the cousin is on the mother's or father's side, is male or female, younger or older, and whether it is a male or female speaking. It is at this point, one may open his mouth and use the proper term. Social scientists point out that an important value in a culture will usually have a rich vocabulary supporting it. The abundance of relationship terms among the Indian people indicates the importance of this value called adjustment to nature.

As the child grew, all day long he was using relationship terms with those with whom he spoke. Although the various relatives among whom he moved all had proper names, he never used the proper names. Unlike today when non-Indians use "Uncle Joe," "Aunt Mary," etc., the Indian child was using father, mother, brother, sister, cousin, etc. With his experience of relating to all people as relatives and using relationship terms whenever he spoke to someone, the child might be well advanced in years before a stranger rode over the hill and right away he would grope for the proper relationship term to apply to him. His early experience that all people are related had developed the enduring attitude that they truly are and, if a relationship is not immediately apparent, there must be one there someplace. Thus, the world view belief that all things, including men, are related is reinforced by the historical experience of relating to everyone in his known world as relatives.

Traditional Indian people, in their dealings with others who were not strictly relatives, did not like to maintain relationships on a strictly friendship basis. Since the proper way to relate with people was as relatives, they would adopt one another at various levels of relationships. Western movies and TV are replete with scenes of Indians adopting non-Indians as "blood brothers" or at other levels of relationship. The point to note is that the Indian meant it (Bryde, 1967).

To this day, traditional Indian people call one another, not by their proper names but by their relationship term. Little Tommy or Joyce is never called as such by grandparents or aunts or uncles but are invariably called "grandson, grandaughter, nephew or niece." Also, to this day, if elderly Indians like another person, Indian or non-Indian, after a while he will stop calling him "friend" and address him as "grandson" or "nephew" or "younger brother," depending on the age of the Indian person.

Whether one chooses to explain it in terms of operant conditioning or classical Pavlovian conditioning, one learns one's behavior largely from the reactions of those closest around him. It is from his initial and continuing experiences within his kinship system that an Indian learns how to be peculiarly an Indian. It is here that he learns how to adjust himself to others as related to them, to stay with and work with and for his group, as the whole group moves vertically or horizontally together. It is within his kinship group that he receives all the verbal, nonverbal and unconsciously given cues to reverence the animate and inanimate nature in the total environment. It is in this kinship group that the Indian value of adjustment to nature is learned. It is this experience of making himself fit in with others that he takes from his kinship group and applies to the larger family of man and the total environment as he moves in and out of both groups.

In the Dakota or Sioux language the word for people is *oyate*. The word *people,* however, does not mean just human people but is applied also to animals who are the animal people. Referring to bees buzzing nearby traditional Indian people will say, "Listen to the little people this morning. They are up early." Probably the only westerner to come close to this appreciative awareness of a relationship to the animate and inanimate environment around him was St. Francis of Assisi who, very Indian-like would refer to and address the birds as "sister bird," animals as "brother wolf" and the sun as "brother sun."

The typical non-Indian attitude toward nature, deriving from the non-Indian value of scientific progress, is that of conquering nature to a maximum degree coupled with the desire to exploit it for maximum profit. Nature is something to be used in order to make *things* better and better and to retain the momentum toward linear progress. The assumption is that by making things better and better people are somehow made better and better. This assumption is not borne out, however, as one views the cultural lag between the advanced technology of the dominant culture and the degraded condition of people in the lowest socio-economic level of this country. The priorities in the dominant culture are: things first, people second. In the Indian society the priorities are: people first, things second. It is more important to get along with people and solve human problems first, then rearrange nature and solve thing problems second.

The writer recently asked a teenage Indian boy who had been born and reared in a large city and who was a complete stranger to the writer, what he thought was one of the main differences between the Indians and the non-Indians. Without the slightest hesitation the young man said, "Indians like nature and people. White men tear up nature and don't care about people." Twenty-two years earlier and about eight years before that young man was born, the writer, many miles away and deep in a reservation was hearing this same idea from elderly Indians for the first time and it has recurred like a theme ever since.

Deep in the jungles of South America there is a small tribe of Indians called the Lengua Indians. In all of their relationships with others, Indians and non-Indians, their total and all pervading social concern is: to respect one's own *innermost* and the *innermost* of others. The innermost in each person is not one's soul or his conscience but is the source of his behavior. One's first concern in life is always to respect and keep in balance one's own innermost. Secondly, one must always respect the innermosts of others. He must then keep his innermost in balance with the innermost of others.

One must never let one's own innermost become upset and one must never upset the innermost of another person because, if he does, they believe grave harm will come to the one causing the upsetting. A new born baby becomes a real person eight days after birth when his ear lobe is pierced with a cactus thorn. From this moment on, the baby is a complete person and every effort is made to keep his innermost calm. Every concession is made to the baby; it is not forced to do anything that might upset his innermost.

A person's gravest social responsibility is to keep his own innermost calm and balanced because this will, in turn, help others to keep their innermosts balanced. Such a good person will not act when his innermost is wavy or upset or if he is excited, or angry and, in this way, he will avoid words and actions that could upset the innermost of another, to which he has a responsibility. Since the Lenguas believe that if they upset the innermost of another person grave harm will come to them, they will say or do anything in order to keep calm the innermost of another. One will even tell another what would appear to be a lie to keep that person's innermost peaceful and calm and to get along with him.

One will never approach another and speak to him without first checking to see whether his innermost is calm. He will then observe the other from a distance in order to ascertain whether that person's innermost is calm. If the other person's troubled innermost should cause one's innermost to become upset, then grave harm will come to the other person. If both innermosts seem calm and balanced, the way is clear to communicate. One never comes right to the point because this can be jarring; one starts far away from the intended topic of conversation, giving gentle hints of the topic to come in order to prepare the other person for it.

Respecting one another's innermost is also the prime consideration in conducting business dealings with one another. For example, if a person needs a horse for his work, he will visit a neighbor who has horses. In selecting one of the horses, he will make his selection by checking his innermost to see which horse his innermost is becoming attached to. Having made his selection, he will begin praising the quality of all of the horses to the owner pointing out repeatedly the one to whom his innermost has become attached. After a while the neighbor will ask him whether his innermost is attached to that particular horse. On responding that it is, the neighbor, not daring to upset the other's innermost, will say, "You may have him." It should be noted that the owner said have instead of buy because without any payment the one needing the horse takes him home.

A few days later, the owner of the horses will drop by the man's place to whom he had given the horse. This man might raise, say, sheep and the former owner of the horse will proceed to praise the other man's sheep, pointing out repeatedly eight or nine which he particularly admires. The man raising the sheep will eventually ask whether the other man's innermost has become attached to those eight or nine sheep. On being assured that it has, the owner of the sheep will say, "Take them. They are yours." In this manner trading and buying take place utilizing the innermost as the basis for doing business.

If a person has done something bad or has a son or daughter that has done something bad or embarassing that would upset others, he will quietly move away and return only after the whole affair has died down. If a community work project should involve all the people and one or two members do not choose to join in, they are never questioned. They know that the currently non-working members will join in their own good time when their innermosts become balanced to the project.

Life becomes very hard for the Lenguas when they are compelled by business or trading or even proximity to deal with and live among non-Indians. Non-Indians, to their way of thinking, have very unsettled innermosts because they are always getting excited, upset and angry, sometimes for no apparent provocation at all. In order to avoid the grave harm that could come to them by upsetting the innermosts of these unpredictable people, the Lenguas will say anything they think the non-Indians want to hear, even if it means stretching the truth, in order to keep them calm.

One of the Lenguas was working for a non-Indian rancher. One day the rancher told the Lengua to go out to the back pasture and and see whether the fence was up and the cattle were in. After a while the Lengua returned and told his employer that the fence was up and the cattle were in. The rancher then assigned him to his work for the day. A short while later, a non-Indian friend of the rancher came by and told the rancher that the fence in his back pasture was down and his cattle were out. The rancher then told his friend that his Indian employee had just checked and had assured him that the fence was up and the cattle were in. The non-Indian friend then told him that it was the same Indian employee who had told him, the friend, that the fence was down and the cattle were out and that he might mention it to his employer if he saw him. The rancher became very excited and wondered angrily aloud and with some heat why his Indian employee had not told him. His friend, who knew the Lenguas better, explained that the employee could not do it because he could not be responsible for upsetting his employer's innermost which, by now, it obviously was, but the non-Indian friend could because non-Indians didn't have much respect for the innermost anyway.

Citing an example of Indian behavior thousands of miles away is not irrelevant because it serves to illustrate one of the most common characteristics running throughout all of the Indian peoples, adjustment to or harmony with nature. The Lenguas call it by a different name but the meaning behind the word is just the same: adjust to and get along with people first, then concentrate on rearranging things.

Closer to home and illustrative of the Indian's perceived difference between the Indian and non-Indian attitude of getting along with others by non-jarring behavior is the word that the Dakota or Sioux Indians selected for white man or non-Indian when they first encountered him. Before the coming of the non-Indian, they had no word in their vocabulary for non-Indians; consequently, when they first met the non-Indians they had to reach back into their existing vocabulary to describe him. The word they chose was *wasicu*. Etymologically, this word came from the verb *iwasicu,* which means to communicate excitedly with many gestures and jumping up and down, and was used sometimes in reference to humorously mischievous spirits. The first non-Indians encountered by the early Dakotas were the French trappers who typically were quite emotional and demonstrative in their communications. This manner of verbal communication was not only humorous but bizarre to the early Dakotas who believed that the proper way of communicating was to talk slowly, calmly and to do nothing to upset the listener. To this day, traditional Dakotas still communicate in this manner.

Some years ago, the writer conducted a survey among forty elderly Indian people who were all over sixty-five years of age. These elderly people were asked what they thought the young Indian people should be taught in school. All of them said that the children needed to learn reading and arithmetic and typing, and in general, whatever they needed to know in order to make a living today. Finally, they were asked what was the *most important* thing of all that a child should learn in school. At this final question, all of these elderly people after a moment of quiet thought would respond, "The most important thing for them to learn is how to get along with one another."

It was already pointed out that these children were learning how to be peculiarly Indian, this "get along" value in their immediate and extended families at home. What was worrying the elderly Indians was that, having learned this type of behavior at home, the disquieting reports of their grandchildren's squabbles and fights with other students and even teachers seemed to indicate to them that something in that mysterious school climate was causing a breakdown in this most important type of behavior learned at home and expected of them. They were, in effect, saying, "We taught them this behavior at home; you should continue this same kind of teaching in school."

Had the elderly people only known, their worst misgivings were well founded about something being "wrong" in the school climate causing a breakdown in the expected Indian behavior of their grandchildren. The school, by promoting individual competition and singling individuals out for praise, thereby cutting the individual off from the group and subjecting him to the ridicule of the group, was teaching a value in direct contradiction to what they were learning at home.

Instead of beginning with the Indian child where he was as an Indian, the school began with him as though he were a little non-Indian in the suburbs with the typical Dick and Jane material for the non-Indian child. The school did not begin with and build up his Indian awareness (the only psychologically feasible way) because it did not bother to look into that which made up his Indian awareness or the Indian value system. In order for the school to have been truly an extension of the Indian home utilizing Indian values, the school would have had to make him aware (not teach) of his Indian values by making him aware that Indians work together as a group; when one person does well, the whole group profits and is praised and individual excellence is appreciated by the group because the whole group profits.

This value conflict between the student and the school is at the unconscious level and continues throughout the total process gradually eroding and destroying the Indian's original sense of prideful identity. By the time the average counselor receives an Indian client the school system has done its damage and the counselor's work is largely therapeutic.

Right in the beginning, the school makes one of its biggest mistakes by not extending the Indian home into the school in not making the Indian children aware of this important Indian value of working with and for the group as something peculiarly Indian. Because of their world view, as well as their historical experiences in the past, the Indians are aware of themselves as a part of and related to the total environment, including man. For this reason, they adjust themselves to the group as a living part to a living whole and the group works together as a whole.

Family Planning in an Exploding Population

John A. O'Brien

How are we to deal effectively with the problem of a population increasing with a speed unprecedented in history? It is especially acute in the underdeveloped countries where the population is exploding, if not like bombs, at least like giant firecrackers. This is the question confronting not only the USA.but also the other nations of the free world.

New developments and a more penetrating analysis of the pluralistic nature of the society in which we live offer well-founded hope for the co-operative action so desperately needed to solve this problem on both the national and international levels. Let us first examine the large area of agreement and see if the differences cannot be further narrowed without compromise of conscience.

Contrary to widespread belief, the Catholic Church does *not* forbid birth regulation. For any serious cause a married couple is exempt from the normal obligation of parenthood for a long time and even for the whole duration of married life. The method sanctioned is rhythm, the use of the infertile or safe period. If the currently available means for predicting or ascertaining the time of ovulation—taking the basal temperature, and the glucose test of the cervical mucus—are carefully employed, the method is estimated to achieve a high degree of reliability. Pope Pius XII expressed the hope that further research will increase still more its effectiveness.

Furthermore, the Church teaches that the primary end of marriage is not merely *procreation* but also the *education* of offspring. This means more than food, clothing and shelter: It means the ability to provide a suitable education and thus open to the child the cultural heritage of the race. In short, it means *responsible* parenthood. This is the note that is being sounded with increasing frequency and vigor by Catholic prelates, priests, educators and lay leaders.

This was the keynote sounded by Father William J. Gibbons, S.J., professor of sociology at Fordham University, at a meeting of the Catholic Sociological

An appeal for understanding, published simultaneously in *Ave Maria* and *Christian Century*, August, 1963. Copyright by John A. O'Brien, 1963. A Research Professor of Theology at the University of Notre Dame, Father O'Brien is the author of 15 books and numerous magazine articles. He is the editor of the book *Family Planning in an Exploding Population*, Hawthorne Books, Inc., New York, N.Y. The opinions expressed in this article reflect personal thinking on this highly controversial subject and he assumes full responsibility for any statement that may be open to possible misunderstanding.

Society in St. Louis in September, 1961. He declared that Catholics in the United States have been oversold on procreation and undereducated on the responsibilities it entails. He believes that too many Catholics think they are being virtuous if they merely refrain from using contraceptives. He points out that the size of the family "should take into account the physical and mental health of the parents, their economic condition, and the society in which they live. When you are faced with such problems as overcrowding, lack of work opportunities and the rest, you need to retreat."

Similarly Dr. Robert Odenwald, formerly professor of psychiatry at the Catholic University of America, points out that in the past too many Catholics have tended to follow, almost blindly, the biblical command to "increase and multiply." But in the light of the new knowledge and because of changing social and economic conditions, "the accent today is rightly placed on responsible parenthood."

"If cogent reasons indicate a limitation of family size," says Msgr. John A. Goodwine, theological censor for the New York Archdiocese, "there should be no difficulty in admitting that the avoidance of pregnancy would be within the bounds of reason and morality." He remarks that the significant change in Catholic thinking on family size that has taken place in the last dozen years "does not seem to be sufficiently understood."

Similar too is the note sounded by Dom Gregory Stevens, O.S.B., professor of moral theology at the Catholic University. Pointing out that the common notion that the Church favors "absolutely a high birth rate" is false, he says: "Indiscriminate procreation is no moral ideal but mere irresponsibility, for the family must make prudent provision for the future welfare of the children both spiritually and physically. The Church considers the primary goal of the natural institution of matrimony to be that of *responsible parenthood.*"

To help parents realize their responsibility, Dom Stevens points out that they "must take into account the present and *foreseeable* future conditions of society. This is demanded for the sake of the children themselves as well as for the common good which all are strictly bound to promote as a matter of what St. Thomas called general justice."

Equally concerned that married couples understand their responsibility in the light of a soaring population, Father Charles J. Corcoran, C.S.C., for many years professor of theology at Holy Cross College, Washington, D.C., warns: "It is unfortunate that in the debates on family limitation, many Catholics forget that the right use of marital rights implies more than the willingness to procreate a child. It implies not only the willingness but also the *ability* to provide for the child's material and spiritual welfare. Correctly understood, this grave responsibility should serve as a potent check on an undisciplined, even if biologically proper, use of sex."

Reflecting this new emphasis upon parental responsibility, Dr. John J. Kane, professor of sociology at the University of Notre Dame, states: "Recent and tremendous social changes in the fields of education, economics and family life place greater strains on American parents than they have perhaps ever faced in the past. Children's expectations have risen dramatically and parents' hopes of meeting such expectations are perhaps stronger than ever. All of this means that the very large family patterns typical of the early part of this century can no longer be realized by most parents if they hope to meet their *real responsibilities*. . . . Considerable thought will have to be given . . . to the practice of some type of family *limitation* in the majority of cases."

Equally explicit is the conclusion reached by Father John L. Thomas, S.J., sociologist of St. Louis University and a recognized authority on marriage and the family: "Granted present nuptiality rates, age at marriage, and advances in health care, no country can long make reasonable provision for its population increase unless a good percentage of its couples take some effective steps to *regulate* family size."

The stress placed by Catholic theologians, sociologists and psychiatrists in America in recent years is mirrored in the writings of their European counterparts. In a recent scholarly work, *Love and Control,* Leon-Joseph Cardinal Suenens, Archbishop of Malines, points out that conjugal love should be guided by reason and a clear consciousness of the duties of parenthood: Procreation should not be a matter of blind instinct. "One of the first and essential things to consider," he says, "when they [married couples] evaluate their circumstances in life is the *education* and *training* to give their children."

Father Stanislas de Lestapis, S.J., professor at the Catholic Institute of Paris and the Vatican's representative at the United Nations World Population Conference in Rome in 1954, says that "there is, in principle, a right, or better, a *duty,* to practice a form of *birth limitation* based on careful thought. . . . There is an optimum number for each family, and each family alone can judge what it is."

The Belgian demographer, Father Clement Mertens, S.J., of St. Albert College in Louvain, calls attention to the "increasing awareness among the leaders of the Church, and among theologians, moralists and others, of the problems which large families now have to face. And there is an increasing awareness of the problems countries have to face, where the population is increasing quickly." He acknowledges that instructions on birth regulation on the pastoral level is not without risks and difficulties.

Nevertheless, he points out: "Risks and difficulties do not justify inertia. . . It is the *duty* of the ecclesiastical authorities in each country to face the problem and see that competent laymen, especially in the best universities, proceed with research which will permit them to cope with different given situations, according to regions or social classes, and to adopt means which will reach a solution."

Probably no other country in Europe has felt so acutely the pressure of population as Holland. This is reflected in the candor, understanding and sympathy with which the Dutch Bishops have discussed the difficult problems facing married couples today. Speaking on a television program in April, 1963, Bishop William M. Bekkers of 's-Hertogenbosch explained that not everyone can reach at once the ideal in marital virtue.

"Those who have entered Christian matrimony," said Bishop Bekkers, "have received from God and under His blessing a mandate of life which is focused first on leading one life together in conjugal love and secondly on founding and building together a good family. Science and its discoveries have enabled man to regulate human reproduction. *The birth rate now falls within man's responsibility.* One can even say that birth regulation, which is quite different from [contraceptive] birth control, is a *normal* part of the total task of a married couple."

Bishop Bekkers then pointed out that *only* the married couple is in a position to determine the number of offspring they can properly rear and educate. This is within the competence of their conscience, and no outsider can interfere with their decision. A physican or a spiritual adviser must respect the private conscience.

Recognizing the imperfections of the rhythm system, the Bishop said: "Not even the rhythm method is without objections. For many people the rhythm method is a solution, but we also know that it causes *insuperable* difficulties for many others. We understand that there are situations where one cannot consider all Christian and human values at the same time. In that case the Church does not immediately think of egoism or luxury.

"She knows that married couples, in well-intentioned love for each other and for their families, sometimes take steps which cannot be considered right steps in the eyes of the Church. But the Church also knows that what one person can reach cannot always be reached by others. She wants to give room for a gradual, perhaps slow and imperfect growing, like that which is possible in all other areas of life − in charity, honesty and piety."

These scholars are but echoing the thoughts expressed by Pope Pius XII on the Feast of the Epiphany in 1957: "When the infant comes into the world, he must have a home to receive him − a home capable of providing him in good health − and to assist him in acquiring those faculties of mind and heart that will enable him to take his proper place in society when the time comes."

Similar is the emphasis placed by Protestant churches in recent years upon responsible parenthood. In the statement on *Responsible Parenthood* issued in 1961 by the National Council of Churches, responsible parenthood is described as weighing "the claims of procreation and the situation of the family in society. In determining the number and frequency of offspring the parents should give careful consideration to the following four factors:

"1) The right of the child to be wanted, loved, cared for, educated and trained in the 'discipline and instruction of the Lord' (Eph. 6:4). The rights of existing children to parental care have a proper claim. 2) The prospects for health of a future child, if medical and eugenic evidence seem negatively conclusive. 3) The health and welfare of the mother-wife, and the need for the spacing of children to safeguard them. 4) The social situation, when rapid population growth places dangerous pressures on the means of livelihood and endangers the social order."

The statement tells parents to remember "that having children is a venture in faith, requiring a measure of courage and confidence in God's goodness. Too cautious a reckoning of the costs may be as great an error as failure to lift the God-given power of procreation to the level of ethical decision."

Probably no religious faith places greater emphasis upon the responsibility of parenthood than Judaism. Reflecting this stress, Rabbi Albert M. Shulman, chairman of the Commission on Marriage, Family and the Home of the Central Conference of American Rabbis, says: "Parents have the serious obligation of regulating the size of their family so they will be able to provide properly for the health and education of their offspring. Procreation should not be a matter of blind instinct but of intelligent and careful planning. This is not only a social obligation but also a moral and religious one."

Re-echoing the note sounded by Jewish religious leaders, Rabbi David H. Wilce declares: "The concept of the sanctity of life is enhanced and the holiness of marriage is given a new dimension when parenthood is freely elected, when children are born wanted, and when family size is determined by conditions of health and well-being for the individual family and for society."

The factors listed in the statement of the National Council of Churches and of Jewish religious leaders are much the same as those which Catholic theologians and sociologists are likewise stressing in their description of responsible parenthood. Here then is a vast area of crucial and strategic importance, where Protestants, Catholics and Jews are in substantial agreement. Here they can work together, with each group following its conscience, to achieve the same important goal.

Here is a key which, if properly used, is capable of opening the door to constructive action in solving the population problem on the national and international levels. That key embodies the two crucial elements to make it work: the prudent *regulation* of births and the clear consciousness of the *responsibility* they entail, which is but another name for family planning.

Father John A. O'Brien has been involved in the dialogue on birth control and public policy for years in various publications ("Look," "The Saturday Evening Post," "Good Housekeeping"), and on the controversial CBS-TV program "Birth Control and the Law." A research professor of theology at the University of Notre Dame, Father O'Brien is the author of 15 books and numerous magazine articles. He is the editor of the book Family Planning in an Exploding Population, (New York, N.Y.; Hawthorne Books, Inc.).

Abortion — or Compulsory Pregnancy?

Garrett Hardin,

The problem of abortion is usually seen as one of justifying a particular surgical operation on the assumption that great social loss is incurred by it. This approach leads to intractable administrative problems: rape is in principle impossible to prove, the paternity of a child is always in doubt, the probability of defective embryos is generally low, and the socioeconomic predicament of the supplicant has little power to move the men who sit in judgment. These difficulties vanish when one substitutes for the problem of permissive abortion the inverse problem of compulsory pregnancy. The latter is a special case of compulsory servitude, which the Western world has agreed, in principle, has no valid justification. Unfortunately, state legislatures are now in a process of setting up systems for management of compulsory pregnancy. The experience of Scandinavia indicates that women do not accept bureaucratic management of their unwanted pregnancies; therefore we can confidently predict that the reform bills now going through our legislatures will have little effect on the practice of illegal abortion. Only the abolition of compulsory pregnancy will solve the erroneously conceived "abortion problem."

The year 1967 produced the first fissures in the dam that had prevented all change in the abortion-prohibition laws of the United States for three-quarters of a century. Two states adopted laws that allowed abortion in the "hardship cases" of rape, incest, and probability of a deformed child. A third approved the first two "indications," but not the last. All three took some note of the mental health of the pregnant woman, in varying language; how this language will be translated into practice remains to be seen. In almost two dozen other states, attempts to modify the laws were made but foundered at various stages in the legislative process. It is quite evident that the issue will continue to be a live one for many years to come.

The legislative turmoil was preceded and accompanied by a fast-growing popular literature. The word "abortion" has ceased to be a dirty word—which is a cultural advance. However, the *word* was so long under taboo that the ability to think about the *fact* seems to have suffered a sort of logical atrophy from

Reprinted with the author's permission from *Journal of Marriage and the Family*, Vol. XXX, No. 2, May 1968. Dr. Garrett Hardin is Professor of Biology at the University of California, Santa Barbara, California.

disuse. Popular articles, regardless of their conclusions, tend to be over-emotional and to take a moralistic rather than an operational view of the matter. Nits are picked, hairs split. It is quite clear that many of the authors are not at all clear what questions they are attacking.

It is axiomatic in science that progress hinges on asking the right question. Surprisingly, once the right question is asked the answer seems almost to tumble forth. That is a retrospective view; in prospect, it takes genuine (and mysterious) insight to see correctly into the brambles created by previous, ill-chosen verbalizations.

The abortion problem is, I think, a particularly neat example of a problem in which most of the difficulties are actually created by asking the wrong question. I submit further that once the right question is asked the whole untidy mess miraculously dissolves, leaving in its place a very simple public policy recommendation.

RAPE AS A JUSTIFICATION

The wrong question, the one almost invariably asked, is this: "How can we justify an abortion?" This assumes that there are weighty public reasons for encouraging pregnancies, or that abortions, per se, somehow threaten public peace. A direct examination of the legitimacy of these assumptions will be made later. For the present, let us pursue the question as asked and see what a morass it leads to.

Almost all the present legislative attempts take as their model a bill proposed by the American Law Institute which emphasizes three justifications for legal abortion: rape, incest, and the probability of a defective child. Whatever else may be said about this bill, it is clear that it affects only the periphery of the social problem. The Arden House Conference Committee (Mary Steichen Calderone (ed.), 1958) estimated the number of illegal abortions in the United States to be between 200,000 and 1,200,000 per year. A California legislator, Anthony C. Beilenson (Beilenson, 1966), has estimated that the American Law Institute bill (which he favors) would legalize not more than four per cent of the presently illegal abortions. Obviously, the "problem" of illegal abortion will be scarcely affected by the passage of the laws so far proposed in the United States.

I have calculated that the number of rape-induced pregnancies in the United States is about 800 per year (Hardin, 1967). The number is not large, but for the women raped the total number is irrelevant. What matters to her is that she be relieved of her unwanted burden. But a law which puts the burden of proof on her compels her to risk a second harrowing experience. How can she *prove* to the district attorney that she was raped? He could really know whether or not she gave consent only if he could get inside her mind; this he cannot do. Here is the philosopher's "egocentric predicament" that none of us can escape. In an effort to help the district attorney sustain the illusion that he can escape this predicament, a talented woman may put on a dramatic performance, with copious tears and other signs of anguish. But what if the raped woman is not an actress? What if her temperament is stoic? In its operation, the law will act against the interests of calm, undramatic women. Is that what we want? It is safe to say also that district attorneys will hear less favorably the pleas of poor women, the general assumption of middle-class agents being that the poor are less responsible in sex anyway (Rainwater, 1960). Is it to the interest of society that the poor bear more children, whether rape-engendered or not?

A wryly amusing difficulty has been raised with respect to rape. Suppose the woman is married and having regular intercourse with her husband. Suppose that following a rape by an unknown intruder she finds herself pregnant. Is she legally entitled to an abortion? How does she know whose child she is carrying anyway? If it is her husband's child, abortion is illegal. If she carries it to term, and if blood tests then exclude the husband as the father, as they would in a fraction of the cases, is the woman then entitled to a *delayed* abortion? But this is ridiculous: this is infanticide, which no one is proposing. Such is the bramble bush into which we are led by a *reluctant* consent for abortion in cases of rape.

HOW PROBABLE MUST DEFORMITY BE?

The majority of the public support abortion in cases of suspected deformity of the child (Rossi, 1966) just as they do in cases of rape. Again, however, if the burden of proof rests on the one who requests the operation, we encounter difficulties in administration. Between 80,000 and 160,000 defective children are born every year in the United States. The number stated depends on two important issues: (a) how severe a defect must be before it is counted as such and (b) whether or not one counts as birth defects those defects that are not *detected* until later. (Deafness and various other defects produced by fetal rubella may not be detected until a year or so after birth.) However many defective infants there may be, what is the prospect of detecting them before birth?

The sad answer is: the prospects are poor. A small percentage can be picked up by microscopic examination of tissues of the fetus. But "amniocentesis"—the form of biopsy required to procure such tissues—is itself somewhat dangerous to both mother and fetus; most abnormalities will not be detectable by a microscopic examination of the fetal cells; and 96 to 98 per cent of all fetuses are normal anyway. All these considerations are a contra-indication of routine amniocentesis.

When experience indicates that the probability of a deformed fetus is above the "background level" of 2 to 4 per cent, is abortion justified? At what level? 10 per cent? 50? 80? Or only at 100 per cent? Suppose a particular medical history indicates a probability of 20 per cent that the baby will be defective. If we routinely abort such cases, it is undeniable that four normal fetuses will be destroyed for every one abnormal. Those who assume that a fetus is an object of high value are appalled at this "wastage." Not uncommonly they ask, "Why not wait until the baby is born and then suffocate those that are deformed?" Such a question is unquestionably rhetoric and sardonic; if serious, it implies that infanticide has no more emotional meaning to a woman than abortion, an assumption that is surely contrary to fact.

SHOULD THE FATHER HAVE RIGHTS?

Men who are willing to see abortion-prohibition laws relaxed somewhat, but not completely, frequently raise a question about the "rights" of the father. Should we allow a woman to make a unilateral decision for an abortion? Should not her husband have a say in the matter? (After all, he contributed just as many chromosomes to the fetus as she.)

I do not know what weight to give this objection. I have encountered it repeatedly in the discussion section following a public meeting. It is clear that some men are disturbed at finding themselves powerless in such a situation and want the law to give them some power of decision.

Yet powerless men are—and it is nature that has made them so. If we give the father a right of veto in abortion decisions, the wife has a very simple reply to her husband: "I'm sorry, dear, I wasn't going to tell you this, but you've forced my hand. This is not your child." With such a statement she could always deny her husband's right to decide.

Why husbands should demand power in such matters is a fit subject for depth analysis. In the absence of such, perhaps the best thing we can say to men who are "hung up" on this issue is this: "Do you really want to live for another eight months with a woman whom you are compelling to be pregnant against her will?"

Or, in terms of public policy, do we want to pass laws which give men the right to compel their wives to be pregnant? Psychologically, such compulsion is akin to rape. Is it in the public interest to encourage rape?

"SOCIO-ECONOMIC"—AN ANEMIC PHRASE

The question "How can we justify an abortion?" proves least efficient in solving the real problems of this world when we try to evaluate what are usually called "socio-economic indications." The hardship cases — rape, incest, probability of a deformed child — have been amply publicized, and as a result the majority of the public accepts them as valid indicators; but hardship cases constitute only a few per cent of the need. By contrast, if a woman has more children than she feels she can handle, or if her children are coming too close together, there is little public sympathy for her plight. A poll (Rossi, 1966) conducted by the National Opinion Research Center in December, 1965, showed that only 15 per cent of the respondents replied "Yes" to this question: "Please tell me whether or not you think it should be possible for a pregnant woman to obtain a legal abortion if she is married and does not want any more children." Yet this indication, which received the lowest rate of approval, accounts for the vast majority of instances in which women want—and illegally get—relief from unwanted pregnancy.

There is a marked discrepancy between the magnitude of the need and the degree of public sympathy. Part of the reason for this discrepancy is attributable to the emotional impact of the words used to describe the need. "Rape," "incest," "deformed child"—these words are rich in emotional connotations. "Socio-economic indications" is a pale bit of jargon, suggesting at best that the abortion is wanted because the woman lives by culpably materialistic standards. "Socio-economic indications" tugs at no one's heartstrings; the hyphenated abomination hides the human reality to which it obliquely refers. To show the sort of human problem to which this label may be attached, let me quote a letter I received from one woman. (The story is unique, but it is one of a large class of similar true stories.)

I had an illegal abortion 2½ years ago. I left my church because of the guilt I felt. I had six children when my husband left me to live with another woman. We weren't divorced and I went to work to help support them. When he would come to visit the children he would sometimes stay after they were asleep. I became pregnant. When I told my husband, and asked him to please come back, he informed me that the woman he was living with was five months pregnant and ill, and that he couldn't leave her—not at that time anyway.

I got the name of a doctor in San Francisco from a Dr. friend who was visiting here from there. This Dr. (Ob. and Gyn.) had a good legitimate practice in the main part of the city and was a kindly, compassionate man who believes as you do, that it is better for everyone not to bring an unwanted child into the world.

It was over before I knew it. I thought I was just having an examination at the time. He even tried to make me not feel guilty by telling me that the long automobile trip had already started a spontaneous abortion. He charged me $25. That was on Fri. and on Mon. I was back at work. I never suffered any ill from it.

The other woman's child died shortly after birth and six months later my husband asked if he could come back. We don't have a perfect marriage but my children have a father. My being able to work has helped us out of a deep financial debt. I shall always remember the sympathy I received from that Dr. and wish there were more like him with the courage to do what they believe is right.

Her operation was illegal, and would be illegal under most of the "reform" legislation now being proposed, if interpreted strictly. Fortunately, some physicians are willing to indulge in more liberal interpretations, but they make these interpretations not on medical grounds, in the strict sense, but on social and economic grounds. Understandably, many physicians are unwilling to venture so far from the secure base of pure physical medicine. As one Catholic physician put it:

> Can the patient afford to have another child? Will the older children have sufficient educational opportunities if their parents have another child? Aren't two, three or four children enough? I am afraid such statements are frequently made in the discussion of a proposed therapeutic abortion. (But) we should be doctors of medicine, not socio-economic prophets (Calderone [ed.], 1958).

To this a non-Catholic physician added: "I sometimes wish I were an obstetrician in a Catholic hospital so that I would not have to make any of these decisions. The only position to take in which I would have no misgivings is to do no interruptions at all (Calderone [ed.], 1958).

WHO WANTS COMPULSORY PREGNANCY?

The question "How can we justify an abortion?" plainly leads to great difficulties. It is operationally unmanageable; it leads to inconsistencies in practice and inequities by any moral standard. All these can be completely avoided if we ask the right question, namely: *"How can we justify compulsory pregnancy?"*

By casting the problem in this form, we call attention to its relationship to the slavery issue. Somewhat more than a century ago men in the Western world asked the question: "How can we justify compulsory servitude?" and came up with the answer: *"By no means whatever."* Is the answer any different to the related question: "How can we justify compulsory pregnancy?" Certainly pregnancy is a form of servitude; if continued to term it results in parenthood, which is also a kind of servitude, to be continued for the best years of a woman's life. It is difficult to see how it can be argued that this kind of servitude will be more productive of social good if it is compulsory rather than voluntary. A study (Horssman and Thuwe, 1966) made of Swedish children born when their mothers were refused the abortions they had requested showed that unwanted children, as compared with their controls, as they grew up were more often picked up for drunkenness, or antisocial or criminal behavior; they received less education; they received more psychiatric care; and they were more often exempted from military service by reason of defect. Moreover, the females in the group married earlier and had children earlier, thus no doubt tending to create a vicious circle of poorly tended children who in their turn would produce more poorly tended children. How then does society gain by increasing the number of unwanted children? No one has volunteered an answer to this question.

Of course if there were a shortage of children, then society might say that it needs all the children it can get—unwanted or not. But I am unaware of any recent rumors of a shortage of children.

ALTERNATIVES: TRUE AND FALSE

The end result of an abortion—the elimination of an unwanted fetus—is surely good. But is the act itself somehow damaging? For several generations it was widely believed that abortion was intrinsically dangerous, either physically or psychologically. It is now very clear that the widespread belief is quite unjustified. The evidence for this statement is found in a bulky literature which has been summarized in Lawrence Lader's Abortion (Lader, 1966) and the collection of essays brought together by Alan Guttmacher (Guttmacher, 1967).

In tackling questions of this sort, it is imperative that we identify correctly the alternatives facing us. (All moral and practical problems involve a comparison of alternative actions). Many of the arguments of the prohibitionists implicitly assume that the alternatives facing the woman are these:

abortion — no abortion

This is false. A person can never do nothing. The pregnant woman is going to do something, whether she wishes to or not. (She cannot roll time backward and live her life over.)

People often ask: "Isn't contraception better than abortion?" Implied by this question are these alternatives:

abortion — contraception

But these are not the alternatives that face the woman who asks to be aborted. She *is* pregnant. She cannot roll time backward and use contraception more successfully than she did before. Contraceptives are never foolproof anyway. It is commonly accepted that the failure rate of our best contraceptive, the "pill," is around one percent, i.e. one failure per hundred woman-years of use. I have earlier shown (Hardin, 1967) that this failure rate produces about a quarter of a million unwanted pregnancies a year in the United States. Abortion is not so much an alternative to contraception as it is a subsidiary method of birth control, to be used when the primary method fails—as it often does.

The woman *is* pregnant: this is the base level at which the moral decision begins. If she is pregnant against her will, does it matter to society whether or not she was careless or unskillful in her use of contraception? In any case, she is threatening society with an unwanted child, for which society will pay dearly. The real alternatives facing the woman (and society) are clearly these:

abortion — compulsory pregnancy

When we recognize that these are the real, operational alternatives, the false problems created by pseudo-alternatives vanish.

IS POTENTIAL VALUE VALUABLE?

Only one weighty objection to abortion remains to be discussed, and this is the question of "loss." When a fetus is destroyed, has something valuable been destroyed? The fetus has the potentiality of becoming a human being. A human being is valuable. Therefore is not the fetus of equal value? This question must be answered.

It can be answered, but not briefly. What does the embryo receive from its parents that might be of value? There are only three possibilities: substance, energy, and information. As for the substance in the fertilized egg, it is not remarkable: merely the sort of thing one might find in any piece of meat, human or animal, and there is very little of it—only one and a half micrograms, which is about a half of a billionth of an ounce. The energy content of this tiny amount of material is likewise negligible. As the zygote develops into an embryo, both its substance and its energy content increase (at the expense of the mother); but this is not a very important matter—even an adult, viewed from this standpoint, is only a hundred and fifty pounds of meat!

Clearly, the humanly significant thing that is contributed to the zygote by the parents is the information that "tells" the fertilized egg how to develop into a human being. This information is in the form of a chemical tape called "DNA," a double set of two chemical super-molecules each of which has about three billion "spots" that can be coded with any one of four different possibilities, symbolized by A, T, G, and C. (For comparison, the Morse code offers three possibilities in coding: dot, dash, and space.) It is the particular sequence of these four chemical possibilities in the DNA that directs the zygote in its development into a human being. The DNA constitutes the information needed to produce a valuable human being. The question is: is this information precious? I have argued elsewhere (Hardin, 1967) that it is not:

> Consider the case of a man who is about to begin to build a $50,000 house. As he stands on the site looking at the blueprints a practical joker comes along and sets fire to the blueprints. The question is: can the owner go to the law and collect $50,000 for his lost blueprints? The answer is obvious: since another set of blueprints can be produced for the cost of only a few dollars, that is all they are worth. (A court might award a bit more for the loss of the owner's time, but that is a minor matter.) The moral: *a non-unique copy of information that specifies a valuable structure is itself almost valueless.*
>
> This principle is precisely applicable to the moral problem of abortion. The zygote, which contains the complete specification of a valuable human being, is not a human being, and is almost

valueless. . . . The early stages of an individual fetus have had very little human effort invested in them; they are of very little worth. The loss occasioned by an abortion is independent of whether the abortion is spontaneous or induced. (Just as the loss incurred by the burning of a set of blueprints is independent of whether the causal agent was lightning or an arsonist.)

A set of blueprints is not a house; the DNA of a zygote is not a human being. The analogy is singularly exact, though there are two respects in which it is deficient. These respects are interesting rather than important. First, we have the remarkable fact that the blueprints of the zygote are constantly replicated and incorporated in every cell of the human body. This is interesting, but it has no moral significance. There is no moral obligation to conserve DNA—if there were, no man would be allowed to brush his teeth and gums, for in this brutal operation hundreds of sets of DNA are destroyed daily.

The other anomaly of the human information problem is connected with the fact that the information that is destroyed in an aborted embryo *is* unique (unlike the house blueprints). But it is unique in a way that is without moral significance. A favorite argument of abortion-prohibitionists is this: "What if Beethoven's mother had had an abortion?" The question moves us; but when we think it over we realize we can just as relevantly ask: "What if Hitler's mother had had an abortion?" Each conceptus is unique, but not in any way that has a moral consequence. The *expected* potential value of each aborted child is exactly that of the average child born. It is meaningless to say that humanity loses when a *particular* child is not born, or is not conceived. A human female, at birth, has about 30,000 eggs in her ovaries. If she bears only 3 children in her lifetime, is there any meaningful sense in which we can say that mankind has suffered a loss in those other 29,997 fruitless eggs? (Yet one of them might have been a super-Beethoven!)

People who worry about the moral danger of abortion do so because they think of the fetus as a human being, hence equate feticide with murder. Whether the fetus is or is not a human being is a matter of definition, not fact; and we can define any way we wish. In terms of the human problem involved, it would be unwise to define the fetus as human (hence tactically unwise ever to refer to the fetus as an "unborn child"). Analysis based on the deepest insights of molecular biology indicates the wisdom of sharply distinguishing the information for a valuable structure from the completed structure itself. It is interesting, and gratifying, to note that this modern insight is completely congruent with common law governing the disposal of dead fetuses. Abortion-prohibitionists generally insist that abortion is murder, and that an embryo is a person; but no state or nation, so far as I know, requires the dead fetus to be treated like a dead person. Although all of the states in the United States severely limit what can be done with a dead human body, no cognizance is taken of dead fetuses up to about five months' prenatal life. The early fetus may, with impunity, be flushed down the toilet or thrown out with the garbage—which shows that we never have regarded it as a human being. Scientific analysis confirms what we have always known.

THE MANAGEMENT OF COMPULSORY PREGNANCY

What is the future of compulsory pregnancy? The immediate future is not hopeful. Far too many medical people misconceive the real problem. One physician has written:

> Might not a practical, workable solution to this most difficult problem be found by setting up, in every hospital, an abortion committee, comprising a specialist in obstetrics and gynecology, a psychiatrist, and a clergyman or priest? The patient and her husband—if any—would meet with these men who would do all in their power to persuade the woman not to undergo the abortion. (I have found that the promise of a postpartum sterilization will frequently enable even married women with all the children they can care for to accept this one more, final pregnancy.) If, however, the committee members fail to change the woman's mind, they can make it very clear that they disapprove of the abortion, but prefer that it be safely done in a hospital rather than bungled in a basement somewhere (Wood, 1967).

What this author has in mind is plainly not a system of legalizing abortion but a system of managing compulsory pregnancy. It is this philosophy which governs pregnancies in the Scandinavian countries (Smith, 1967), where the experience of a full generation of women has shown that women do not want their pregnancies to be managed by the state. Illegal abortions have remained at a high level in these countries, and recent years have seen the development of a considerable female tourist trade to Poland, where abortions are easy to obtain. Unfortunately, American legislatures are now proposing to follow the provably unworkable system of Scandinavia.

The drift down this erroneous path is not wholly innocent. Abortion-prohibitionists are showing signs of recognizing "legalization" along Scandinavian lines as one more roadblock that can be thrown in the way of the abolition of compulsory pregnancy. To cite an example: on February 9, 1967, the *Courier,* a publication of the Winona, Minnesota Diocese, urged that Catholics support a reform law based on the American Law Institute model, because the passage of such a law would "take a lot of steam out of the abortion advocate's argument" and would "defeat a creeping abortionism of disastrous importance" (Anonymous, 1967).

Wherever a Scandinavian or American Law Institute type of bill is passed, it is probable that cautious legislators will then urge a moratorium of several years while the results of the new law are being assessed (though they are easily predictable from the Scandinavian experience). As Lord Morley once said: "Small reforms are the worst enemies of great reforms." Because of the backwardness of education in these matters, caused by the long taboo under which the subject of abortion labored, it seems highly likely that our present system of compulsory pregnancy will continue substantially without change until the true nature of the alternatives facing us is more widely recognized.

Dos and Don'ts for a Tomorrow

Lonna E. Reinecke and Donald R. Scoby

INTRODUCTION

If people feel sincere concern about the destruction of the environment and wish to become active in shaping a future that may allow the survival of man and other forms for some time to come, there are things to be done, attitudes to adopt, and most important, things not to be done. It takes a well-developed maturity to reduce one's life style in the face of apparent affluence, and it takes diligence, stress and time to do the ecologically better but harder and more time-consuming thing when those about you do not. But "martyrdom" is not the goal—influencing others to de-escalate life styles is. To aid you in offering alternative life styles to others and as a reminder to you, the following list is presented. It should be obvious that this list of dos and don'ts could go on indefinitely. The object however, is to "prime the pump" after which the list can be improved and added to in ways to fit individuals.

This compilation includes selections from Stony Brook-Millstone Watersheds Association, P.O. Box 171, Pennington, N.J. 08534, ideas and items from numerous other sources, as well as our own contributions.

Attitudes to develop:

Improve your style of living to make it more compatible with a good environment. Don't just talk about it.

Worry about long term accumulative effects of countless chemicals that are thrown into our environment to maintain our current high life style. Do what you can to reduce them.

Instill in your children the desperate need for understanding and caring for our environment and set a good example yourself.

Redefine the standard concept of progress and success so that future generations might not make the same mistakes.

Consider any modern man-made product more than a potential danger to the environment until proven innocent.

Keep informed on new developments in ecology research. Educate your family as well as yourself.

Written for this volume. Lonna E. Reinecke is a graduate student in entomology at North Dakota State University, Fargo, North Dakota.

Be willing to pay more taxes to finance the fight against pollution.

Urge that money be spent on biological control of pests rather than on the use of pesticides. Be willing to put up with some pests.

Prepare for a no-growth economy, no-growth GNP, no-growth cities, no-growth nation, and a no-growth population. These supposedly "bad" things represent a needed steady-state situation.

Do not begrudge the loss of goof-off time when doing without a time-saving luxury.

Do not equate reduction or avoidance of physical labor to success. You are probably polluting the environment and lowering your state of health if you do.

Make Christmas a religious holiday—not an indulgent buy-in.

Do you really need that electric knife, electric scissors, electric toothbrush, electric mixer, electric shaver, electric can-opener, electric broom, electric manicuring set, electric hair-dryer, etc?

Take pride in the fact that you do not have an automatic dishwasher, clothes dryer, etc.

In spite of what commercials tell you, your clothes don't need to be the whitest white and fragrant—only reasonably clean.

Object to public commercials pushing products directly and indirectly destructive to the environment—also those directly or indirectly advocating large families or that you need things—new things, bigger things, better things, which you don't.

An effort should be made to deglamorize the automobile—cars should be low-powered, utilitarian and long-lasting.

Support and invest in companies that clean up and recycle.

Industry must include in its price the cost to the environment. We must know the real cost of consumables. We should pay as we go.

Be willing to pay more for products which have been developed with good environmental precautions. Avoid the cheaper but more detrimental products.

There is a link between population size and affluence—the greater the general affluence desired, the less population can be supported and vice versa.

Remember, a larger population means more housing developments, more autos, and more congestion, which in turn means higher taxes for schools and other facilities in our stressed environment.

Consider laws that would fix the limits of cities as they now stand so that open land not already covered with concrete will be preserved. Builders will have to make better use of land already in use.

Stop at two children or if too late, encourage others to do so.

Look for ways to change the burial fetishes practised by the undertakers' business and supported by social attitudes.

Talk to your friends, neighbors. Spread your knowledge around. Help others to understand "the Problem."

Stifle that inner voice that says this little bit won't hurt. Multiply it by 203,000,000.

Even a small excess of cleaning products makes a difference. Assume 500,000 families used an ounce more detergent per day to wash dishes than needed. This adds 11,680,000 pounds per year to the pollution burden.

Consider small farming a desirable, wholesome vocation. Support legislation that will encourage and maintain the small farm.

Make some aspect of pollution part of your career. There are opportunities for business men in pollution control: developing plants, devices, parts, etc; installing them; constructing them; servicing.

This one has been around, but is one of the best. Make it do. Use it up. Do without.

Politics to encourage:

Keep the addresses of your representatives handy. Write them and send telegrams (request delivery) to let them know of your attitude on legislation that concerns our environment.

Encourage politicians to act in favor of our environment.

Demand that politicians make environmental action a strong plank in their political platform.

Discourage the building of unnecessary highways, dams, factories, etc.

Use your voting power to support ecology-minded congressmen and legislation.

Let your representative know they have your support when confronted by strong anti-environmental interests.

Write:

> President Richard M. Nixon
> The White House
> 1600 Pennsylvania Avenue
> Washington, D.C. 20500.

> The Honorable Russell Train
> Chairman, White House Council on Environmental Quality
> 1600 Pennsylvania Avenue
> Washington, D.C. 20500.

> The Honorable Rogers C. B. Morton
> Secretary of the Interior
> C Street at 18th and 19th Streets N.W.
> Washington, D.C. 20240.

on the following:

a. Enforcement of current water pollution laws. Passage of new, stronger laws and stricter fines.

b. Prohibition of dumping raw sewage, oil, herbicides, and garbage in all bodies of water, particularly the ocean.

c. State your opposition to the size of the super oil tankers.

d. Prohibition of oil drilling along the Atlantic Coast.

Push for compulsory conservation education (teachers, adults, and youths) in public schools.

Set up telephone trees to alert people during local and national conservation legislative crises.

Encourage tax incentives to business men to encourage them to curb pollution.

Exert pressure on high factory officials to clean up.

Write: state officials, local newspapers and Board of Health about pollution infringements. (Write original letters, not form letters.)

Write your state and local officials about evidence of pollution in your area.

If there is a bond issue for a waste treatment plant, air clean-up etc., vote for it.

Support municipal open space and conservation commissions. Open space in the long run saves money.

Prepare and pass out leaflets on conservation issues such as local pollution problems, misuse of land.

Voice your support for mass transit rail systems rather than more highways and airports.

Promote world-wide co-operation on mutual problems—such as saving the oceans, clean atmosphere, radiation pollution, etc.

Make a blacklist of people, companies, and organizations impeding pollution control.

Things to stop:

Don't try to keep up with the Joneses.

Many products in our society are not necessary to maintain a good life—recognize these, don't use them.

Complain to store managers if such items as bananas, cucumbers, and peppers are unnecessarily plastic wrapped. Buy unwrapped produce where you can.

Don't use paper towels, cups, diapers, napkins, kleenex, etc. Use articles of reusable material.

Don't use aluminum wrap or cans unless your community collects and recycles them.

Don't purchase non-domesticated furs and hides, i.e. alligator shoes, etc.

Don't buy excess clothes just to keep in fashion.

Don't use full amounts listed on detergent boxes for dishwashing and clothes washing.

Don't burn it.

Don't smoke.

Don't use mercury-treated seeds, paints, cosmetics, etc.

Don't pollute your mind with drugs.

Don't use fertilizer containing pesticides. They poison the soil along with your crab grass, dandelions, etc.

Don't use inorganic fertilizers—run-off following rain pollutes our streams and water table. (Use natural organic fertilizer derived from plants and animals.)

Don't put heavy paper, clothes, rags, disposable diapers, grease, solvents, into water systems.

Don't flush garbage down sink disposals—it adds to the already heavy organic load at the disposal plant.

Don't waste water on lawns. Only water vegetables and trees during dry spells.

Don't flush unnecessarily.

Don't leave your car engine running.

Don't support the SST or similar ventures.

Don't fly or drive—take a train or bus.

If you have a snowmobile or any land rover type vehicle, do not use it in the wilderness. If you don't have one, don't get one.

Never litter. Beverage can rings are even damaging when they are tossed in the water where fish strike the shiny objects and die after ingesting them. Also bad for wildlife are film scraps from the handy camera—these discards kill fish and other wildlife.

Things to start:

Plant trees, for they make the summer cooler, the winter not so cold, the air cleaner, the soil stay put, the water run off slower, the wildlife stay and the ugliness disappear.

Shovel snow by hand or hire someone to do it that way. It provides a job (or exercise for you), cuts noise pollution, cuts production pollution, and cuts fuel pollution.

Get a new or used hand lawn mower and use it.

Try to remember that you do not need and should not have a snowmobile or land rover and neither should our dwindling wilderness.

Grow your own vegetables in a home garden, and use organic methods.

Can your own fruits and vegetables—at least until commercial canning industry uses reusable containers and uncontaminated food.

Use sand instead of chemicals on icy walk ways.

Use a fly swatter instead of a pesticide.

Help support a wildlife preserve instead of keeping a pet.

Walk or bike.

Take a city bus.

Organize neighborhood car pools for shopping, transportation to work, and transportation to schools.

Use and encourage the use of public transportation systems.

Keep your car in good running condition. It will get more mileage and last longer.

Buy a used car instead of a new car and try to make it a small one.

Be willing to pay for the slightly more expensive lead-free or low-lead gasolines.

Move to a smaller house—it will require less heat, electricity, furniture, etc.

Close off rooms you're not using in winter or summer to cut down on fuel for heating or cooling.

Make certain doors and windows are tight so less fuel will be necessary.

Use less electricity, turn down your thermostat, and cut out unnecessary lights.

Turn down your air conditioner—don't use at all if possible. If you don't have one, don't get one. Draw shades on south and west windows in summer to keep heat out of house and plant trees.

Turn off radio and TV when not listening or watching.

Adopt if you want more children.

Promote separate recreation areas for people who like crowds, others who like solitude. Urge that strip-mined areas be turned into recreation areas, sanitary landfills and rock quarries.

Promote legislation to assure the restoration of areas that will be mined in the future.

Organize or join a clean-up group to clean up an area or a stream.

If you need a boat, get a canoe or sailboat.

See that your library has books on conservation, population, environment, etc.

Promote library displays (school, college, public) on environmental problems.

Encourage industry in every way you can to make durable products. It costs more to make a poor product several times than one good long-lasting unit.

Try to support small industry rather than the giants, thus reducing the concentration of pollution.

Use local products of food, etc. to cut down on national transportation.

Use a soap shaving mug rather than an aerosol container. The difference should be obvious.

Wash clothes in washing soda (such as Arm and Hammer) and biodegradable soap (such as Ivory Snow). Together they clean as well as detergents. Yellowing can be prevented by stripping clothes of detergent residue by washing in 4 TBS washing soda to a tub of hot water the first time that washing is done with soap.

If you must use detergents obtain those low in phosphates and not containing enzymes. Phosphates help algae and weeds grow at an unnaturally high rate; the decomposition which follows reduces the oxygen level, killing off other life forms. Remember some pollution is normal, it is the fantastic rate that man has induced which causes the problem.

Obtain a current list of detergents and other products that assesses the type and quantities of detrimental components. Encourage others to shop with this information available.

Hang out your laundry in good weather and use lines in your basement in bad weather.

Wash dishes and/or run your dishwasher once a day.

Use untreated fabrics, Permanent pressed fabrics are produced with chemicals we don't need in our environment.

Cut back on the use of all paper products such as napkins, plates, cups, etc. Use only those that are white, thereby reducing the amount of dye being placed in our water.

Use rags or sponges to wipe up spills instead of paper towels.

Keep rags and handkerchiefs handy—perhaps in a small nice-looking box— where you now have your paper towels and other tissues. You grab for what's handiest.

Use wax paper and cellophane instead of plastics and foils.

If you continue to buy plastic film and aluminum wrap products, reuse them over and over.

Save—Christmas wrappings, string, etc.

Use a market basket or tote bag instead of disposable paper or plastic sacks.

Buy products which conserve on wrappings—you pay for wrappings.

Reduce your subscriptions to magazines. Use the public library and share current printed matter with friends.

A neighbor can share a newspaper with you—especially in apartment buildings.

Give newspapers and clean cardboard boxes to the Salvation Army or other recycling agency.

Use white toilet tissue—dyes pollute.

Avoid plastics—buy wooden or cloth toys, ceramic or glass mixing bowls, cloth coats, wood and cloth furniture, etc.

Always look for ways of reducing your trash volume below the national average of over 5 lbs per person per day.

Only buy beverages in returnable bottles. Advocate returnable bottles for other products.

Urge the use of Tin-Free Steel (TFS) cans for both foods and beverages (they're more easily recycled).

Be willing to separate paper, cans, glass, garbage, and yard litter when recycling processes are available.

Encourage recycling centers for paper, aluminum, etc.

Make compost heaps (individual and community).

Resist catering to style makers in clothing, cosmetics, furniture, cars, etc. Style changes encourage waste.

Help "the Joneses" overcome their compulsion to over-indulge.

Miscellaneous:

Plant trees as they reduce noise, are aesthetically pleasing to look at, absorb carbon dioxide, produce oxygen, screen dust, provide habitat for wildlife. The evapotranspiration from one well-watered tree releases a cooling effect of over one million BTU's per day—the equivalent of 10 room size air conditioners operating 20 hours a day.

Do not use long-lived pesticides, chlorinated hydrocarbons, such as DDT, dieldrin, aldrin, endrin, heptachlor, chlordane, lindane.

Short-lived pesticides such as malathion, rotenone, Off are available; however, their breakdown products are not fully understood and may be extremely dangerous to the environment.

Voice objection to your Board of Health about mass spraying by mosquito control commissions, particularly near areas such as lakes, ponds, marshes, etc. Introduce lady bugs, gambusia (mosquito-eating fish), praying mantis, and dragonflies in such areas.

Reduce the amount of water you pollute by reducing the amount of water you use. Use less in your bath—you can bathe effectively in less than a bucketful of water. Wash and rinse dishes in a pan full of water instead of under running water. Get a suds saver on your automatic washer or better use the old-fashioned wringer type where wash and rinse water are used over and over.

Encourage co-operation between neighbors in the use of home equipment. One object shared by 2 families is better than needless duplication.

Promote regional sewage disposal system, with tertiary treatment or its equivalent.

State your opposition to junk mail and refuse to accept it.

Determine ways to reduce the level of noise produced by man.

Keep muffler in good repair.

Do not sound horn except in emergencies.

Check community ordinances governing noise. Does it cover construction equipment, trucks, bulldozers, motorcycles?

Remember that power saws, snowmobiles, and lawn mowers are prime sources of noise.

Staff conservation booths at fairs.

Show movies available from various sources, including almost any conservation or population organization.

Schedule lectures on environmental problems for college and professional clubs, social and church organizations.

Some organizations to join:

Zero Population Growth, Inc.
Los Altos, California 94022.

Sierra Club
1050 Mills Tower
San Francisco, Calif. 94104.

Friends of the Earth
30 East 42nd St.
New York, N.Y. 10017.

National Wildlife Federation
1412 16th St. N.W.
Washington, D.C. 20005.

Nature Conservancy
1522 K Street, N.W.
Washington, D.C. 20005.

National Audubon Society
1130 Fifth Avenue
New York, N.Y. 10029.

The Wilderness Society
729 Fifteen Street, N.W.
Washington, D.C. 20005.

Personal Convictions

Introduction

Our religious humanitarianism, *as we now practice it,* is one of the main contributors to our potential destruction. This may seem to be an especially heretical statement; however, far too often our humanitarian concerns are geared to solve the problems faced by man thousands of years ago and are only adding to present problems. Since we place such a "halo of good" around death control and a "halo of bad" around birth control, we are setting the stage for the eventual starvation and illness of millions. Death control is not bad (although we do, in many cases, take the dignity out of dying); however, it is a disaster when in our pious attitude we cannot insist on birth control measures to allow the population to live within the natural limits of the carrying capacity of the area.

This final section is not a scientific presentation but one where religious convictions and ecological principles have been allowed to ferment in the minds of the individual contributors. Therefore, the thoughts expressed are "common sense" to the authors while being highly controversial and (perhaps) offensive to others with a different set of background experiences. It should again be emphasized, however, that these background experiences are all man-made and not divinely dictated.

Ecology, God and Me

J. Frank Cassel

The stench on the Red River of the North was a "more-than-usual" stench. The stench of rotting fish rose above the usual odors. The flow rate of the river was the lowest in years and its oxygen content was even lower. Lacking this essential to life, death resulted. Do these fish prophecy the fate of man in our deteriorating world? Many are sure they do—and before long!

"The heavens declare the glory of God and the firmament shows his handiwork" (Psalm 19: 1). That smog? What God is this? In the seriousness of our plight, the Christian, especially since he is being blamed by many for the state of things, must give thought to himself in relation to Nature and its God.

Several years ago Lynn White (1967), a historian, proclaimed in a much-quoted speech that the historical roots of our ecological crisis lie in the Judeo-Christian concept of man's right to dominate the earth. White, like many other Christians, sees God as transcendent and man as exploiting Nature by God's command (Genesis 1: 28). He suggests that the mitigation of the crisis can be achieved only if man sees himself as an integral part of nature—the brother of all other organisms. Strangely enough Francis Shaeffer (1970) in his recent book on the Christian view of Ecology, though being somewhat critical of White, ends in essential agreement with him. The thesis of this paper is that neither White nor Shaeffer understand either the essential nature of man nor of God. In their effort to return man to Nature, it seems to me, they do not even recognize the nature of Nature.

THE NATURE OF NATURE

"The heavens declare the glory of God ..." (Psalm 19: 1) "I will lift my eyes unto the hills from whence cometh my help ..." (Psalm 121: 1) " ... the invisible attributes of God ... have been plainly discernable through the things which he has made and which are commonly seen and known" (Romans 1: 19). Christ is "both the first principle and the upholding principle of the whole scheme of creation" (Colossians 1: 17). What is this creation through which we can know God—its Creator?

Written for this volume. Dr. J. Frank Cassel is Professor of Zoology at North Dakota State University, Fargo, North Dakota.

We talk about the ecosystem and trace the energy of the sun as it powers the structure of nature. Through photosynthesis green plants provide themselves and animals with food for reconversion to energy. Some animals feed on plants, some on other animals, and some like you and me on both. Organisms occur at different places in many complex aggregations all of which are continually converting and reconverting energy as it "flows" through the system. The study of these astounding and intricate interrelationships with the *web of life* is *ecology*.

Dare we say that here we see an energizing God, a God of intricate precision, and of astounding variety, an integrating God, a God at once of parsimony and of abundance who "conserves" energy as He makes it productive?

But how is energy flow in the ecosystem sustained? Through *eating* and *being eaten*. For some to live, some must die! Do we say then that God is a God of destruction? Or is He a God who brings life out of death? Do we condemn the cow for eating grass, or the cat for eating mice?

THE NATURE OF MAN

By the same token, I doubt that we can reasonably say that the roots of blame for destruction of an aspen grove by a beaver dam lies in the beaver's religious heritage. The nature of the species called "beaver" is to build dams in which he builds his lodge, stores his food and on which he floats the aspen cuttings which he uses for both. Just so, as Richard Wright (1970) has recently observed, the nature of man is to dominate the natural communities of which he is a member regardless of his religious heritage or current persuasion, *Homo sapiens* can be called a *super dominant,* not only because he is dominant in otherwise undisturbed habitats, but also because he can alter the environment to suit his needs and desires.

Just here, perhaps, is a unique character of man—he desires. We do not need the Bible to point out that often these desires center on ourselves rather than on good for others. The Bible does point out, however, man's responsibility for his environment, as a good steward and husbandman (Genesis 2: 15, etc.).

THE NATURE OF GOD

On the other hand, through the Bible we learn of Jesus Christ and find that God would direct our desires outward, not inward—that good would replace selfishness with love (I Corinthians 13). We learn also, however, that God is not only "out there," transcendent and apart from Nature and Man but also "in here," immanent and a continually essential dynamic of the Universe and the Biosphere as well as the potential internal dynamic and identity of each individual man (Colossians 1: 15-17, 27).

Scripture calls us first to harmony with God through Jesus Christ (Colossians 2: 10). Only in this completeness of commitment to the God of Nature can we hope to achieve the harmony with Nature that White and Shaeffer deem so important. And only, it seems to me, through the love of God in Jesus Christ, and by the Holy Spirit loving through me, can I hope to overcome the greed that tempts me to use the environment to my own ends regardless of the ultimate effect upon you.

PIE-IN-THE-SKY?

Yes, but pie-down-here, too. I can change the world only to the extent that God changes me and then motivates me to do His will—*today*. My role in the environmental crisis is to live a non-polluting life physically, mentally, morally—but within the scope of my manhood. I will still eat. I will still go to the toilet. I will still try to mold ideas. But, oh God, teach me to love!

Despite my love, oh God, keep me from copping out. Keep me aware of problems and sensitive to the needs not only of the people I know but also of the biotic community of which I am a part. Stimulate me through study to increase my knowledge and widen my understanding that I may act and vote intelligently and constructively and be at peace with nature, with my friends, with myself and with You.

BIBLIOGRAPHY

Shaeffer, Francis. 1970. *Pollution and the death of man.* Wheaton, Ill.: Tyndale House.
White, Lynn, Jr. 1967. The historical roots of our ecological crisis. *Science* 155: 1203-1207.
Wright, R. T. 1970. Responsibility for the ecological crisis. *BioScience* 20: 851-853.

Will Population Controls Allow Man to Outsmart the Dinosaurs?

Donald R. Scoby

As the stark realities of the results of overpopulation become clearer each day, man comes face to face with the realization that he is now on the list of endangered species. "Impossible," we may think. How can *Homo sapiens,* a species with the ability to reason, communicate and think about the "truths" of nature, be on the point of extinction after only one or two million years, when the dinosaurs, a group with much lower intelligence, survived for over 150 million years? As we look at the population problem and determine reasons for its existence and growth, we may end up wondering which is smarter—man or dinosaur.

The symptomatic treatment of our damaged environment is not the way to assure the survival of man. Today's adults may possibly provide the treatment necessary to improve the air, water and soil and thus temporarily remove man from the endangered species list. The danger, however, will return in years to come simply because the heart of the problem lies in overpopulation. The control of the problem must unfortunately rest upon future generations because the attitudes of today's generation are detrimental if not fatal to human existence.

Historically, it was necessary to have a high birth rate (natality) to compensate for the high death rate (mortality). Large families were necessary to assure the continuation of the species. Because of the need for survival, man has created and perpetuated a "halo of good" surrounding the concepts of death control, charity to the poor, and large families. These values have thus been inherited by the generation which is presently in legislative power and which is setting the stage for the extinction of man in the near future.

Every area of human existence is endangered by these concepts of "good." Technological advances in the area of medical death control have resulted in the pollution of the genetic make-up of man. Genetically inherited conditions, such as phenylketonuria, open spine and even certain mental conditions, can be treated in the present generations but when the genes carrying these conditions are passed on through heredity without natural controls, they will increase

Written for this volume.

society's burden of the future. It is quite humanitarian to keep alive those with serious genetic disorders but it does effect the human gene pool to allow these individuals to reproduce. Every effort should be made to retain all possible genetic combinations because a certain combination might be the only one capable of breaking up toxic chemical substances, otherwise acting as potential killers of the entire human race. For this reason I do not favor complete genetic selection of only the physically fit, but rather a program of genetic counseling whereby individuals normally doomed to die before reaching reproductive age would be sterilized. This procedure of sterilization would be more in keeping with natural laws which would have prevented the passage of "bad" genes through an early death.

Political policies of tax exemption and welfare payments may win votes for political candidates, but they also encourage larger families and result in a great national economic strain due to the complete dependence of the poverty-stricken upon society. Food for additional millions is projected through agricultural production based on the concept of bigger yields through greater use of fertilizers, pesticides, and herbicides. However, this cycle threatens to destroy our habitable environment. Industrial giants support as a major goal an increasingly high gross national product (GNP). Even though money may seem to make the world go around, it can eventually stop progress through increased pollution by industry which can create an environment fatal to man. The deadly cycle of progress based on the belief that more people create bigger markets that lead to more profit enabling more men to make more progress thus goes back to the hopelessly dated "halo of good" and is based on the assumption of unlimited space and resources.

Is it any wonder that the superiority of man over dinosaur is in question? Through our advances, the death rate has dropped from somewhere around 45 per thousand to approximately nine per thousand in technically advanced countries. However, the birth rate, even though dropping in some countries, has not dropped accordingly. Common sense should tell us that from the zygote (fertilized egg) to the corpse, man inhabits a world limited both in space and resources. Biblical verses can also be interpreted to advocate the changes which are necessary for our survival. As an example, when Christ, prior to his crucifixion, was attempting to prepare his disciples for his departure, He said (John 16: 12-13) "I have yet many things to say to you, but you cannot bear them now. But when the Spirit of truth comes, he will guide you into all truth." (RSV). Science has revealed many truths that Christ spoke of but could not reveal because of circumstances surrounding the need for survival during his time. The science of ecology which deals with the relationships within nature has many truths to tell us. One basic truth is that man is an integral part of nature and as such he *must* live in harmony with his environment. In order to accomplish this he must change his living habits and patterns. Since this is 1971

A.D. with a different set of conditions than 35 A.D., it is mandatory to balance the death rate and the birth rate.

Of course, balancing the death and birth rates requires that we change our values of "good" associated with unlimited reproduction and the unlimited transformation of our environment. Man should, rather, accept the attitude of being a steward of his world living in harmony with nature. Hopefully, it is this idea of Christian stewardship, free of greed and selfishness, that will be accepted by the young. If today's adults would face the center of the problem, overpopulation, the responsibility would be lifted from the shoulders of the young. But since the adults seem to be unable to face the central problem squarely, they must at least permit medically feasible birth control devices to be widely used and establish pollution preventives effective enough to assure a healthy environment for their grandchildren. The grandchildren, hopefully, will have the "guts" enough to establish realistic laws regulating reproduction and assuring man a compatible environment for millions of years to come rather than the short one or two million years that man has been a species. Only by living in harmony with nature can man hope to better the dinosaur's record of survival.

Who Shall Inherit the Earth?

Donald R. Scoby

"And God saw everything that He had made, and behold, it was very good."

Genesis 1: 31

Many men will dispute the above and deny there is a God and that He created a world which, when He had completed His work, He could look upon as good. If these men are judging from the condition of the world today they have many examples to support their beliefs. Indeed pollution and overpopulation have spoiled the world to the degree that the human race may not be able to exist upon the earth for much longer.

It is my personal conviction that the strongest evidence available to prove the existence of God lies within man himself, as well as in the world in which he lives. Within nature organisms exist in various levels of complexity. Man occupies a high level and is one of the most complex. Not only is man complex, but he possesses free choice, which is the only quality making him unique in comparison with other organisms. If there were no God, man would exist only in nature. He would not have the power to choose how he lives in relation to the rest of his environment.

At the present time it is clearly evident that man possesses freedom of choice and that he has made ample use of it. His efforts to improve the world in which he lives have ironically resulted in a polluted and nearly ruined environment. Nature's balance is so thwarted that many species are becoming extinct in an abnormally short time. Thus far man's use of his freedom of choice has endangered his very existence. But man still has some hope for a future. Two paths remain open. He may either ignore the pollution resulting from his actions and continue on his path toward annihilation, or he may choose to change his actions and attitudes in order to preserve the human race.

If man makes the latter choice, the responsibility will rest with each individual. No one person may indulge in the luxury of expecting change from others but not from himself. The condition of the world today is not the creation of God; it is the result of man's folly. It is time man realized the full worth of the world which God created and which was, as a balanced system, a

Written for this volume.

quality environment favorable to man. Stewardship in the '70s will have to be exercised by all or man will suffer far greater losses than he has already experienced. He will lose his very chance for survival.

At the present time many conditions of pollution threaten man. Among these is a problem probably little known to most. Man through his technological advances for the betterment of the world is upsetting the balance of nature. As a result he is creating an environment unnatural for the organisms within it. Not only does he demand adjustments from these organisms but also from himself. The changes are occurring too fast for man to cope with them. The results are strengthening many organisms detrimental to man while man himself is deteriorating. The following example will illustrate this premise.

Each part of nature exists to serve a specific yet interrelated function. The air, water and land support all organisms, and these organisms in turn support one another. A system of checks and balances was supplied to insure the safety of all. One system, whereby one group of organisms is gradually replaced by another group, is called ecological succession. Within each group of many species the organisms reproduced, died, decomposed and created an environment which tended to be detrimental to themselves but conducive to the life of the organisms in the higher levels of complexity. I had always thought of man as the highest level, who, through his free choice was able to change his environment for what he thought was the better. Through man's knowledgeable changes of nature, however, organisms that previously were controlled through natural means are now thriving and will eventually rob man of his world. The insect is a prime example.

To rid himself of these pests, man has, with little if any thought of future consequences, used tons of pesticides. The purpose of these products was to eliminate the insect, but they failed. For example, each time DDT was used to kill mosquitoes, a few possessing higher immunity to it lived. Stronger doses of the pesticide only produced stronger resistance until use of DDT is dangerous because it is affecting the life systems of many non-target species in the world today. Man is strengthening the mosquito and its physiological make-up while weakening his own. Through medicines and surgical practices man is lengthening the lives of those who would normally die at birth. These individuals eventually reproduce and pass on their weaknesses to their children, thus populating the world with an ever weaker human race. As man strengthens the insect, he weakens himself. Therefore, it may be asked, "Who or what will inherit the earth?"

If this situation continues, man surely will not inherit the earth. There are three things man can do when the environment changes. He can adapt, move, or die. Since man cannot physically adapt fast enough and has nowhere to move, it seems he has no choice but to exist at a sub-human level or to die. And die he will unless he updates his archaic attitudes of the past and remedies the conditions existing in the 1970s.

Of course, man must stop technology's upsetting of the natural conditions of nature, but he must take steps to strengthen his own species. The first step toward accomplishing man's survival lies in the development and acceptance of a thorough genetic counseling system, its success necessarily aided by legalized abortion. Through these steps, man would eventually be able to eliminate the birth of individuals with inherited defects such as mongolism and the genetic pool of man would thereby be strengthened. Man would not only strengthen the human race, but also provide better care for those presently disabled if he were not continually burdened with additional defective persons.

We do not question that we as humans value life enough to care for those whose lives are nearly useless to themselves and others. But would it not be better to stop bringing these lives into the world? Who suffers more from our supposed kindness than the disabled individuals? A far more generous and realistic approach would be to eliminate the birth of the defective rather than to encourage the nursing of those who are unfit for a productive and satisfying life in this world. Genetic counseling would help to eliminate the more degrading forms of inherited genetic disabilities and together with abortion would provide a safe and constructive solution for parents who choose not to bear a severely disabled child which would only be a burden for all of society.

Of course such a beneficial program is not possible because of current attitudes toward abortion. Many people are violently opposed to abortion and consider it murderous. Others are uncertain, plagued by concern for the human race on the one hand and moral convictions on the other. But what man must realize is that his attitudes are based on man-made principles proposed many years ago when the world did not have to face the problems of overpopulation and an overabundance of genetic defects. Genetic defects were formerly taken care of by natural means; whereas, today the severely defective face only a hopeless vegetable existence.

Historically man has always wrestled with the question of abortion, the reason being his uncertainty about when the embryo actually becomes an individual with life of its own. Many claim this occurs at the time of conception. Others believe the life of the child is present when a heart-beat is detected. In my own mind I feel that when the embryo exists upon the hormonal support of the placenta (three months) and not directly upon the mother, he becomes a self-determining individual. For years the church remained in a quandry with no absolute views on abortion. But in 1869 the Roman Catholic church took a definite stand on abortion and declared it morally wrong because life began at conception. But the conditions of 1869 are far different than those of 1971, and to use an old cliche, times have changed.

It will do no good to develop a genetically sound race if the immense numbers of that race will cause its own extinction. At the present time the free choice of man invested by God has been removed by requiring every potential parent to bear the conceived child unless a condition exists which endangers the life of the mother. It is time to allow man to exercise his ability of free choice and to aid in the survival of man. He should be able to choose legal abortion and exercise positive measures to limit the population. Should he choose the path of destruction through overpopulation, his free choice would eventually be limited by the government or more drastically by natural means of starvation, disease and war. By requiring sterilization for those not practicing effective birth control, the government would be forcing man to accept the positive and necessary goal of saving the human race. Common sense and economic incentives for small families should have the desired effect through individual choice; however, if this does not occur required sterilization will be necessary.

Aristotle and Plato recommended abortion as a population control measure and a therapeutic remedy. In direct contrast, Hippocrates spoke against abortion and set the example for physicians in years to come. At present, man would be better to follow the recommendations of Aristotle and Plato, for abortion is now a necessary remedy for the genetic and population problems of the world.

Sadly enough, free choice will not operate effectively in our situation of overpopulation. For successful completion of such a remedial program based on changed attitudes, each individual must play a large part by changing his own life. But as has been proven by past actions, man does not readily accept individual responsibility but rather places it upon the shoulders of everyone but himself. Many individuals have no concern for the problem, many are ignorant, and many are hindered by social or religious attitudes. Therefore, other incentives must be employed to encourage man to make wise choices for his future.

Presently, the largest influence on man is probably money. Should economic practices be designed to limit rather than to enlarge families, man may be able to curb the population explosion. Improved welfare and tax programs should reward people for having fewer children, not for having more as they do today. Families under welfare should be given adequate aid to support two children. However, working people support the welfare recipient; should they not therefore have the right to demand sterilization after two children are born? Granted, those who have large families now should not be cut off from support, but this type of economic pressure and government control should be employed to stop the poor from unwittingly having large families or in many cases of actually earning a living by having children. Welfare programs should be oriented to eliminate the need for welfare rather than the present programs which tend to perpetuate welfare.

It is not only the poor who seemingly benefit economically by having many children. The middle and upper classes also benefit through the tax exemptions now provided by the government. Individuals or families with less than the median number of children are forced to subsidize families with more than the median number of children. Should the exemptions for children be increased to $1,000 for one child, $500 for the second, and a sliding penalty based on income for each additional child be introduced, many people would stop at either one or two and aid zero or even a negative population growth. In order for there to be no discrimination the third child should be on a sliding scale: that is to say, if the income of a person was $3,000 then the -$500 would be fine. However, if the person was a millionaire the third child should cost that individual $500,000 per year. No one person should have any more right to have a large family than another. For those who still desire a large family, adoption is the answer. Morally speaking it is the only right way. It makes better sense to provide for those individuals already here rather than to populate to the point of destroying all of mankind.

These steps of genetic counseling, legalized abortion and economic remedies are bases for the beginning of a cure for the problem, but social attitudes must change before any of those steps may be accepted. The most logical place to begin these changes is in the schools and churches. The indoctrination of the value of large families begins in early childhood and continues through the rest of man's life. Children's stories, instead of portraying youngsters who go to the farm to visit Aunt Jenny and their five cousins, should portray youngsters visiting Aunt Jenny and their one cousin. Rather than honor families who have many children achieving high goals in their lives, we should reprimand these families for their size and the resulting danger to the human race. And as a final example, the mother-of-the-year in the future should be chosen for her foresight in limiting her family size rather than her ignorance in aiding the problem of overpopulation by having more than one or two children. At present, man continues to believe children are "cheaper by the dozen," but the actual price he pays is the eventual ruination of his environment. He is contributing toward a low quality of life plus the possibility of a premature grave for his children and grandchildren.

Invested in man is the one quality which will determine his existence—his free choice. Which way will he go? Will he choose bias, prejudice and archaic rules to guide his living while stumbling blindly toward his doom, or will he face the results of what he has done to the environment God gave him and decide to change his attitudes in order to assure a quality environment for the human race? One of the greatest sins occurring every day is the misuse of the world which God could once look upon and call good. No man can shake off the guilt of this direct disobedience to the call of stewardship. Each individual committing the acts of pollution and contributing to the problems of overpopulation is responsible. Only by changing his own life style may he expect change in others.

The question of who will inherit the earth can be answered. Man will inherit the earth, but only if he will take positive steps toward his and its preservation. As it has always been, the choice is up to him. It is yet to be seen which way he will go.

The Double Decade of Dalliance

Donald M. Huffman

And it came to pass in the days of the mid-twentieth century that the great wisemen of all the great nations of all the world, having forsaken the battlegrounds of the second of the great world wars, did engage in competition calculated to both expand the limits of the universe and to more precisely resolve the lower limits of the universe. And so, as the "new wisemen of the new biology" spoke of molecular structure of biological units, and the "new wisemen of physics" turned their gaze outward to begin their assault on space, there was great excitement and much anticipation. And lo, when one great power did orbit Sputnik 1, the leaders of the other power of the land of the eagle did smite themselves upon their breasts, and there was much weeping, and wailing, and gnashing of teeth, for indeed this loss of face caused great consternation in the land. And the wisemen of that nation having not yet launched their space vehicles were distressed and sore afraid, and they said to one another, "What is this catastrophe which has come to pass?" And straightway they formed committees of all manner, and began to accuse all manner of men of incompetence, and brother turned against brother, and submarine experts became great critics of educational systems, and all did say to their leaders, "Give us alms that we may gird our loins, do battle, and bring up our young wisemen so that we may again assert our supremacy. For are we not the richest nation in all the world, yet we have not done those things which we ought to have done, and we have done those things which we ought not to have done, and there is no strength in us. Let us therefore straightway intensify the training of our youth that this tragedy might not repeat itself, that our greatness may be known to our children and to our children's children." And thus it was that from one end of the land to the other there went up a great cry and many pompous decrees, and the coffers of many institutions were filled, and the purse strings of mighty foundations were opened, and the land of the purple mountain majesty above the fruited plains did flood alms in to all manner of educational institutions (not all of them bad), and a great cry went abroad, "We must revise our curricula, and must dedicate ourselves to a great challenge, for man cannot

Paper presented at the Association of Midwestern College Biology Teachers, University of Northern Iowa, October 9, 1970. Dr. Donald M. Huffman is Chairman of the Department of Biology at Central College, Pella, Iowa.

serve both pleasure and progress." And it came to pass, because of this massive effort (or in spite of it) that great masses of wisemen did engage themselves in research (not all of it worthless), and a great multitude of foundation programs were established and the cup of scientific resources did overflow, and great were those golden years for the wisemen who by crafty grantsmanship did successfully beseech the multitude of foundations for financial support. And great and mighty edifices of learning arose, and the ranks of the wisemen were swelled with eager young proteges of great promise, and the leaders of that country saw what had been created, and along with the wisemen they said, "It is good, it is very good."

And thus it eventually came to pass that the land of the eagle did propel more and larger satellites into the heavens than did the land of the bear, and behold the leaders of the red, the white, and the blue (but seldom black), were proud and puffed up, and the alms continued to flow, and the country prospered, and the young wisemen found great demand for their services, and throughout the length and breadth of the land there arose a feeling of great joy.

And about that same time in that same country there arose a few prophets who prophesied in diverse manner and predicted great calamity if the leaders of that land failed to perceive that there were yet other problems which demanded attention. But their voices alas fell on deaf ears, and their words were as sounding brass and tinkling cymbal. And that country became entangled in great battles abroad, though as their leaders explained, there were not really battles, but holy wars against the encroachments of the devil of the land of the bear. And there arose great strife within, because as the prophets had foretold, there were many inequities in that land, and neglect had opened great festering sores in the national body, and a greater fever was rising within. But for a time the wisemen grew sleek and fat, and failed to see that the golden egg had begun to tarnish, and the goose from whence it came was becoming exceedingly thin. Then did the internal strife intensify, and the foreign entanglements become more costly, so that even the wisemen in ivy-covered research labs perceived that all was not well and that the consequences thereof might be far reaching. And there arose in that land a great financial famine (though the leaders assured the people that it was merely a minimal recession on the road to a more healthy economy), and the purse strings of the mighty foundations were first drawn tighter, and the massive flood of alms subsided to a gentle flow, then to a mere trickle, and there was much weeping, and wailing and gnashing of teeth, for indeed the loss of funds caused great consternation. And thus it came to pass that no longer might new edifices for research be constructed, and the AYI, the URP and like programs became only faint memories of the once lush diet of alphabet soup of the great foundations.

And at that selfsame time, the young wisemen were emerging from their apprenticeships and did seek gainful employment, and lo, there were insufficient positions in which to place these young wisemen, and in those days the desks of departmental chairmen and deans were inundated by requests from these young wisemen. But, alas, budgets were tight in every realm, and there were no places for the young wisemen to lay their heads, and there was again weeping, and wailing, and gnashing of teeth, for indeed great was the consternation and many of the young wisemen had families, and these families were sore distressed. So it was, that the wisemen of all manner did perceive this deplorable situation, and did beseech their leaders for more alms, but alas, their pleas fell as sounding brass and tinkling cymbal, because a great hue and cry had been raised in the land, and the youth of the land were asking for withdrawal from foreign entanglements, and there were also demands for granting of alms to feed the poor, clothe the naked, and bring comfort to the disadvantaged. And the leaders did confer with the wiseman, and differences of opinion were rampant, and some leaders spoke of "effete snobs" and "supercilious cynics," and it was implied that the institutions of higher learning had become a hotbed of political activism. And it was even rumored abroad in those days that the great Mickey Mouse did wear a Spiro Agnew wrist watch; and the strife continued, and great heat was generated but little light shed on the problems of that land.

And, at that same time in that very country there was a rediscovery of some great neglected prophesy, and ecology became first a whisper, then a shout, and finally a deafening roar, and there was much great joy among wisemen, for they said, "Is it not as we have prophesied—all nature must remain in balance, and if we are to exist at all, we are to exist in harmony with our environment." And lo, there arose a great cheer from all the people (with the exception of a few economists), and the wisemen once again did strike one another on one another's back, and the leaders joined the rejoicing, though it was often difficult to determine whether they knew whereof they spoke. And thus it was that a great Simian was removed from the backs of the leaders. But the conflicts abroad continued to rage, and the internal strife continued, and the great foundations continued their slow trickle in somewhat different directions.

And thus it is that we come to this moment in time, and the same problems exist, though we wisemen claim to see a faint glimmer of light at the end of the long tunnel, and we continue to prophesy and to beseech our leaders for alms. But there rings in our ears the odd echo, "our faults lie not in our stars, but in ourselves." And it appears that the greatest fault of all is to know we have a fault without trying to do anything about it. We wisemen have a job to do, and we must be about our business soon. Today is upon us and tomorrow is rushing toward us, and if yesterday's faults have blinded us to reality, grant us the wisdom to do what we may for tomorrow. For if we fail to learn from the past there may be no tomorrow.